AZZEDINE ALAÏA'S
DIOR
COLLECTION

AZZEDINE ALAÏA'S
DIOR
COLLECTION

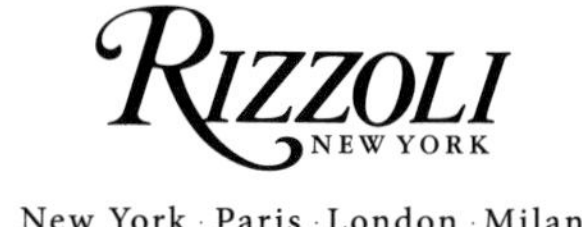

New York · Paris · London · Milan

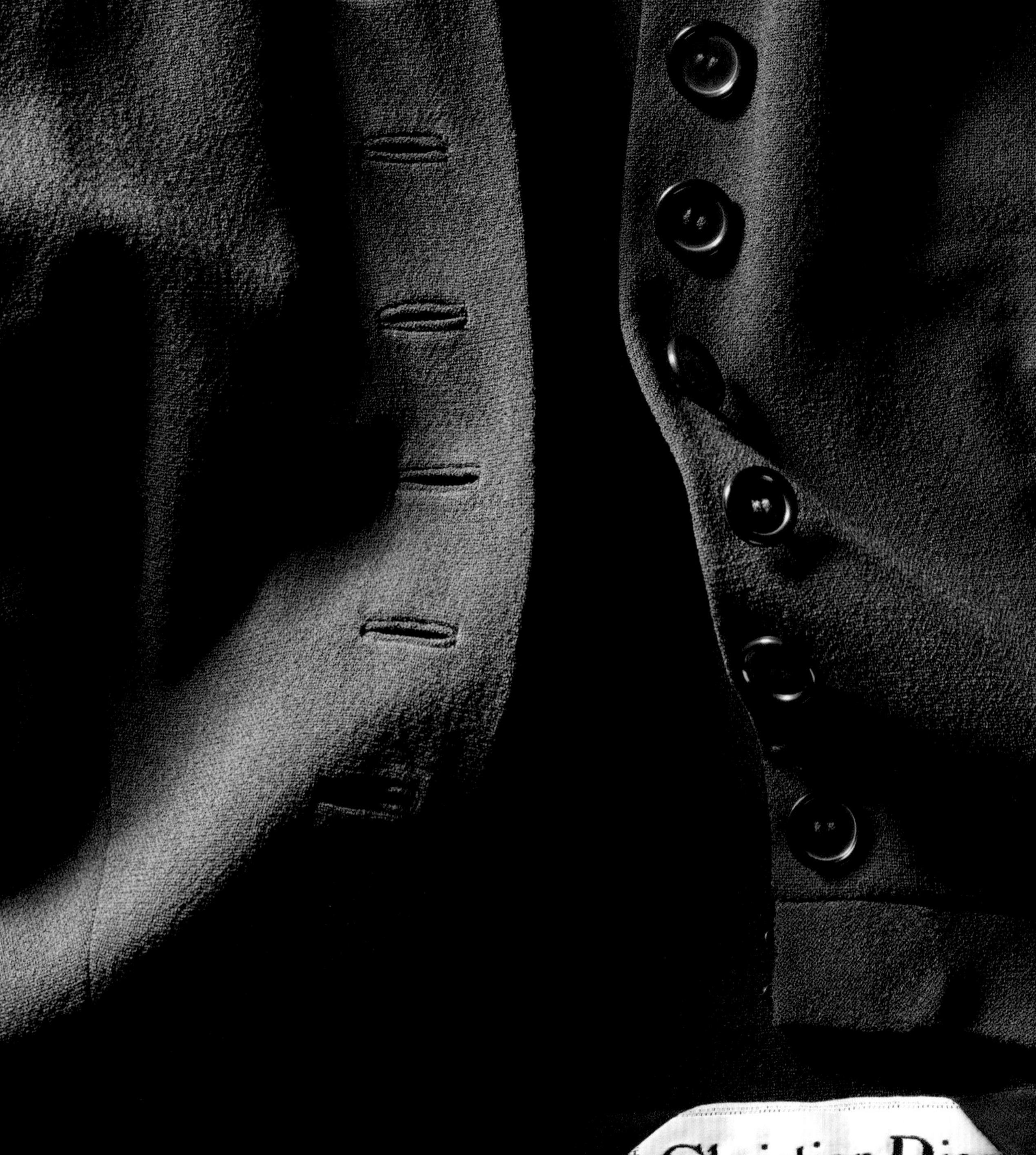

Christian Dior
PARIS

Christian Dior
Chérie

En taille dress in wool crêpe
(detail), Spring–Summer 1948
haute couture collection, *Envol* line.
Paris, Fondation Azzedine Alaïa.

So-called *en taille* dresses were
"designed for the wearer to
be able to go outside without
a coat or jacket," according to
the press release.

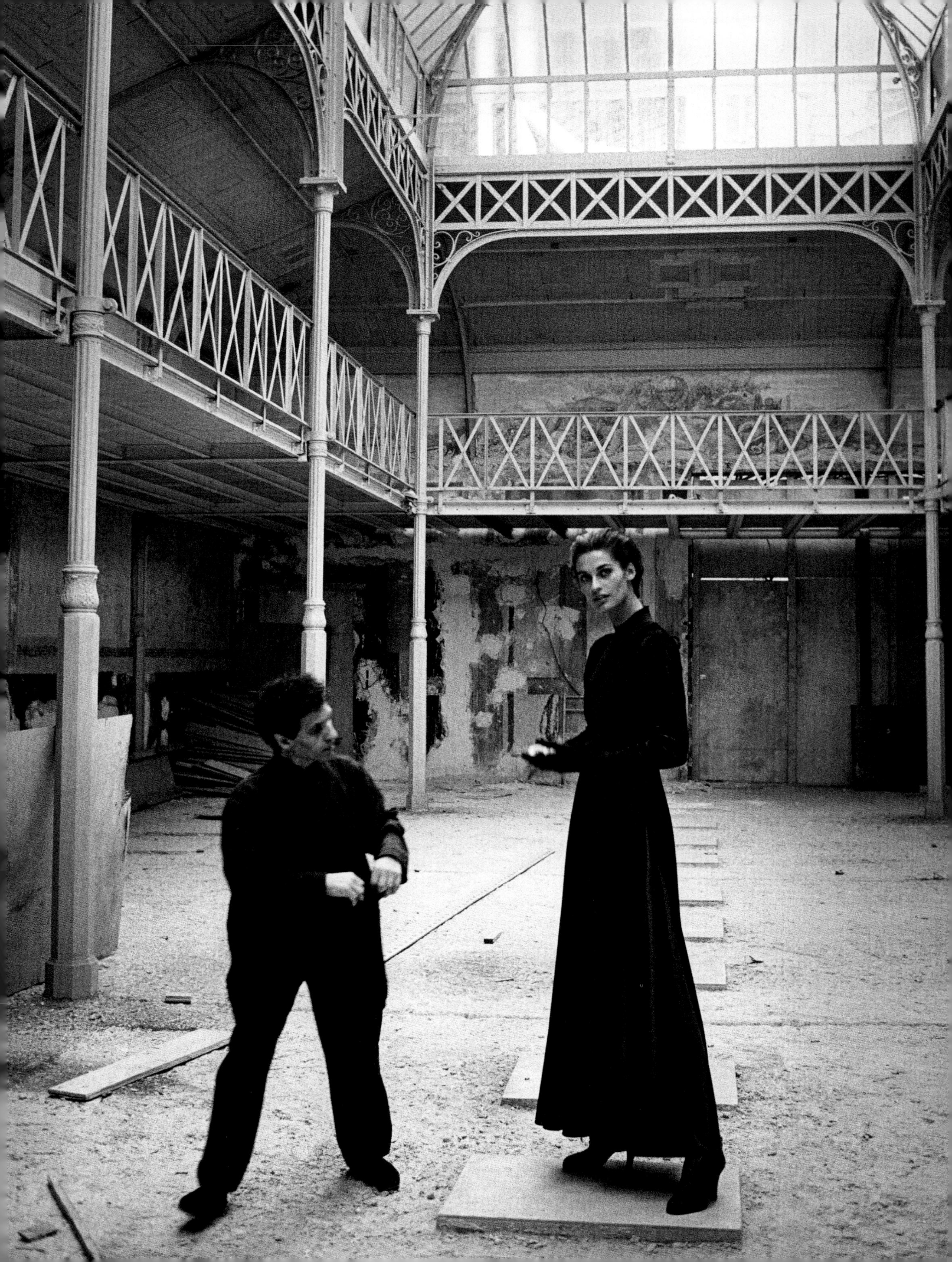

PREFACE

OLIVIER SAILLARD

Ever since the 1950s, entire successive generations of fashion designers have longed for the same thing: to become Christian Dior. Having become so synonymous with the epitome of couture, Dior is no longer merely a name but a force for success—four letters that have consequently shaped happy destinies for many.

After the death of the New Look's creator in 1957, aspiring couturiers dreamed of taking on the same mantle. Azzedine Alaïa was no exception. In his native Tunisia, where he was working as an assistant to a midwife named Madame Pineau, who had taken him under her wing, he would conjure up worlds in his mind as he looked through fashion magazines that she brought him from France. He long spoke of how intrigued and captivated he was by the fullness of the Christian Dior dresses in the photographs. They seemed to "stand up all by themselves."

Later, when he arrived in Paris in 1956, he had a fleeting glimpse of the ateliers at Avenue Montaigne, having secured a few days' work through recommendations from Habiba Menchari and from Zeineb Lévy-Despas, a faithful haute couture client. The experience was not to last, but Alaïa came away from it with an unbridled admiration for Christian Dior and for French excellence, as embodied by the House of Dior. He would never forget the plush, genteel atmosphere of the place, or the atelier's high standards. More than that, he never stopped measuring himself against that level of fashion ambition that comes to dominate life so much that it overshadows everything else. Constantly singing the praises of Christian Dior's oeuvre, his dazzling design skills, and the sumptuousness of both the fabrics and the cuts, Alaïa secretly amassed an archive of objects that testify to this passion.

From 1968, he started to take stock of the legacy of those he most admired, with Christian Dior at the top of the list. Numbering into the hundreds and soon into the thousands, the result is the largest private collection of fashion archives, which is now held by the Fondation Azzedine Alaïa. Whenever he was not in his atelier cutting

Azzedine Alaïa on the premises of his couture house, which became the headquarters of his foundation at 18 Rue de la Verrerie, Paris, 1989. Photograph by Peter Lindbergh.

fabrics, assembling a sleeve, or perfecting the detail of a garment, he had only one thing in mind: to head to the auction rooms and buy pieces as souvenirs of the men and women who wrote the history of fashion. Initially scattered around various locations where he carefully preserved his treasures, which rival those of the great museums, he acquired a total of 596 House of Dior dresses, suits, and coats, which are brought together today in all their glory.

The oldest ones date from 1947, the year of the first collection that launched it all, from scandal to being embraced by an entire era. Saved for the fashion world and for French heritage, the collection includes several hundred different models from the 1950s. It also represents the various creative directors who succeeded Dior himself: Yves Saint Laurent, Gianfranco Ferré, John Galliano . . . The founder-couturier's pieces bear witness to how much the French-of-Tunisian-descent couturier coveted Dior's work. Seeking out the mysteries of the dresses, and of the delicate structures that make diaphanous skirts "stand up," Alaïa deftly acquired the objects of his youthful daydreams.

Having been identified, traced, and inventoried through invaluable collaboration with the House of Dior archives themselves, they now form the core of an unprecedented exhibition at Rue François Ier, at La Galerie Dior. It goes without saying that Alaïa would have been moved by this, and would no doubt have been supremely proud—he himself a virtuoso couturier who internalized the lessons of the great Christian Dior. The exhibition pays tribute to a sharing of knowledge and expertise that Alaïa likewise amassed and constantly espoused.

Dior staff record of Azzedine Bénalaïa
(as Azzedine Alaïa was then known),
June 26–29, 1956. Paris, Dior Héritage.

BÉNALAÏA

Prénoms : *Azzeddine*

Nom de Jeune fille :

Adresse : *15 avenue Elisée Reclus Paris 7ème*

Né le : *26 - 2 - 1935* à *Tunis (Tunisie)*

Personne à prévenir en cas d'accident :

N° Sécurité Sociale : *?*   M^{le} Caisse de Compen^{tion}

CÉLIBATAIRE	MARIÉ	VEUF	DIVORCÉ

N° Pointage		ENFANTS				DATE DE RÉVISION	
		Noms	Nés le	Noms	Nés le	Prim. ancien^{té}	Congés payés
Emploi *?*	1			5			
	2			6			
	3			7			
H F	4			8			

Mineur

Apprenti avec contrat

Français

Étranger

Mutilé %

Enfants

SITUATION MILITAIRE

SERVICE. Armé _ Auxil. Ajourné _ Exempté

Réformé T _ Réformé D

Classe recrut^t :   mobili^{on} :

Arme :   Grade

Affectation :

SITUATION D'ÉTRANGER

Carte N° :

Date :   Validité :

Profession inscrite :

Préfecture :

SITUATION DANS L'ENTREPRISE

Date Chang^t Situation	Service	Poste	Date	Remuner^{on}	Prime ancienneté	Date	Rémunér^{on}	Prime ancienneté
?								

Date d'entrée : *26-6-56*

Ancienneté

Malade

Blessé

Congé

Abs s/motif

Frédéric

STATISTIQUE		ABSENCE					
Année	M	AT.	C.P.	P.	S.M.	D.	

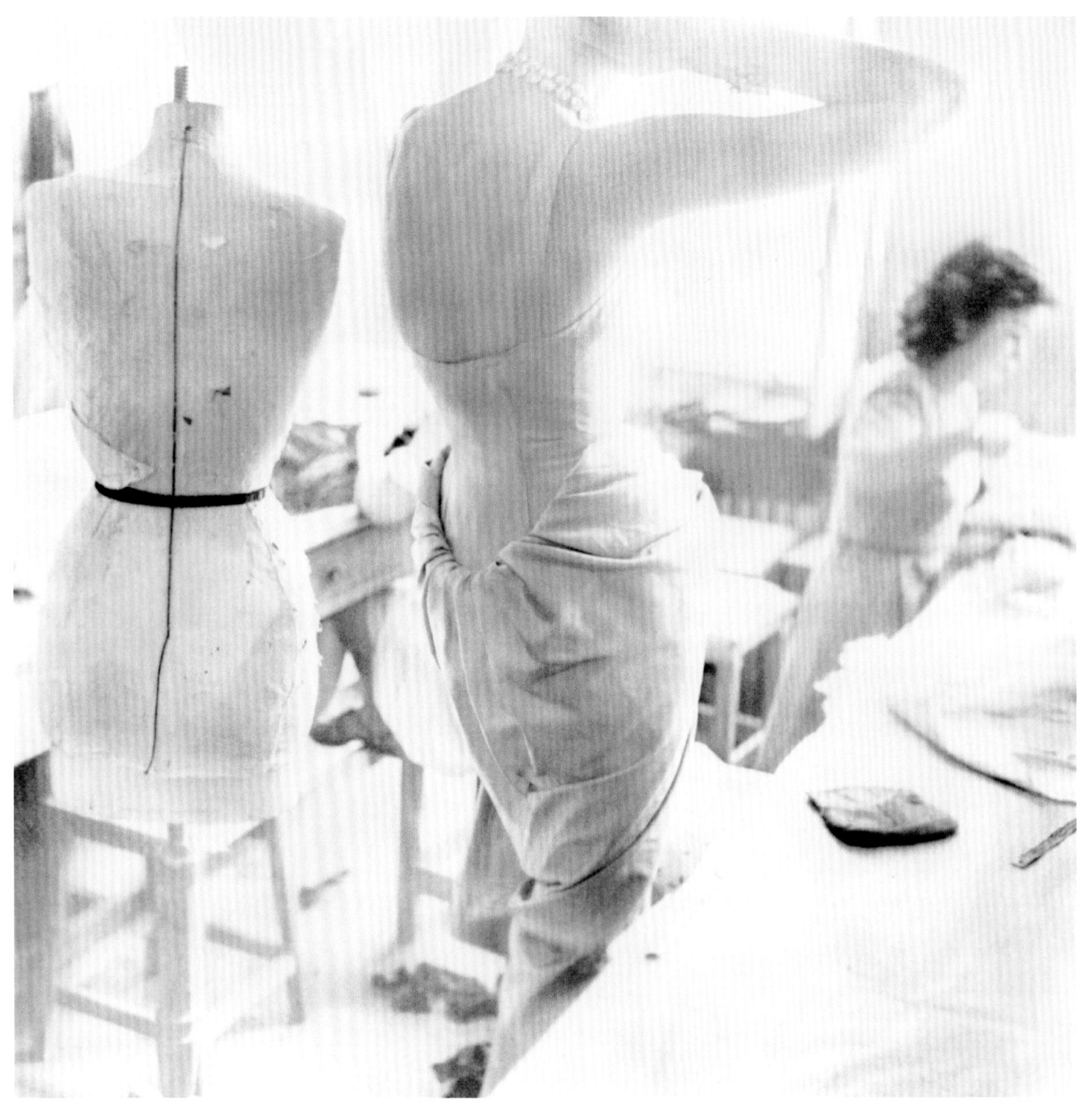

Workroom, House of Dior, August 1947.
Model wearing the *Zerline* gala dress, by Christian Dior,
Autumn–Winter 1947 haute couture collection, *Corolle* line.
Photograph by Richard Avedon, published
in *Harper's Bazaar*, October 1947.

THE CRAFT
OF THE DIOR ATELIERS

LAURENCE BENAÏM

LINES TO THE LETTER

Gathered like surgeons in a consultation room, the *premières* and *premiers d'atelier* (workroom forewomen and foremen) examine the pieces in the House of Dior archives, turning them over, unpacking the secrets of their cut, shape, and construction. Emerging from its box with a rustle of tissue paper, the beautiful *Astarté* cocktail dress (pp. 40–41)—from Christian Dior's Spring–Summer 1955 haute couture collection, *A* line—looks brand-new, as if it had never been worn. Inside the skirt, the black tulle has two layers of crinoline to give it volume: the top one stiff and lace-like, the underlayer softer. "It's a tradition here to produce the *Corolle* style and maintain its rounded form," explains one of the *premières*.

Experts in action, they go on to analyze the five billowing layers of black fabric, weighing them up and turning them this way and that. They all share not only a passion but also techniques that, like a crinoline petticoat, constitute its structural framework: the Dior spirit. A particular way of expressing a vision of the female silhouette in a single piece. It is clear to see in the sketches in the collection charts; "a sketch must suggest both attack and allure; it must already suggest a living silhouette; it must be redolent with movement."[1]

Considered the founder of haute couture, Charles Frederick Worth reinvented the "princess dress"—with no stitching at the waist—as well as a dress with a bustle supported on an undergarment that could take different forms. From a simple cushion to an assembly of little metal rings, the bustle would be held in place by ties and worn underneath starched petticoats to show off the small of the back. Innovating and standing out. In a similar vein, the Dior line sets the direction, and the craftsmanship goes hand in hand with it. Reviving the technique of pleating while at the same time bringing

---

1   Christian Dior, *Dior by Dior: The Autobiography of Christian Dior* (London: V&A Publishing, 2025; orig. published in 1957), 86.

more roundness at the hip; matching the volumes to the body: Dior craftsmanship is faithful to the couturier's motto, adding interfacing without causing a sense of heaviness, notching a lapel, slimming the silhouette without a break at the waist, in a quest for harmony between the curve and the line. It is a style of handwriting as much as a summation of secrets passed down through the generations. It is not especially about being hieratic, as with Cristóbal Balenciaga, but rather about a way of setting a "creative idea" in circulation through all the ateliers, which "reaches the apprentices and then *'les petites mains'* and then the fingers that run over the *toiles*, the fingers that are pricked by a needle or hesitate over a design, the fingers that are creating the styles of tomorrow."[2]

Christian Dior wrote of how sketching could have the effect of "an electric shock."[3] The sketch is never a technical specification, but it does announce a look: "You see the body and the way it will carry the garment," remarks one *première d'atelier*. In the realm of architecture, designing a suspension bridge requires complex calculations; in haute couture, Dior craftsmanship internalizes something beyond geometrical norms when creating the patterns, positioning them on the fabric, and making the *toiles:* here, it is a matter of spirit, intuition, and sensitivity. "Although the *couturier* is naturally anxious to sew and cut well, he feels all the time this desire to express himself. For all its ephemerality, *couture* constitutes a mode of self-expression which can be compared to architecture or painting. Even if expression is the initial and primary goal, a collection can only be successful if it is also well cut and sewn, just as a beautiful house can only exist if it is well constructed."[4]

A SCHOOL OF STYLE

Flattening a collar, manipulating it back into shape, stretching it along the bias, and releasing it to the point that it will not go slack. Masking or emphasizing concavities, judging the fabric width needed for a pleated skirt, folding diagonally from the straight grain to establish the bias. With its three meters (ten feet) of lining fabric (for the jacket), and four times as much for the skirt, the iconic *Bar* suit set the tone for an enterprise that was conceived like a school of dress and deportment. When Christian Dior opened his couture house to launch the New Look, on February 12, 1947, he not only created a style but also reinvented the body through gowns that—thanks to a "return

---

2   *Ibid.*, 88.
3   *Ibid.*, 85.
4   *Ibid.*, 87.

to long-forgotten techniques"[5]—conveyed the message of it being reinvested with a sense of rediscovered honor. The *Corolle* dress? As *Elle* magazine commented in March 1947, it "masks slightly heavy hips. Flatters legs. Makes the wearer look younger. Appeals to men." With "rounded shoulders, full feminine busts, and hand-span waists above enormous spreading skirts,"[6] Christian Dior reset the intentions of the profession itself—a school of discipline that Worth had already defined in his motto "obtain and maintain." While advocating an end to uniforms, Dior had no hesitation in using military terms in relation to his couture house, describing his staff as his "*état-major*"[7] and the evening before a collection's launch as the "eve of the battle."[8]

"EVEN IF EXPRESSION IS THE INITIAL AND PRIMARY GOAL, A COLLECTION CAN ONLY BE SUCCESSFUL IF IT IS ALSO WELL CUT AND SEWN, JUST AS A BEAUTIFUL HOUSE CAN ONLY EXIST IF IT IS WELL CONSTRUCTED." CHRISTIAN DIOR

A master of dancing volumes, his brand brought together a sense of splendor and excess—in the *Emba* coat with its 91 meters (300 feet) of white mink, or the famous *Chérie* dress with its 80 meters (262 feet) of immaculate faille—along with a sense of orderliness and discipline. "In order to give my models more 'presence' I lined nearly all of them with cambric or taffeta, thus reverting to an old tradition."[9] At his side was the "fairy-fingered"[10] Marguerite Carré. As the House of Dior's technical director from 1947 to 1960, she had *fallen* into couture when she started to work at the House of Worth at the age of sixteen. But it was in Jean Patou's couture house that she mastered her art, becoming a *modéliste* (designer); she remained there for eighteen years. Christian Dior dubbed her "Dame Couture" and confided that "over the years she has become part of myself—of my 'dressmaking'

---

[5]   *Ibid.*, 24.
[6]   *Ibid.*
[7]   *Ibid.*, 12.
[8]   *Ibid.*, 134.
[9]   *Ibid.*, 24.
[10] Interview with Raymonde Zehnacker, in *Dior. Cahiers du patrimoine*, no. 4, 2009, 88.

self."[11] The question that she systematically asked him speaks volumes: "Have I expressed you correctly?"[12]

Attitude! Every aspect is crucial in holding the whole together—just like in these highly technical creations: made to last, and with a wealth of know-how to be gleaned from studying them. These days invisible zippers have replaced metal hooks, but the clean lines of some models reveal specific obsessions—as with the *Accacias* suit from Spring–Summer 1949 (*Trompe-l'œil* line, p. 23), given a distinctive air of modernity by its jacket with naturally rounded shoulders and its wrap skirt with delicate edging on the pockets.

> # "IT IS PERFECTLY VALID TO SPEAK OF THE ARCHITECTURE OF A DRESS. A DRESS IS CONSTRUCTED, AND IT IS CONSTRUCTED ACCORDING TO THE DIRECTION OF THE FABRICS [...] THAT IS THE SECRET OF COUTURE, AND IT'S A SECRET THAT DEPENDS ON THE FIRST LAW OF ARCHITECTURE: THAT OF OBEYING GRAVITY."
>
> **CHRISTIAN DIOR**

A shawl collar, notched and yet made of a single piece of fabric, hand-stitched to the interfacing and hand-"folded" so that, when ironed, it gives an illusion of natural movement, avoiding any flattening effect. No side seams—a lesson in harmony between propriety and freedom, line and softness, which the press release for the collection in question described as "a lot of loose-fitting but clean-lined jackets and paletots, with very long lapels." Is there any fashion house other than the House of Dior where a "markedly offbeat, unfixed, shortened silhouette" could spark such fascination? There is clearly a structural "skeleton" in the basque of the jacket but, like the integrated *toile* and the invisible stitching of the pocket trim, it remains an enigma.

---

11   Dior, *Dior by Dior*, 13.
12   *Ibid.*, 87.

It just makes you want to wear it, because it is so weightless and slips on so easily. As one of the Dior *premiers d'atelier* affirms, "Minimizing the quantity of seams is very couture."

THE ARCHITECTURE OF A DRESS

Moods, whims, feelings: the romanticism of a restored golden age comes together with an absolute sense of line, a rigor that is guaranteed by Dior craftsmanship. Christian Dior constructed not only dresses but also bodies, whose architecture is indissociable from the couture techniques. This is exemplified in the *Marcel Pagnol* evening dress from the Spring–Summer 1952 collection (*Sinueuse* line, pp. 46–47), where the "soft, casual silhouette" announced in the press release translates into a fully pleated long skirt. Here again, the two layers of pleating—one straight, the other sunburst—provide the desired look: neither a fluted stem nor an overly flared corolla, the folds do not restrict movement but invite it.

It was always a pressured atmosphere in the ateliers at 30 Avenue Montaigne, although in 1948 the Spring–Summer collection's *Zig-Zag* line, with its "spirited, sketch-like aspect," brought a new airiness—without turning its back on structure. As the collection's press release explained, "The fabrics are treated as a mass, with practically no darts or cuts. The effects are obtained solely through their orientations, which emphasize the fluidity of the body's movements with maximum grace." It was not about letting go, or uncontrolled evanescence. With Christian Dior, even chiffon, organza, organdy, and lace were subjected to the science of proportions, far beyond the vagaries of fluidity. There was even a proposal for "organtweed." Where else than at Dior would there be talk of "newness in the cut, the constant focus of our efforts"?[13]

Parallel pleats meticulously positioned along the exact line of the weave. A *Vivante* line for Autumn–Winter 1953. A "hippy" silhouette for the *H* line in Autumn–Winter 1954. The anatomy was aligned with an alphabet, and the alphabet with a syntax of skills. Returning to Marguerite Carré, "an utter perfectionist with a deep love for the profession, she was the one who mastered the science of poise, of the bias, of the drape; the one in charge, who knew how to divide the workload across the various ateliers depending on their respective competencies; the patron saint of miracles, thanks to whom a décolleté has the appearance of living water flowing from the basin of a fountain, or five layers of flounces give the impression

---

13   Press release (in French), Spring–Summer 1953 haute couture collection, *Tulipe* line.

15

of swallows taking flight, or a pleat seems to snap shut as if whipped into place."[14]

Because, here, it is as if the art of volumes and their construction formed a single whole, bound together by an invisible force that stands the test of time. "I wanted to be an architect; being a fashion designer, I am obliged to follow laws, principles of architecture. One of the materials you spoke about earlier and that I have access to—fabric—constantly brings me back to it. It is perfectly valid to speak of the architecture of a dress. A dress is constructed, and it is constructed according to the direction of the fabrics [...] that is the secret of couture, and it's a secret that depends on the first law of architecture: that of obeying gravity."[15]

Some eighty years later, everything has changed, and yet nothing has changed. Shapewear has long replaced garter belts, and *toile de laine* (woolen fabric) has given way to lighter *toile de soie* (silk). And doubtless because haute couture pieces are worn more than once, bias-cut organzas offer greater comfort, caressing the skin. As required for versatility, basque structures are removable, allowing jackets to curve outward over a skirt or to skim the hips when worn with jeans . . . The craftsmanship is so very much alive that it "speaks," continuing to fashion an ideal. Sewing a line of stitches; creating a skirt slit for ease of movement; ensuring a neat finish; structuring a piece; re-aligning a seam; stitching to a vanishing point to adjust a dart.

Most moving of all is that the *premières* and *premiers d'atelier* never have a negative word to say about Christian Dior. In a dialogue of movements, he is forever present through dresses that seem to say: "The fabric is alive on the shoulders. The waist is alive beneath the fabric."[16]

---

14   Marie-France Pochna, *Christian Dior: Destiny – The Authorized Biography,* (translated by Kate Robinson, Paris: Flammarion, 2021), 367.

15   Christian Dior, speech given at the Sorbonne University, Paris, August 3, 1955, published in *Conférences écrites par Christian Dior pour la Sorbonne, 1955–1957* (Paris: Éditions de l'Institut Français de la Mode/Éditions du Regard, 2003), 43.

16   Press release, Autumn–Winter 1953 haute couture collection, *Vivante* line.

Christian Dior designing at his desk at 30 Avenue Montaigne, Paris, in February 1948. Photograph by Michael Ochs.

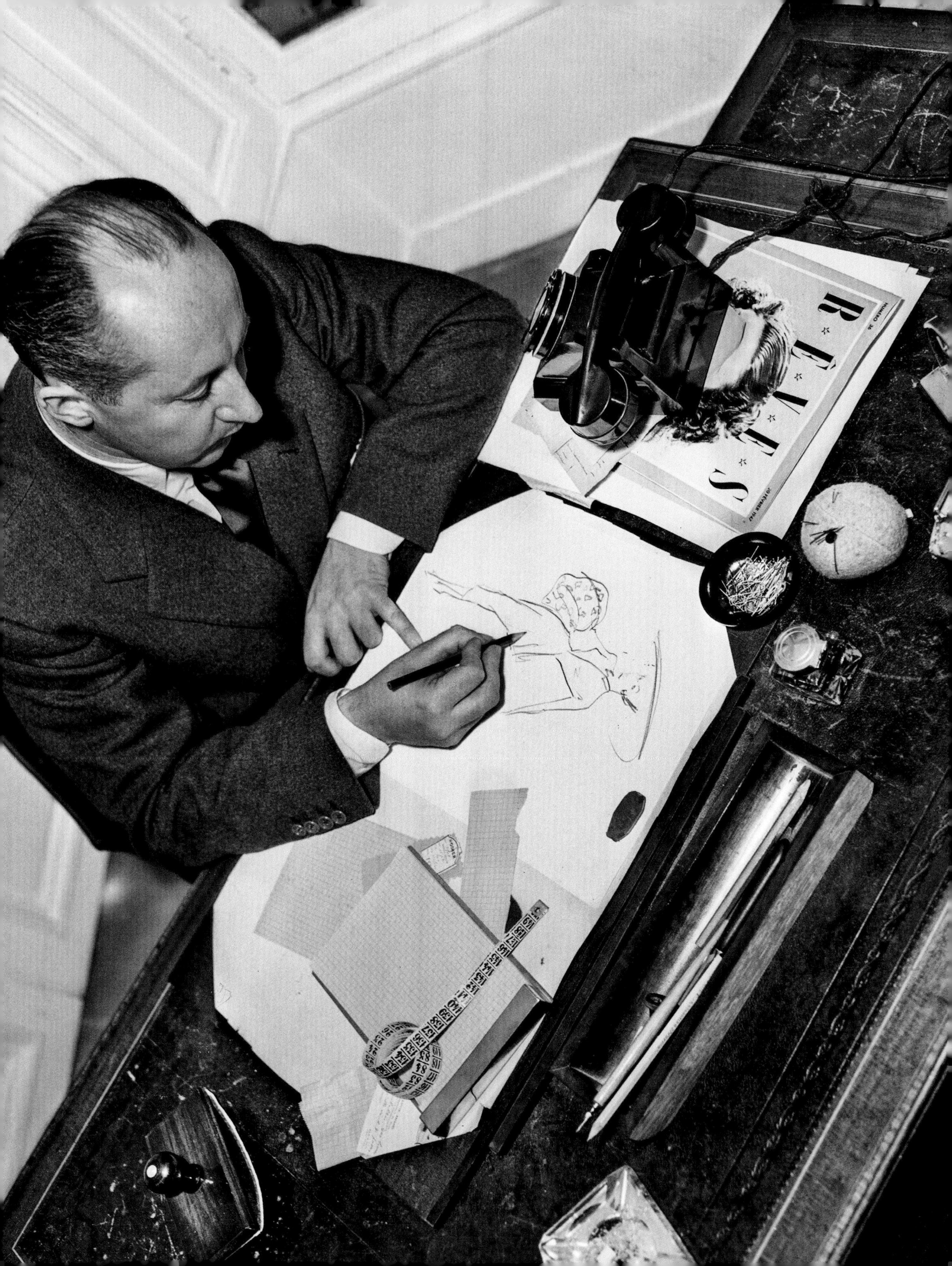

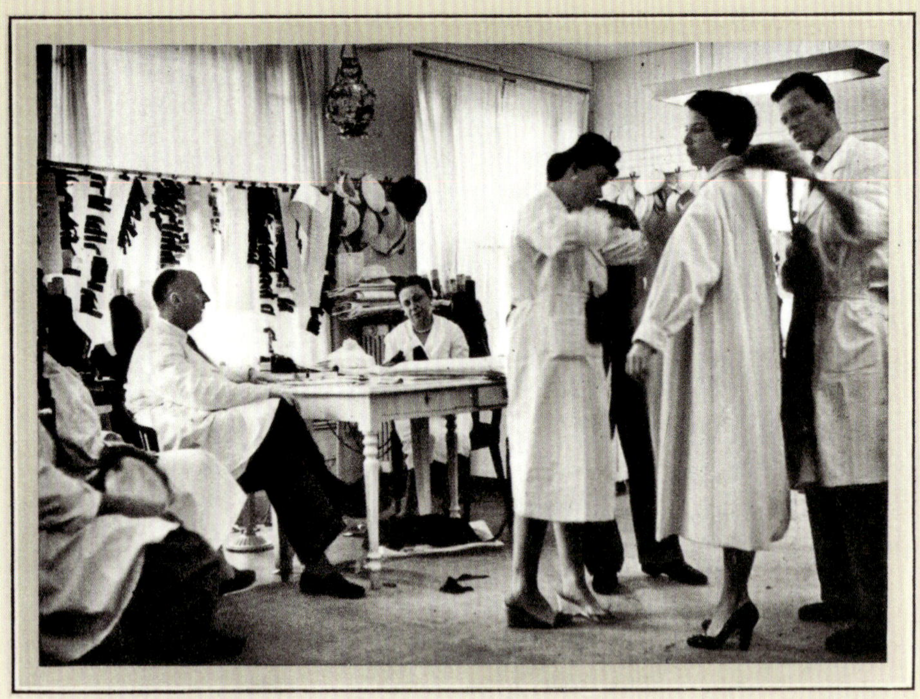

Christian Dior, prenant un peu de champ, dirige un essayage

LA MARCHE D'UNE COLLECTION

| 1. dessins | → | 2. studio | → | 3. atelier exécution des toiles | → | 4. essayage |

| 5. répétition de travail | → | 6. répétition générale | → | 7. présentation | → | presse / acheteurs / clientes |

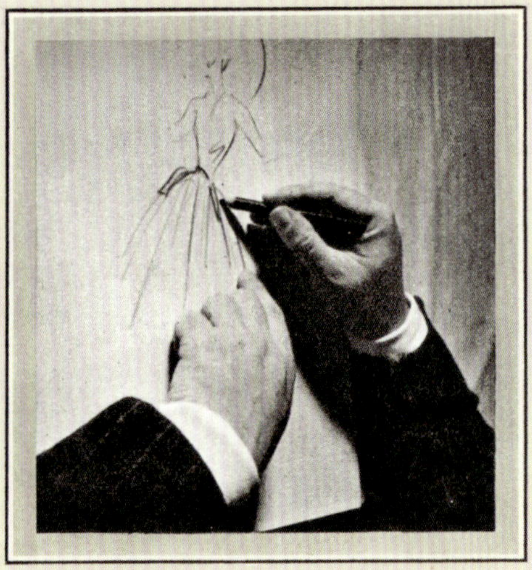

Croquis de travail

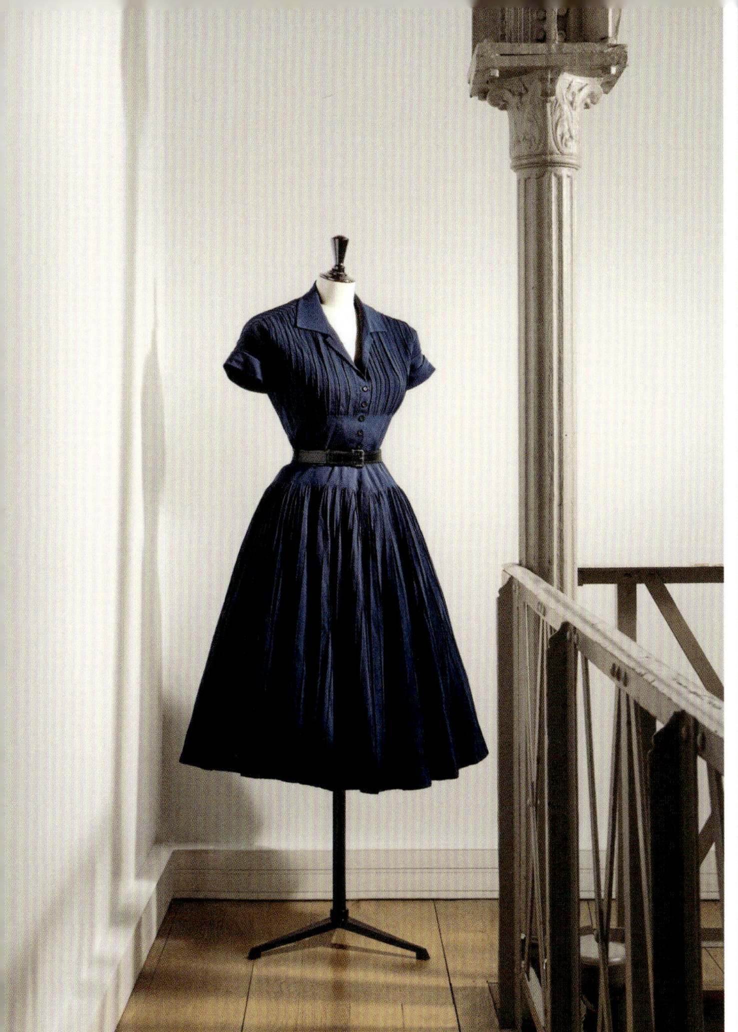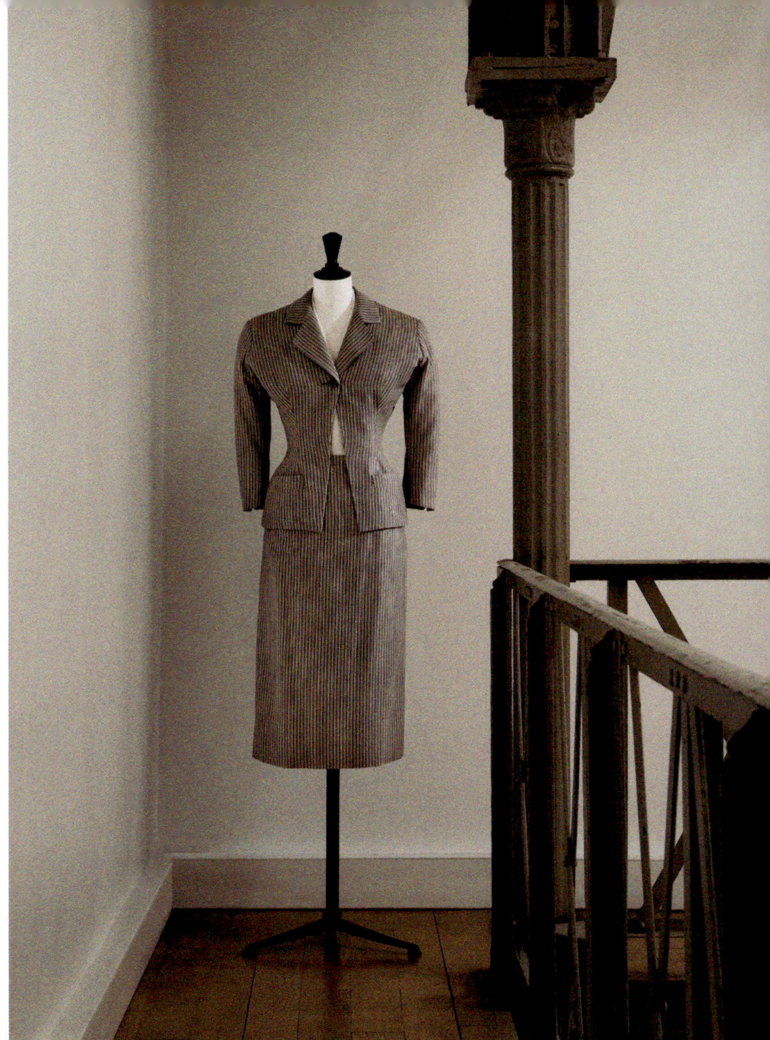

"Comment Christian Dior crée ses robes"
(How Christian Dior creates his models),
page from the presentation booklet
for the couture house produced under
the direction of Geneviève Perreau, Paris,
Christian Dior, 1953. Paris, Dior Héritage.

This document describes the set-up
of a collection: 1. Sketches; 2. Studio;
3. Workroom where patterns are made;
4. Fitting; 5. Work rehearsal; 6. Final
rehearsal; 7. Presentation, press,
professional buyers, private clientele.

Christian Dior
Cocotte

Dress in wool crêpe,
Spring–Summer 1953
haute couture collection,
Tulipe line. Paris,
Fondation Azzedine Alaïa.

Christian Dior
Oxford

Afternoon suit in striped cotton
canvas, Spring–Summer 1953
haute couture collection,
Tulipe line. Paris,
Fondation Azzedine Alaïa.

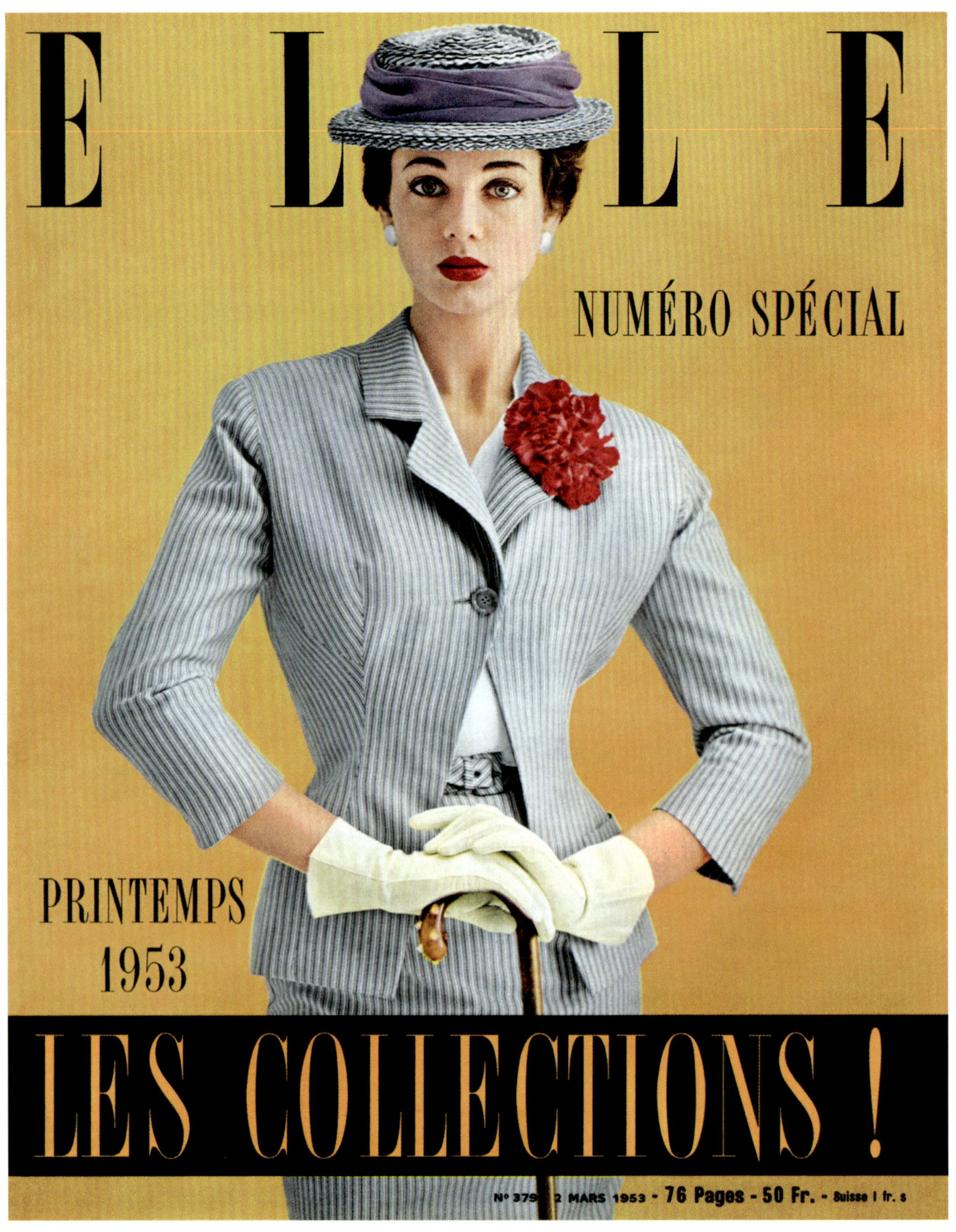

Cover of *Elle* magazine showing
the *Oxford* afternoon suit by Christian Dior,
Spring–Summer 1953 haute couture collection,
Tulipe line. Photograph by Jean Chevalier,
published in a special issue from Spring 1953.

Models wearing the *Oxford* afternoon suit.
Photographs of the model Renée by
Regina Relang (above left) and by Willy Maywald
(bottom left); photograph by Philippe Pottier,
published in *L'Officiel*, April 1953 (above right);
photograph by Georges Saad, published
in *L'Art et la Mode*, Spring 1953 (bottom right).

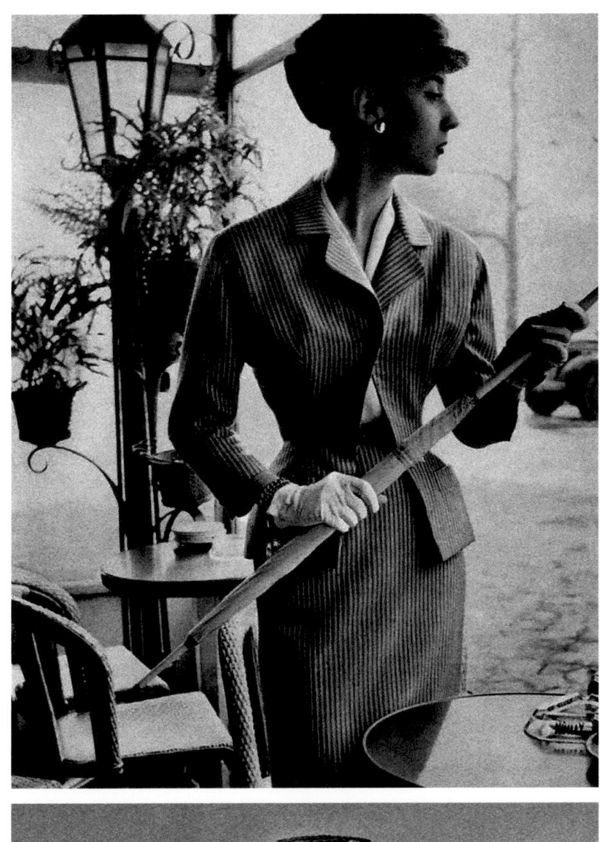
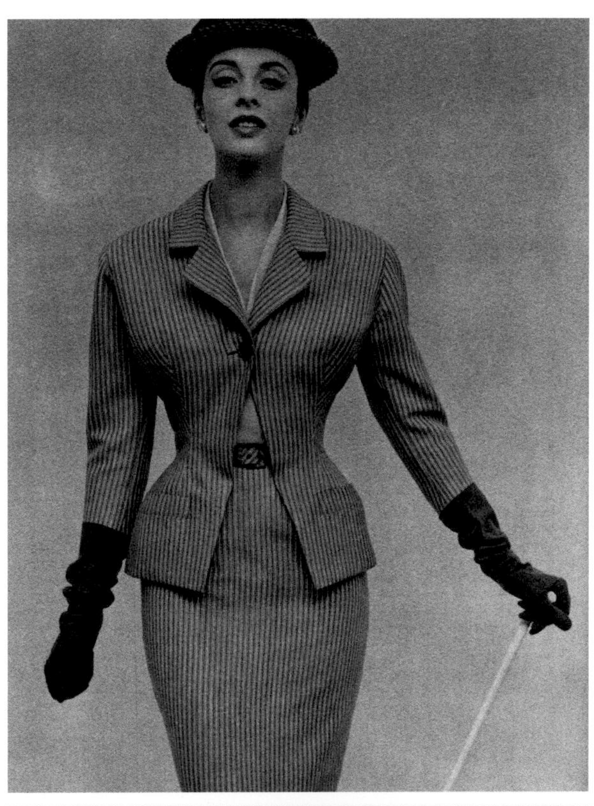
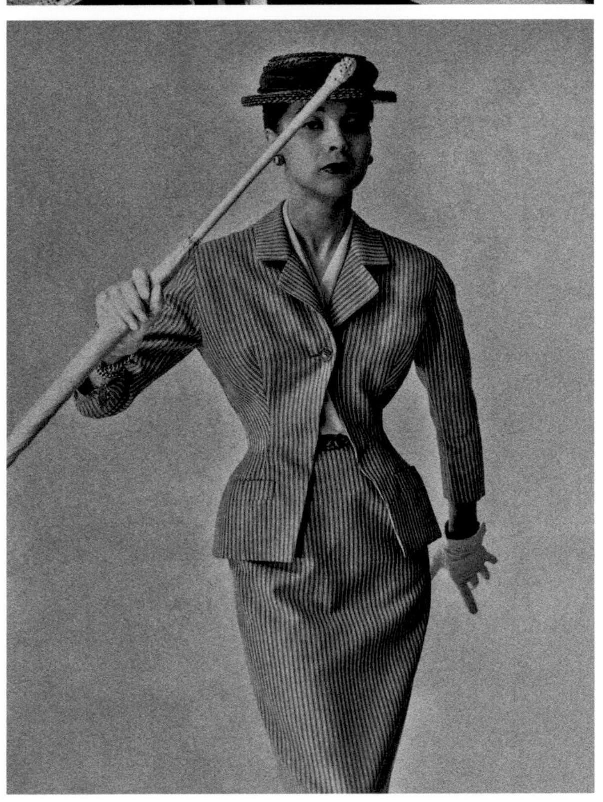
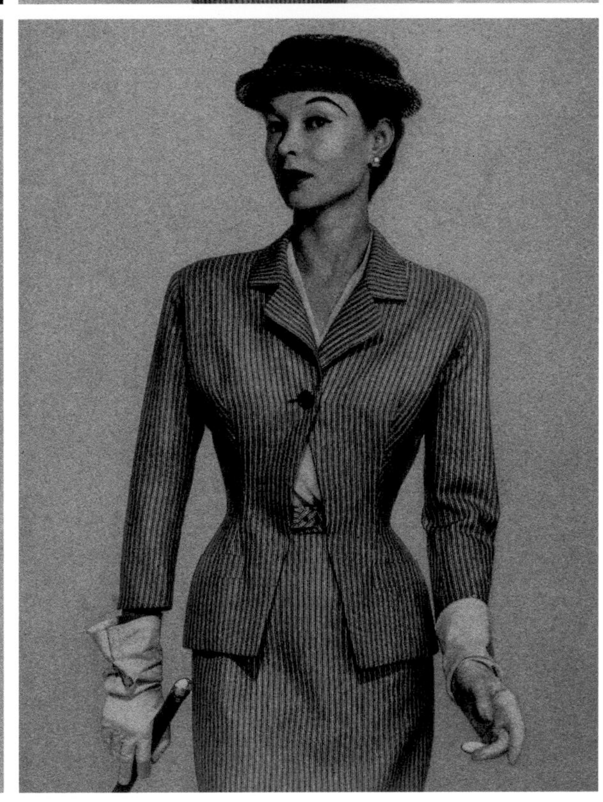

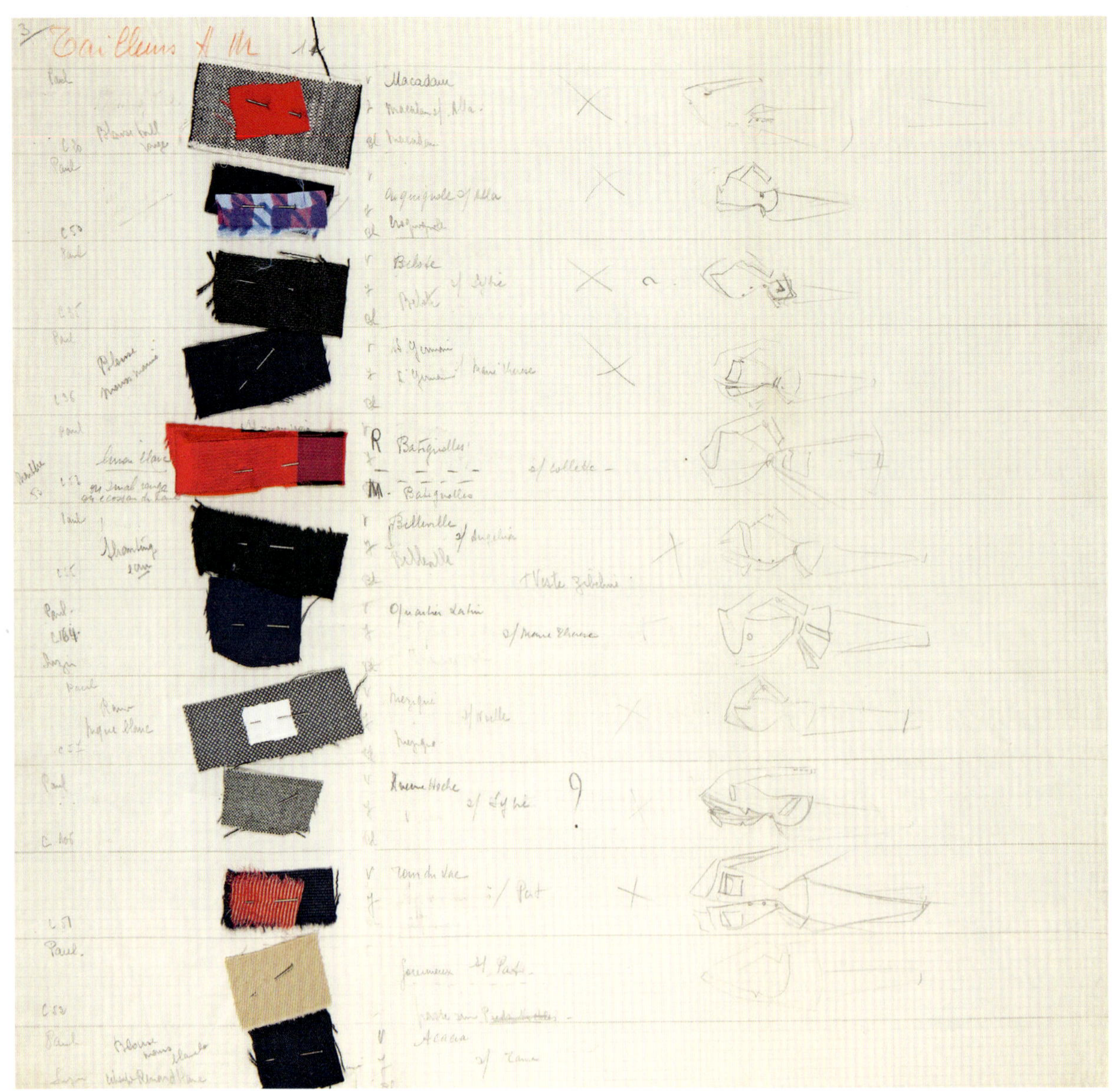

"Afternoon suits" page from the chart for
Christian Dior's Spring–Summer 1949 haute couture
collection, *Trompe-l'œil* line. Paris, Dior Héritage.

The chart enables the couturier to have an overall vision
of the collection, to balance out the garment models by type.
It lists all the information on the garment models with their
names, sketches, fabric samples, the names of the *premières*
and *premiers d'atelier* (workroom forewomen and foremen) who
supervised the production of the garments, and the first names
of the models who wore them at the presentation show.

Christian Dior
Accacias

Classic suit with "fairground" lapels
in wool crêpe, Spring–Summer 1949
haute couture collection, *Trompe-l'œil* line.
Paris, Fondation Azzedine Alaïa.

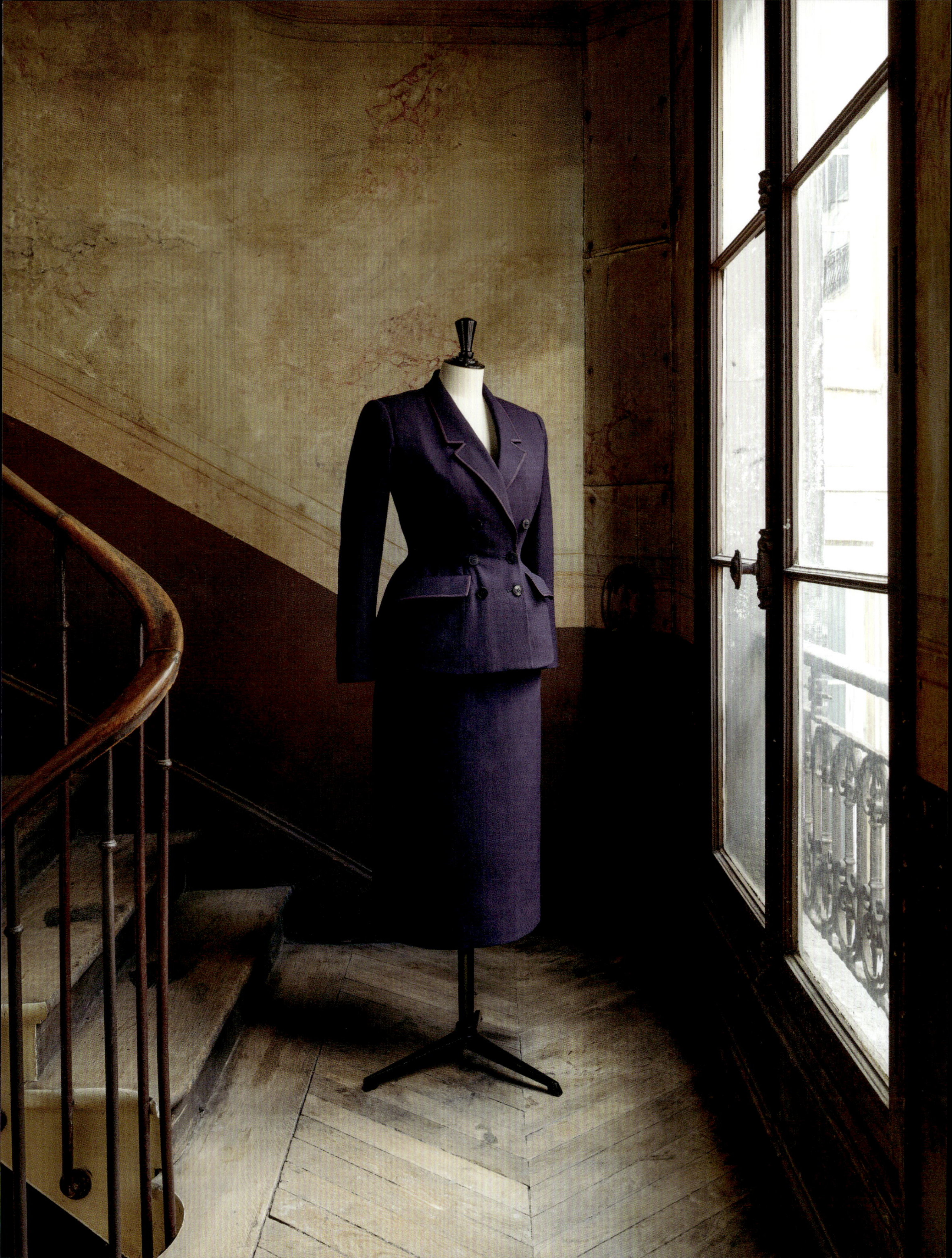

" CHRISTIAN DIOR "

COLLECTION PRINTEMPS-ETE 1949

I	ACCACIAS	Tailleur classique marine - revers "forain" - Tour de cou renard blanc.
2	AMBASSADEUR	Ensemble du soir - manteau et robe faille rose.
3	AMBIGU	Tailleur du soir court en ottoman blanc brodé de rubis et de cristal.
4	ATHENEE	Ensemble de gala - cape d'hermine et renard blanc - robe de satin blanc brodée de passementerie et de diamants.
5	AUTEUIL	Robe-chemisier en foulard imprimé beige et blanc.
6	AVENUE FOCH	Manteau vison d'élevage royal pastel.
7	AVENUE HOCHE	Tailleur classique - revers "forain", fil à fil gris - blouse en piqué blanc - cravate zibeline de Kamtchatka.
8	AVENUE MONTAIGNE	Robe après-midi en alpaga et gros grain noir jupe et corsage ligne "trompe l'oeil".
9	BAGATELLE	Ensemble de cocktail en broché fleuri sur fond noir -
IO	BAGNOLET	Robe lainage jaune primevère - jupe "trompe l'oeil".
II	BAL MUSETTE	Robe de cocktail en marquisette blanche et marine.
I2	BASTILLE	Robe-chemisier de ville blanche ceinture daim mauve - mouchoir citron.
I3	BASTRINGUE	Manteau lainage jaune.
I4	BATEAU-MOUCHE	Deux-pièces en lainage marine - col marinier -
I5	BATIGNOLLES	Ensemble d'après-midi - manteau surah écossais coquelicot et noir - robe surah noir doublée du même écossais.
I6	BELLEVILLE	Tailleur en lainage noir ligne "trompe l'oeil".
I7	BELOTTE	Tailleur lainage - ligne "trompe l'oeil".
I8	BERCY	Manteau-robe en toile pourpre garni de toile marine.
I9	BISTRO	Tailleur d'été en toile bleu-pied d'alouette.
20	BOEUF SUR LE TOIT	Deux-Pièces de dîner en faille marine - ceinture de lézard vert.

.../...

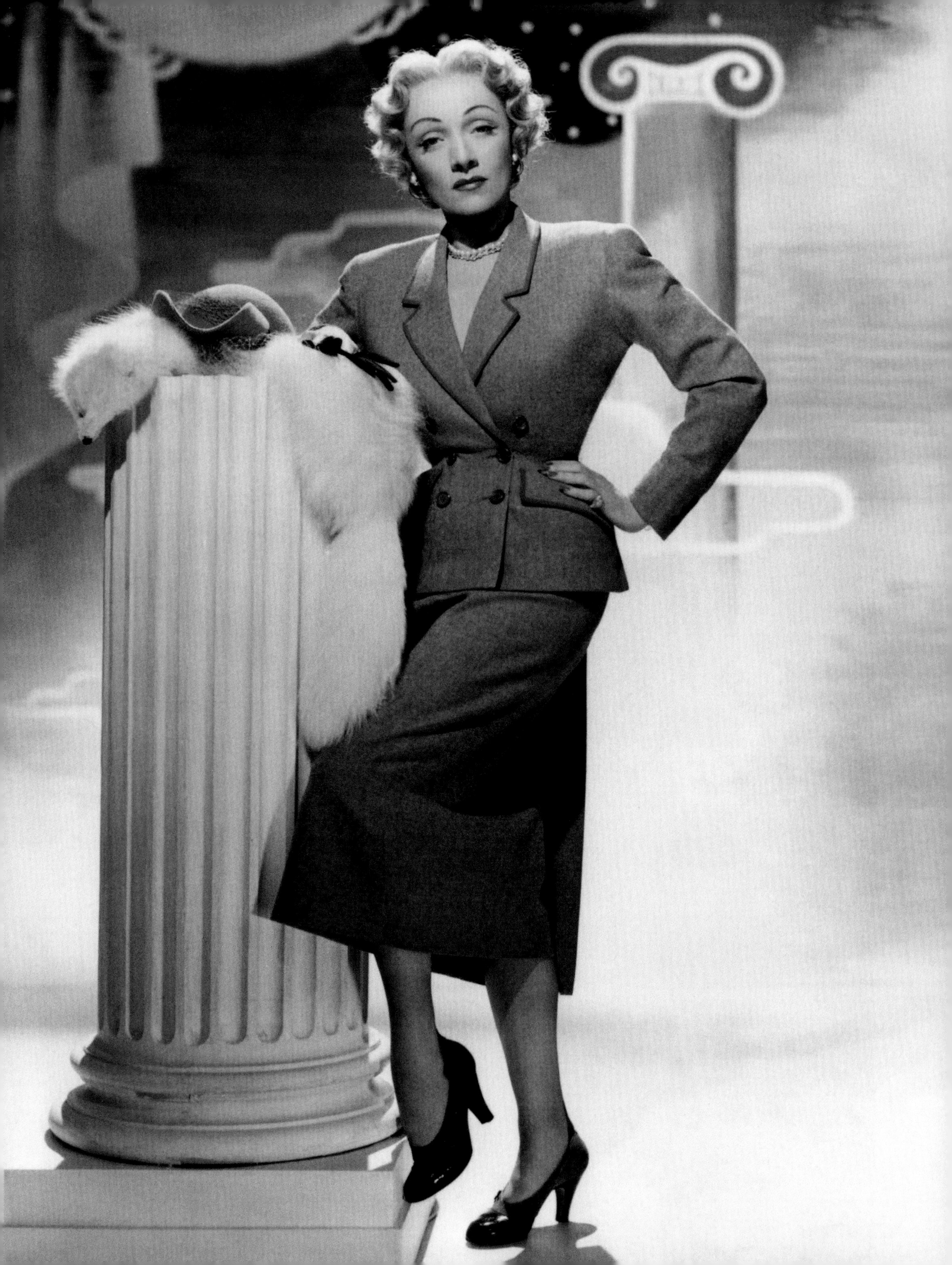

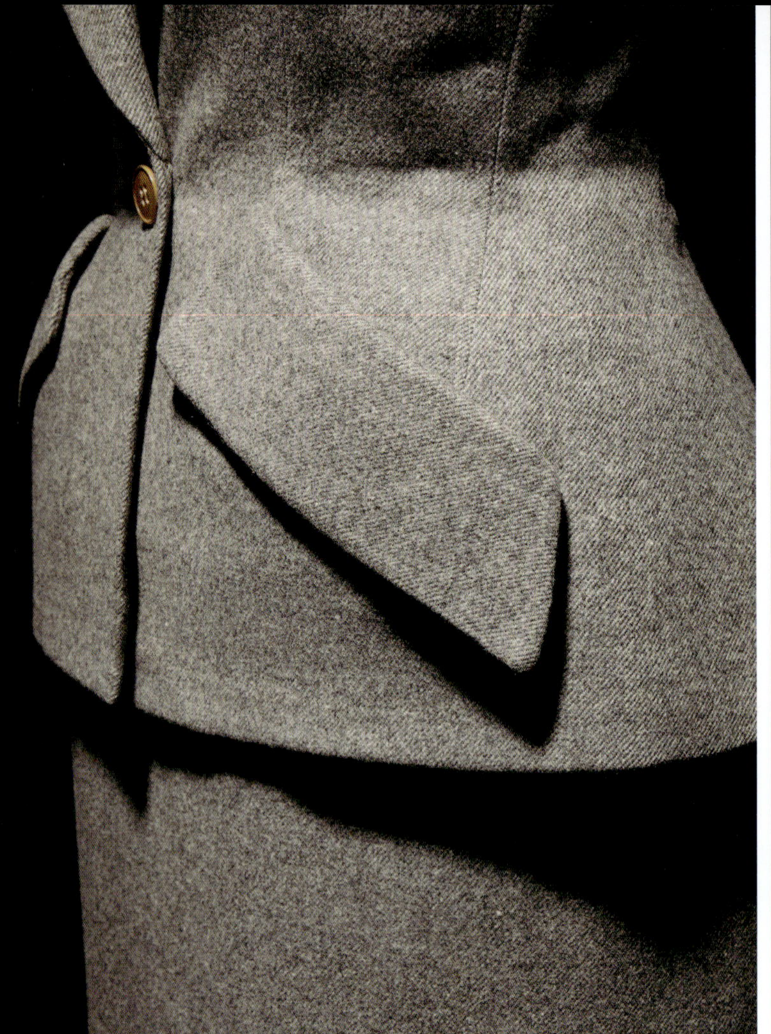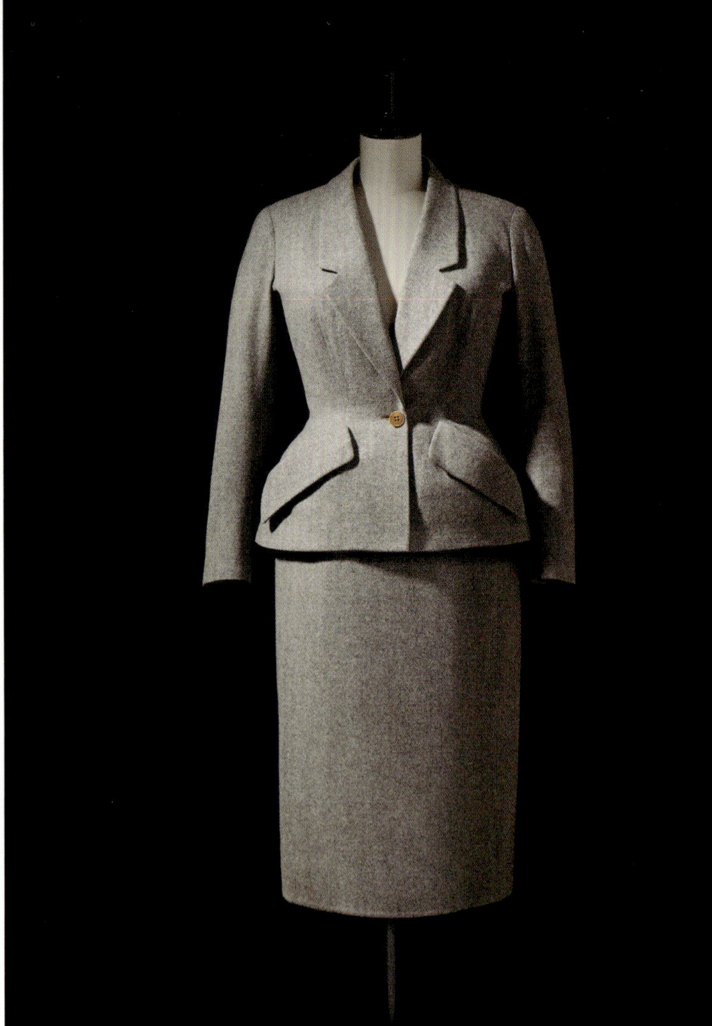

Christian Dior

Dress suit with "scissor" lapels in flannel
(with detail), Autumn–Winter 1949 haute
couture collection, *Milieu du siècle* line.
Paris, Fondation Azzedine Alaïa.

This suit is an adapted version of
Christian Dior's *En avant* model,
Autumn–Winter 1949 haute couture
collection, *Milieu du siècle* line.
The original version is in black wool,
with a slightly different neckline.

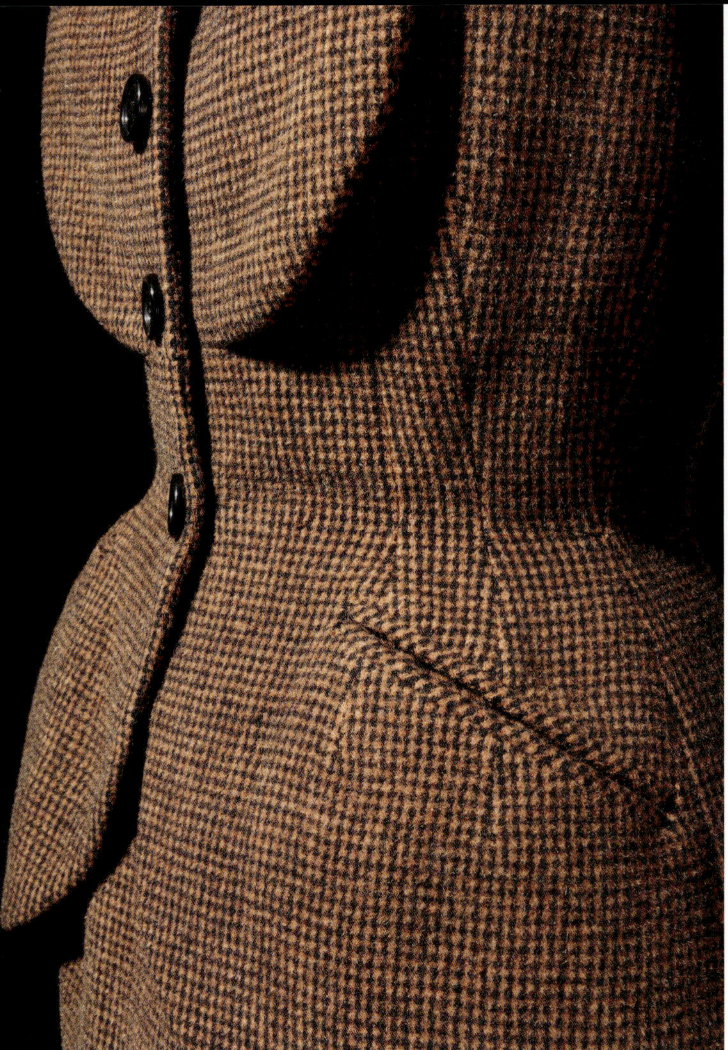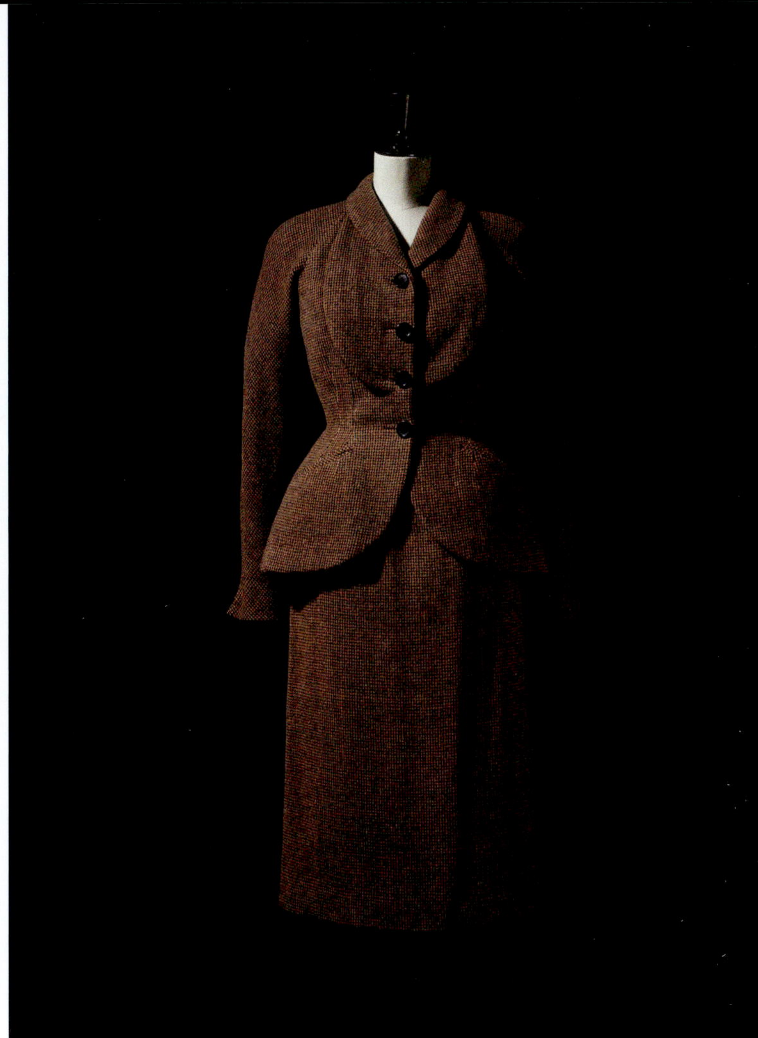

"THE COLLECTION *MILIEU DU SIÈCLE*, WHICH FOLLOWED THAT WINTER WAS VERY EXPERT: IT WAS FOUNDED ON A SYSTEM OF CUTTING, BASED ON THE INTERNAL GEOMETRY OF THE MATERIAL, STRAIGHT GRAIN AND BIAS CRISSCROSSED, RADIATED LIKE WINDMILLS." **CHRISTIAN DIOR**

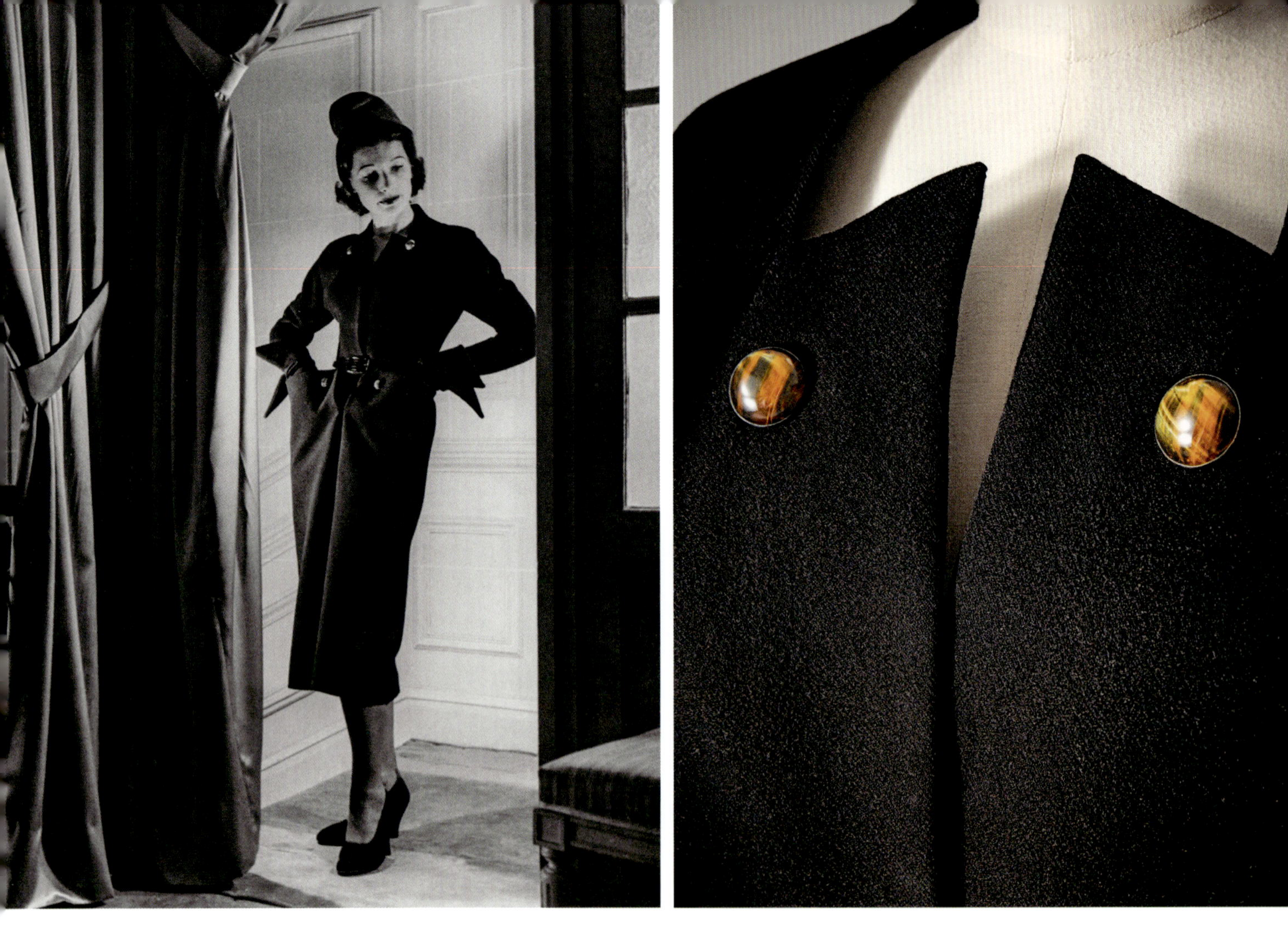

ABOVE LEFT
Model wearing the dress of
the Christian Dior *Dandy* ensemble
in the salons at 30 Avenue Montaigne,
Paris. Photograph by Willy Maywald.

ABOVE RIGHT AND OPPOSITE
Christian Dior
Dandy

Dress in wool (with detail),
Autumn–Winter 1948
haute couture collection, *Ailée* line.
Paris, Fondation Azzedine Alaïa.

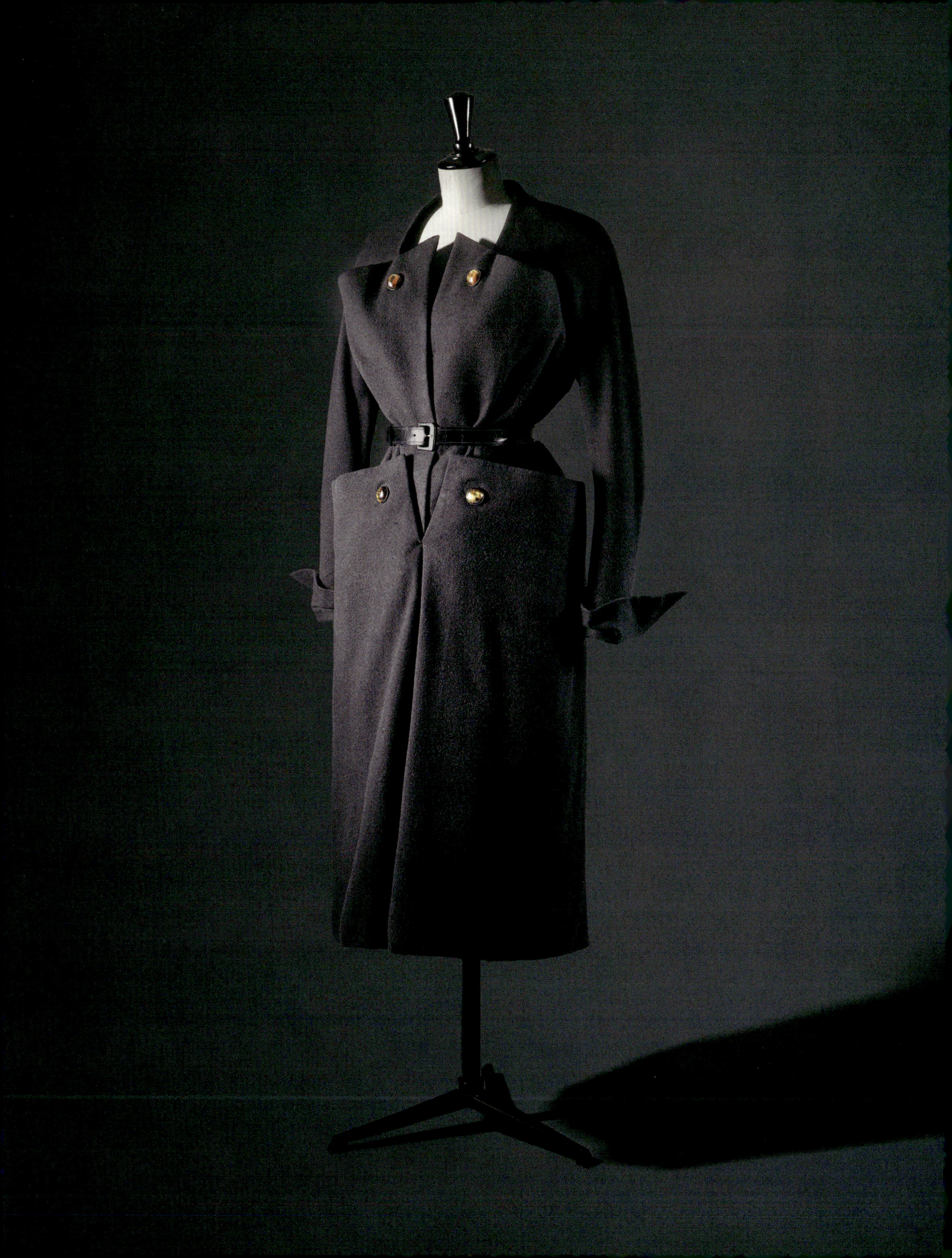

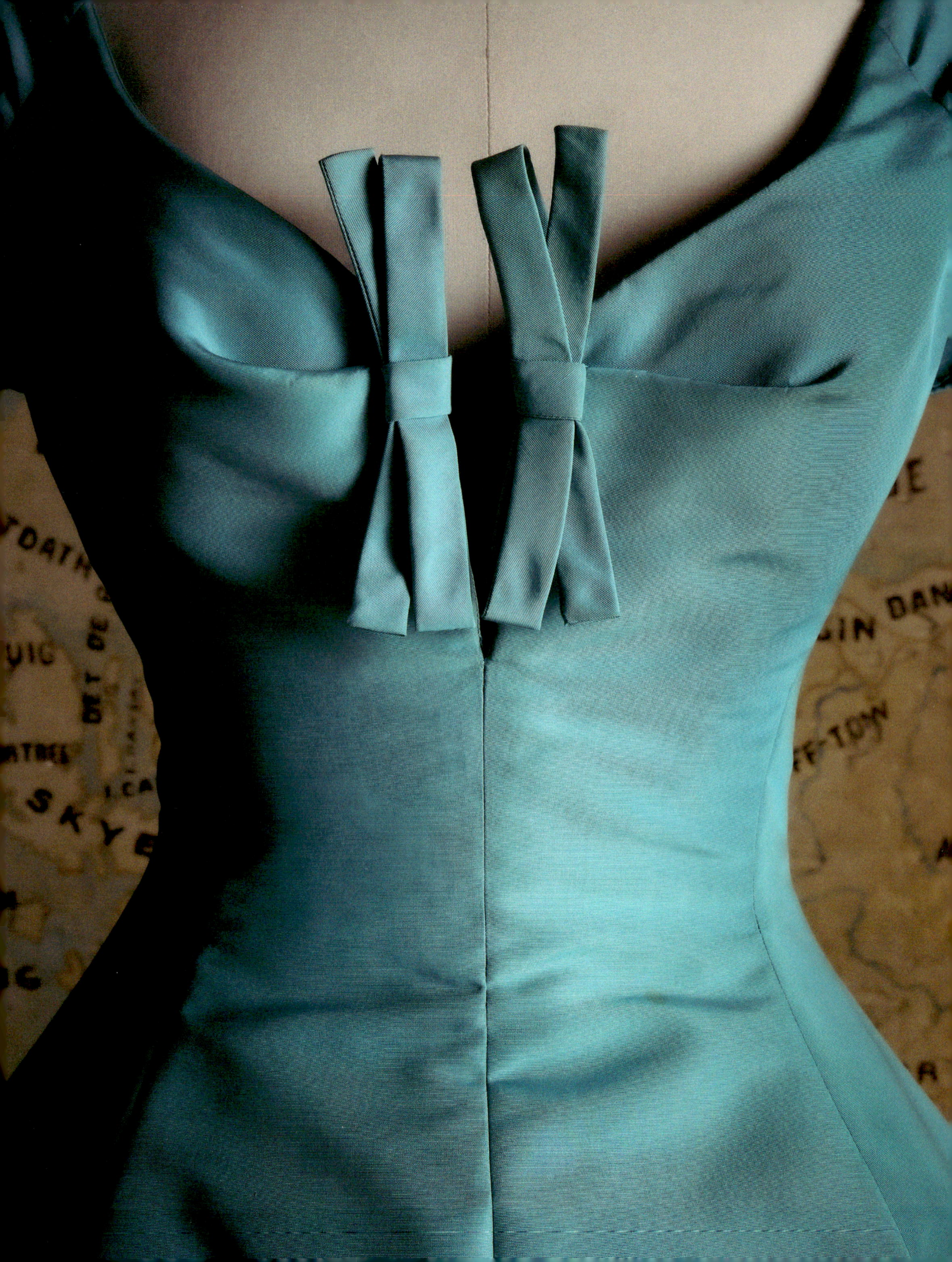

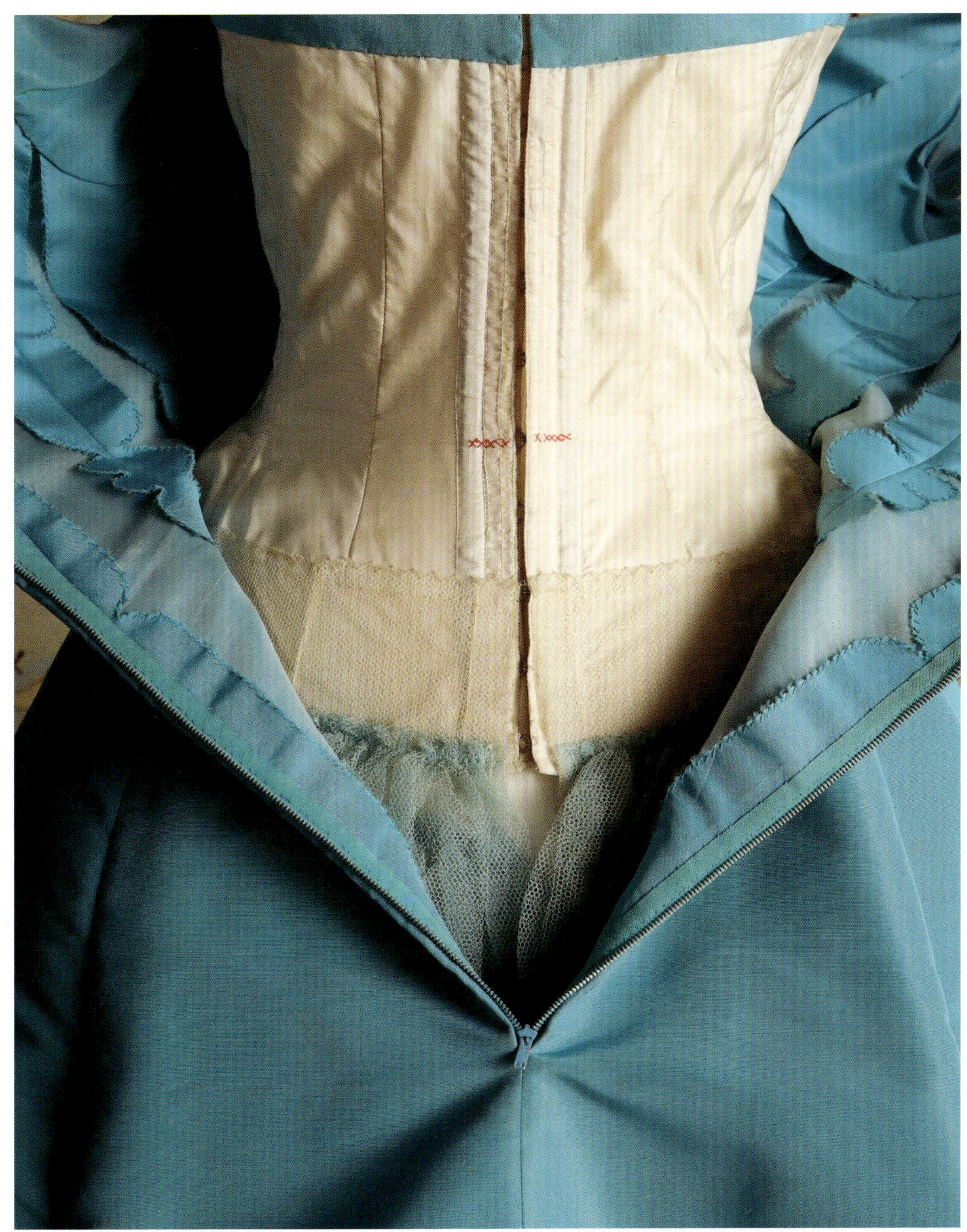

Yves Saint Laurent for Christian Dior
Madrid

Early-evening dress in Aleoutienne (with inside
detail), Spring–Summer 1958 haute couture collection,
Trapèze line. Paris, Fondation Azzedine Alaïa.

The original version of this model is in "black diamond."

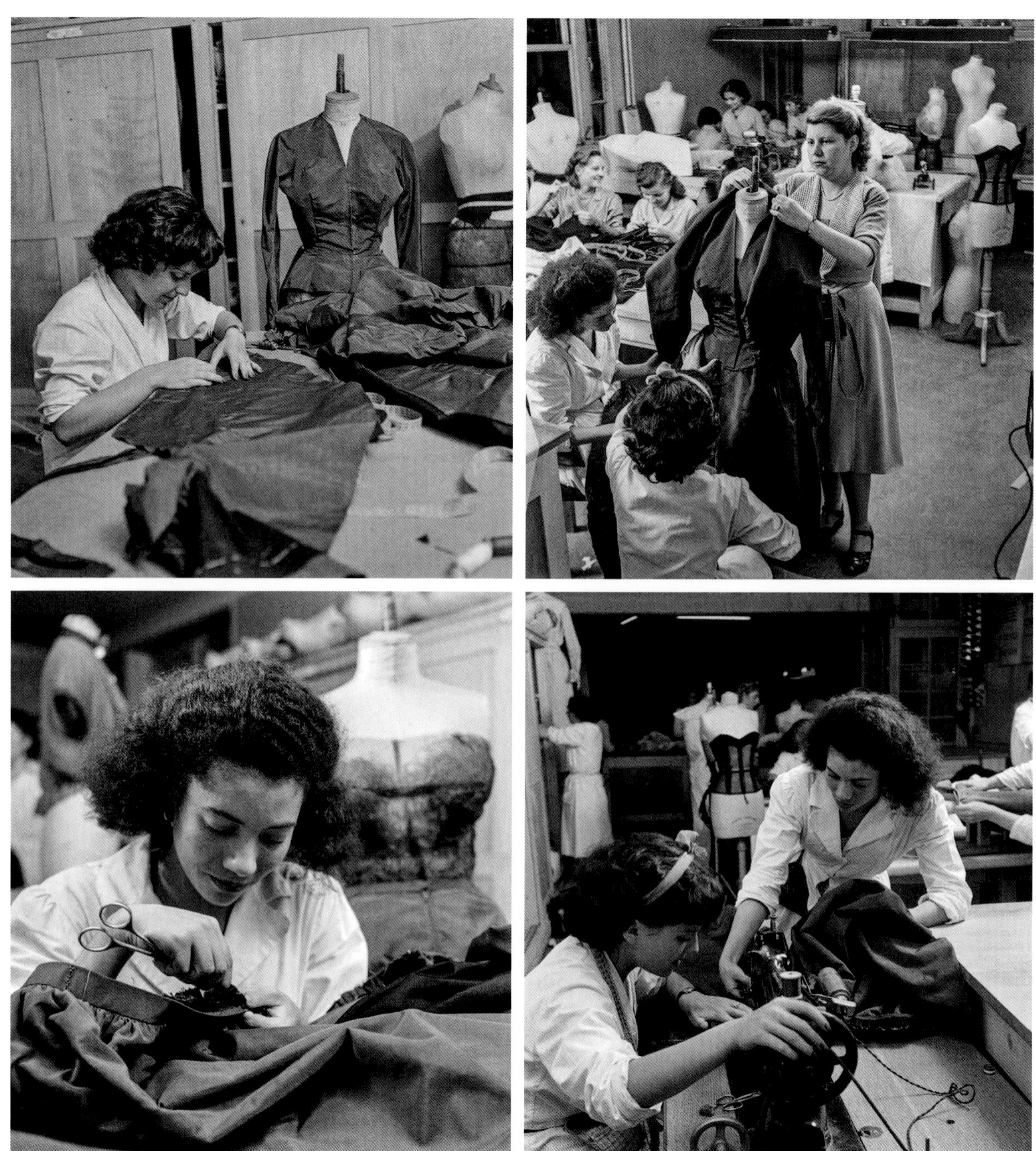

Making and fitting a dress in
the ateliers and a fitting room of the
Christian Dior couture house, Paris, 1950s.
Photographs by Eugene Kammerman.

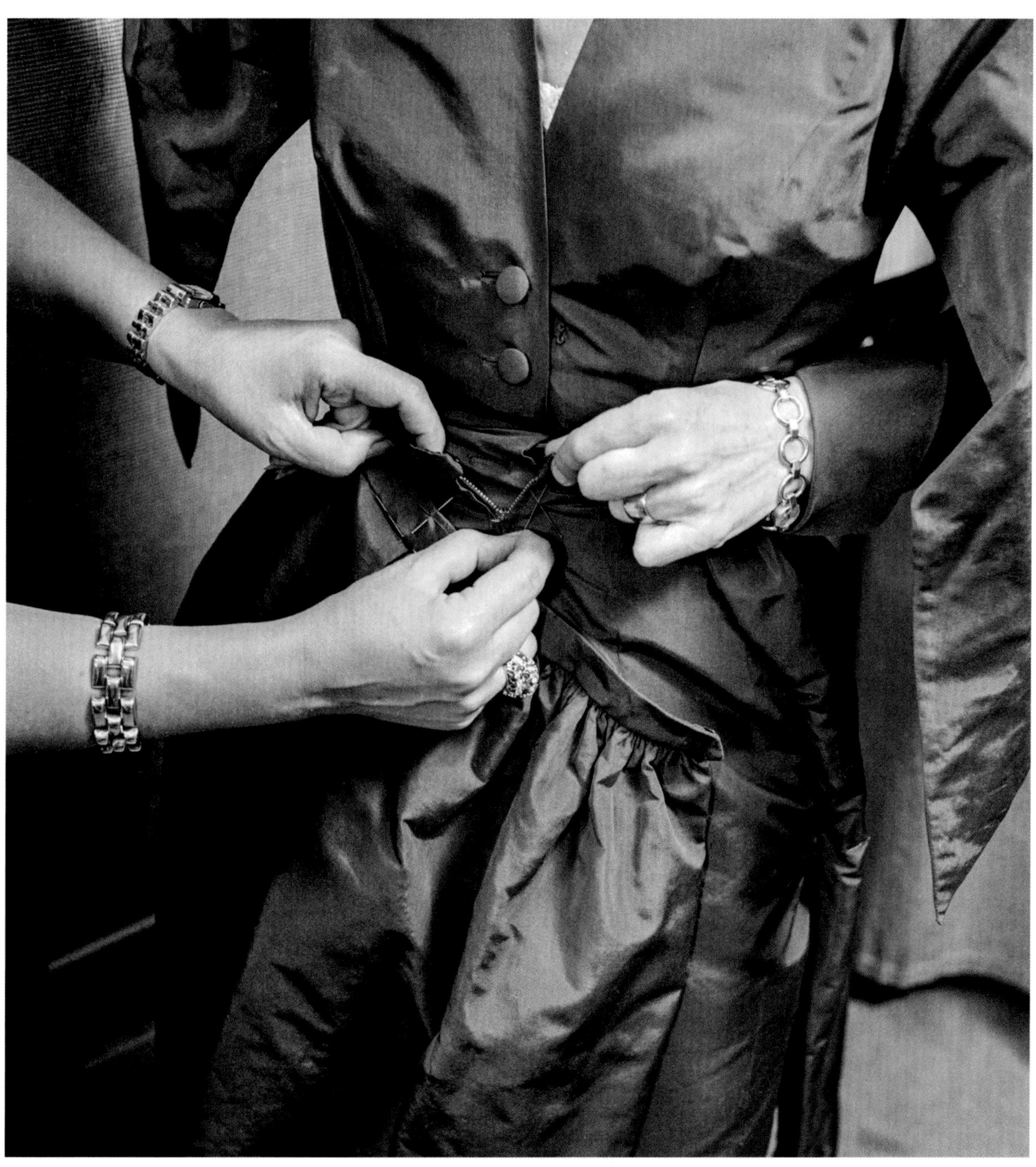

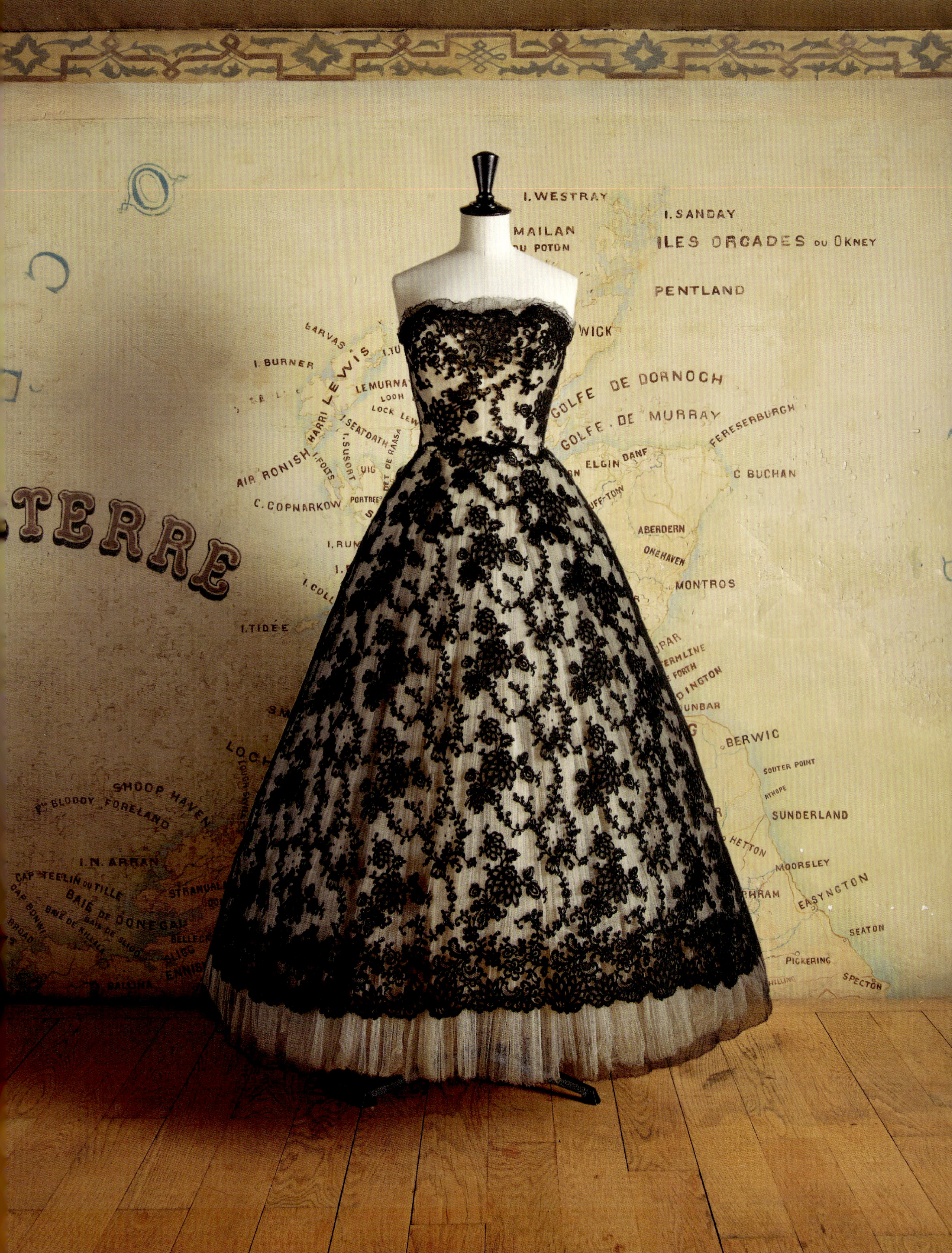
I. WESTRAY
MAILAN
DU POTON
I. SANDAY
ILES ORCADES DU OKNEY
PENTLAND
WICK
GARVAS
I. BURNER
LEWIS
LEMURNA
LOOH
LOCK LEW
GOLFE DE DORNOCH
GOLFE . DE MURRAY
FERESERBURGH
AIR RONISH HARRI
I.FOLTS
I.SEATDATH
I.SUSORT
VIG
ELGIN DANF
C BUCHAN
C. COPNARKOW
PORTREES
DET DE RAASA
ABERDERN
ONEHAVEN
I. RUM
MONTROS
I. COLL
I.TIDÉE
TERRE
UPAR
ERMLINE
E FORTH
DINGTON
UNBAR
BERWIC
LOCH
SOUTER POINT
RYHOPE
SHOOP HAVEN
F. BLODDY FORELAND
SUNDERLAND
HETTON
MOORSLEY
I.N. ARRAN
CAP TEELIN DU TILLE
PHRAM
EASYNGTON
BAIE DE DONEGAU
BAIE DE SAIGO
SEATON
BAIE DE NILALA
STRAMUAL
BELLEC
PICKERING
SLIGO
BROAD
SPECTON
BALLINA
ENNIS

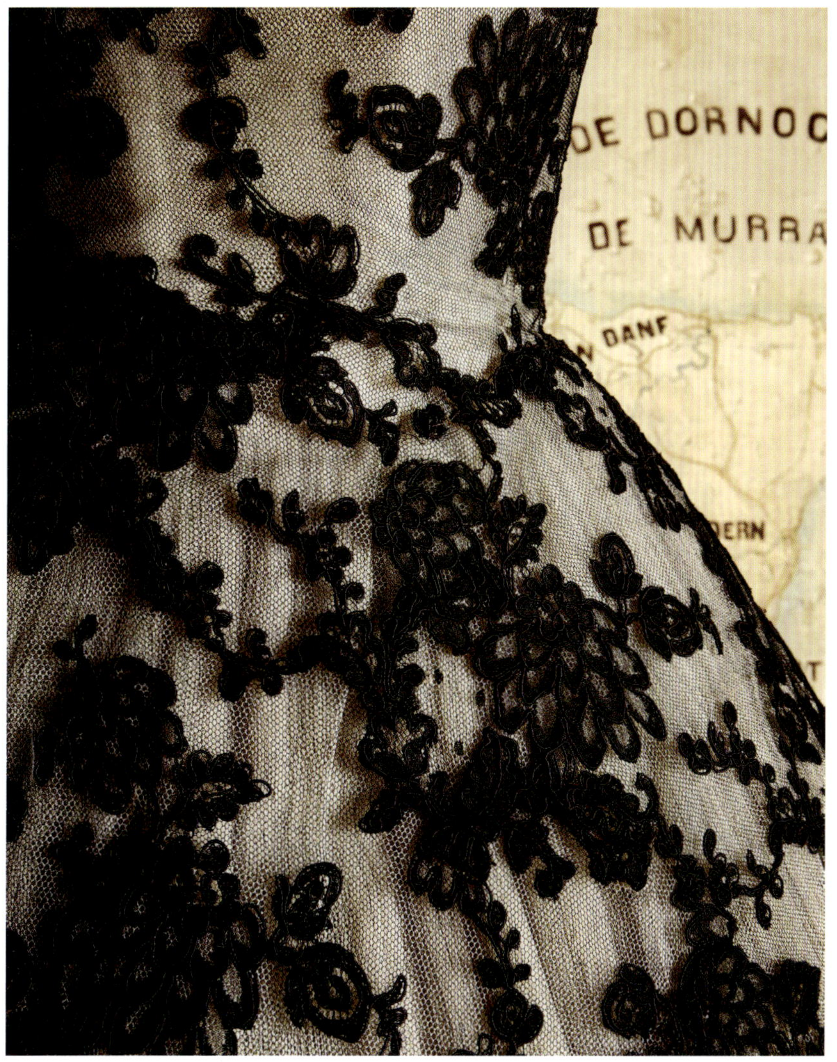

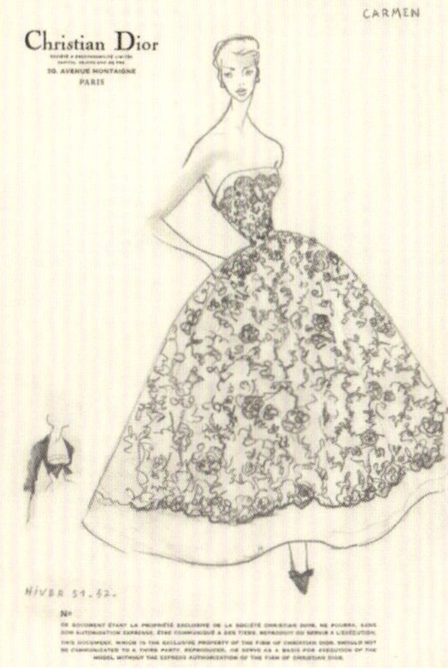

Christian Dior
Carmen

Early-evening dress in lace
over tulle (with detail),
Autumn–Winter 1951
haute couture collection,
Longue line. Paris,
Fondation Azzedine Alaïa.

Press sketch for the Christian Dior
Carmen early-evening dress.
Paris, Dior Héritage.

The press sketch, produced by
one of the studio's draftspeople,
was intended to illustrate the final
design in greater detail
for the press and clients.

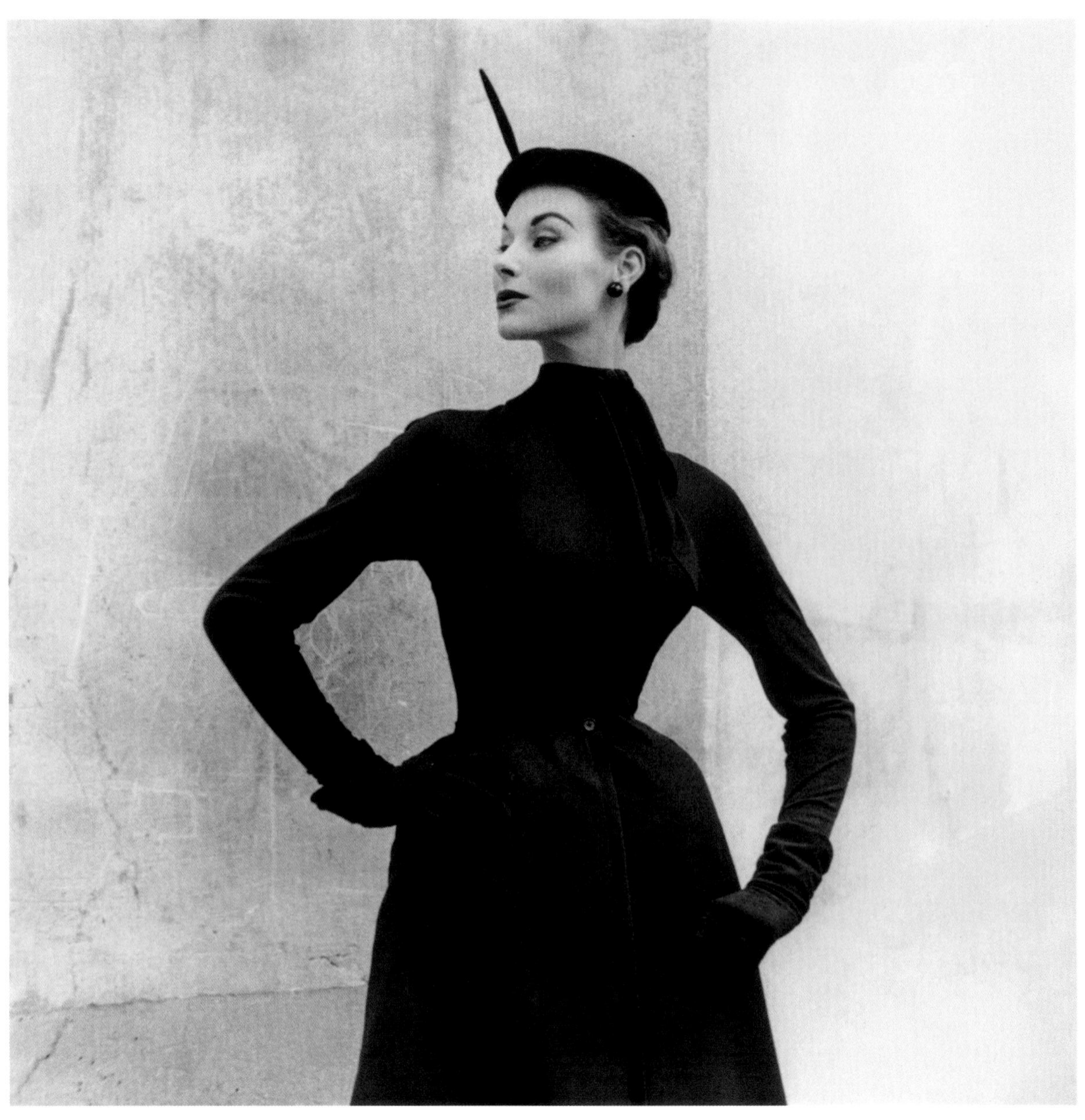

Model wearing the Christian Dior
La Fourmi ensemble, Autumn–Winter 1952
haute couture collection, *Profilée* line.
Photograph by Frances McLaughlin-Gill,
published in *Vogue*, September 1952.

Gala dress in embroidered
silk velvet, Autumn–Winter 1952
haute couture collection,
Profilée line. Paris,
Fondation Azzedine Alaïa.

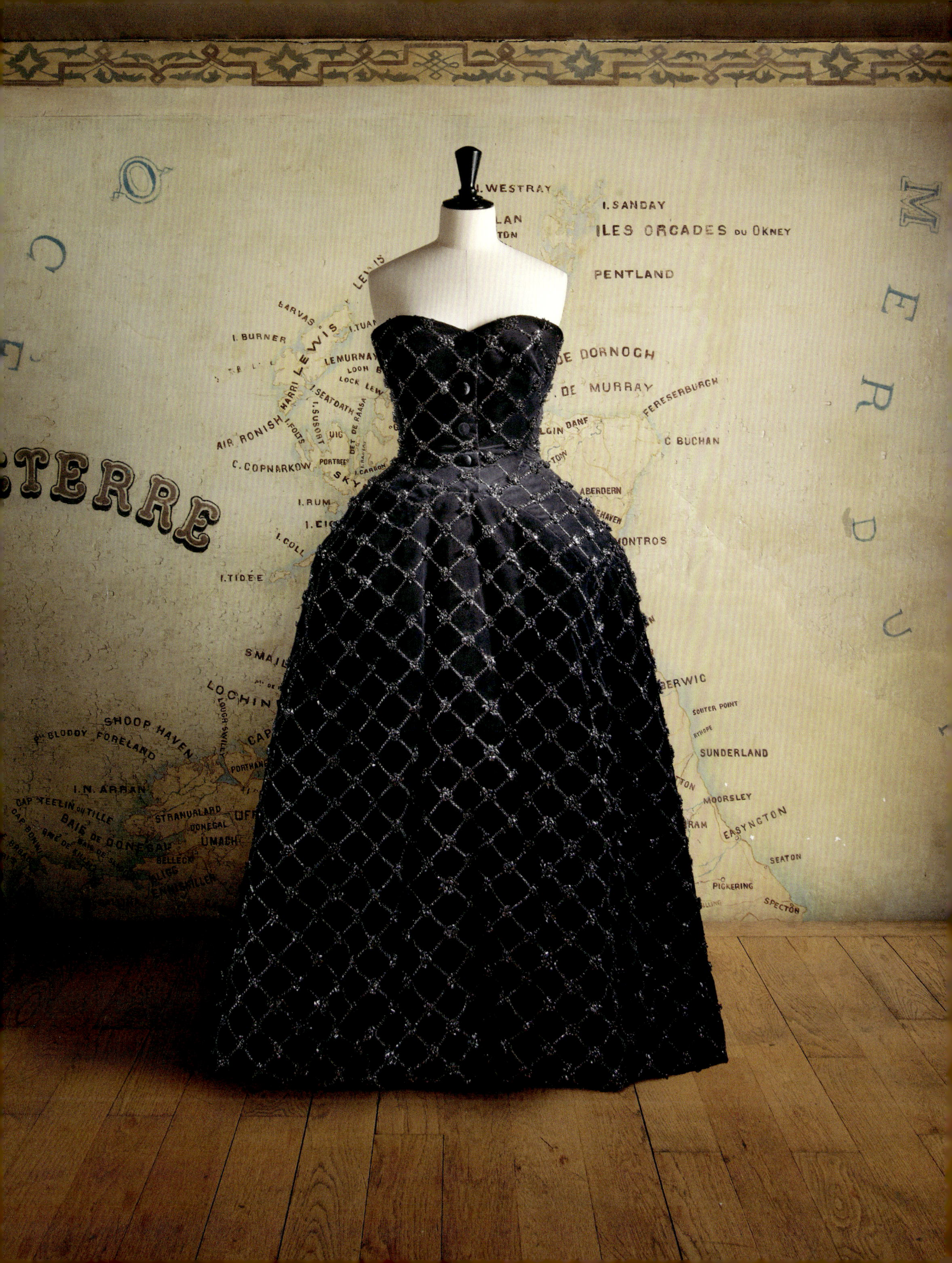

I. WESTRAY
I. SANDAY
ILES ORCADES ou OKNEY
PENTLAND
ETERRE
I. BURNER
LEWIS
LEMURNAY
DE DORNOCH
DE MURRAY
FERESERBURGH
C BUCHAN
AIR RONISH
C. COPNARKOW
ABERDERN
I. RUM
MONTROS
I. COLL
I. TIDEE
SHOOP HAVEN
FORELAND
I.N. ARRAN
SOUTER POINT
SUNDERLAND
MOORSLEY
EASYNGTON
SEATON
PICKERING
SPECTON

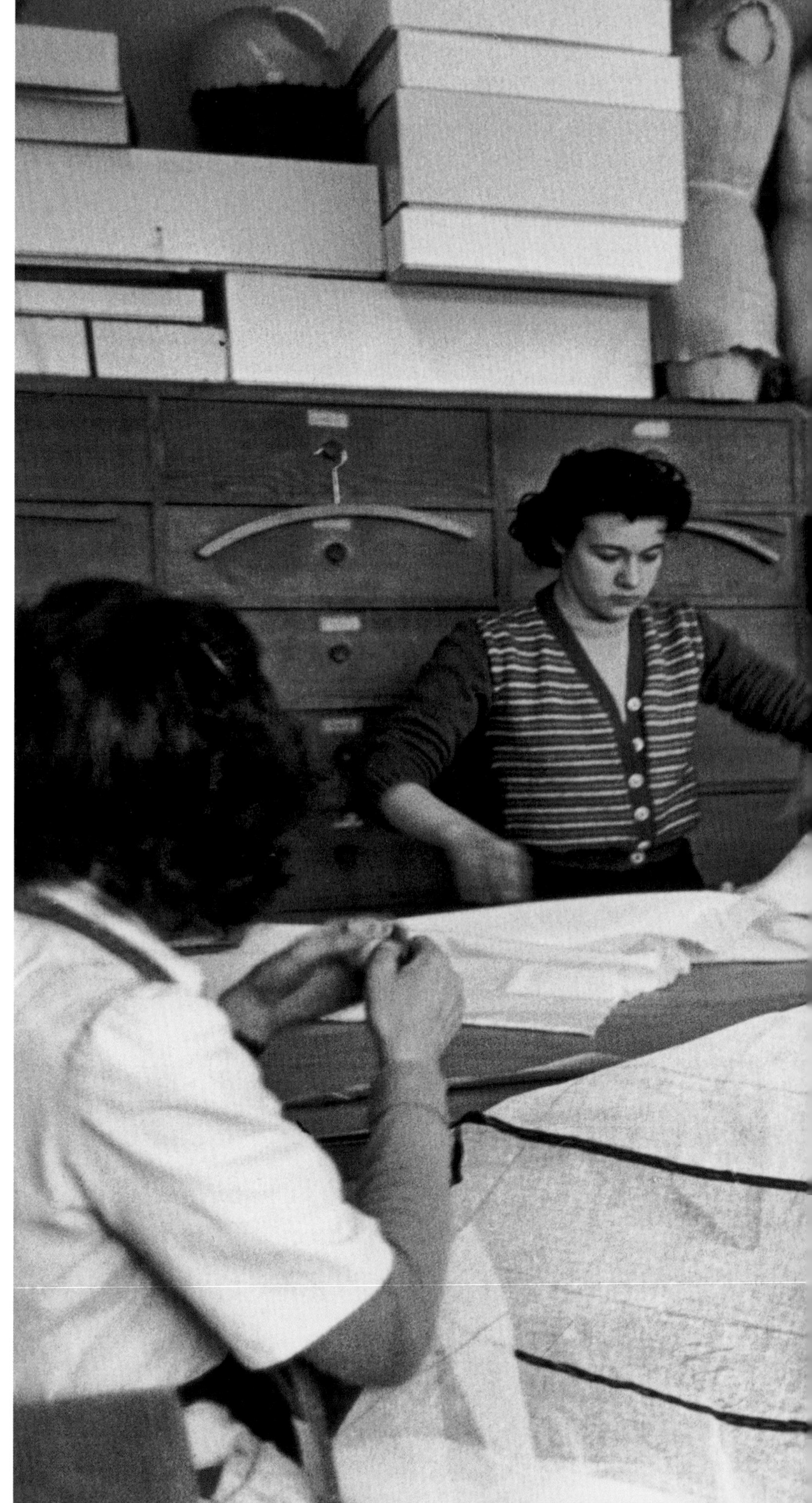

Atelier at
the Christian Dior
couture house, Paris,
circa 1947. Photograph by
Henri Cartier-Bresson.

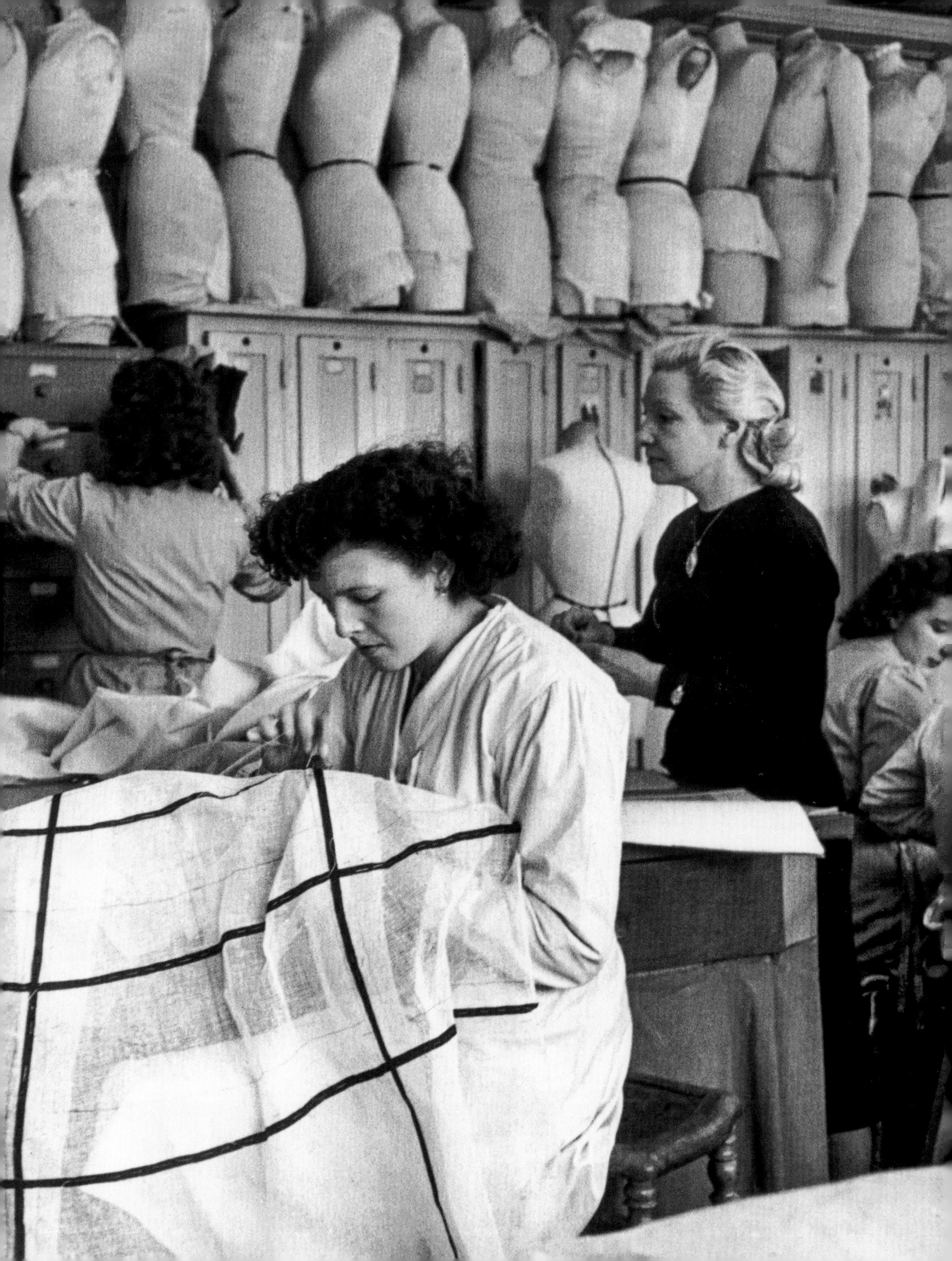

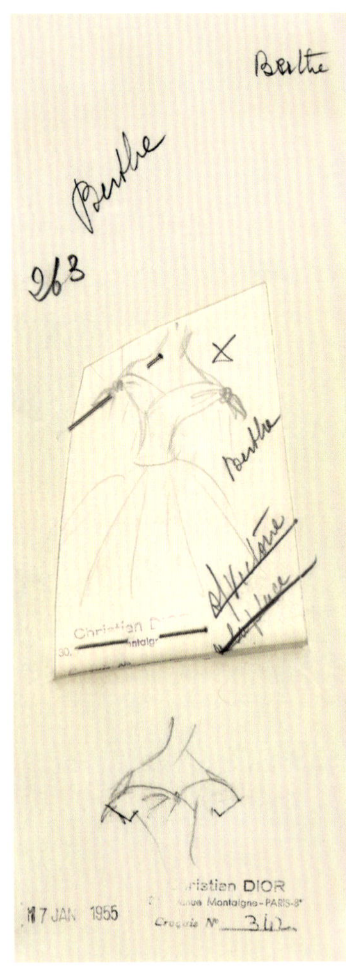

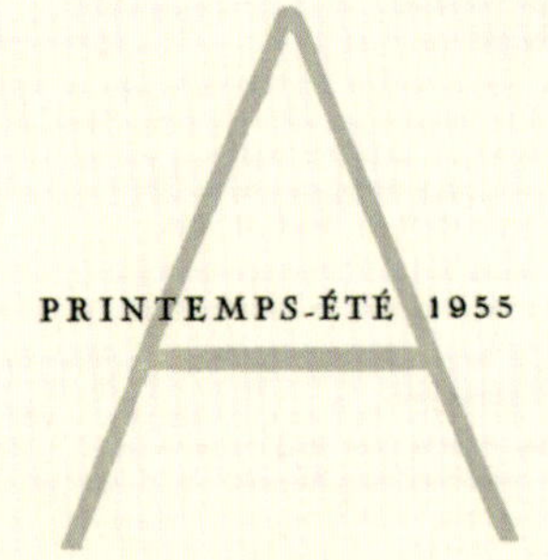

Christian Dior

PRINTEMPS-ÉTÉ 1955

LIGNE A

JEUX DE TAILLE

A la rigueur de l'hiver, au parallélisme de la ligne H, la silhouette de ce Printemps substitue une ligne plus libre, plus évasée, que symbolise parfaitement la lettre **A**, de construction très proche de l'H, mais basée sur l'**infléchissement** de **deux diagonales** dont l'angle est susceptible de mille variations.

En résumé, **évolution** sensible mais non **révolution** d'une silhouette générale dont les possibilités sont loin d'être épuisées. Si l'effet d'**allongement** du buste reste la ligne dominante, la barre transversale de l'**A** est essentiellement mouvante, bien que la taille souple et peu appuyée conserve, sans trop la marquer, sa place naturelle.

La ligne idéale qui l'indique, qu'elle soit ceinture, bouton, nœud ou empiècement peut par contre aussi bien se placer sous la taille que sensiblement au-dessus, parfois même sous la poitrine, qui demeure très haut placée.

Les **jeux de taille** sont un des points essentiels de la mode de ce Printemps, aussi capricieuse que la saison.

Les **épaules** restent naturelles.

Les **manches** sont en général courtes, comptent peu et sont même souvent absentes.

Les **cols** sont peu importants, ils aiment la forme d'un ruban plus ou moins large, non cousu au corps de la robe et plongeant dans le dos. Quelques cols chemisiers.

Les nombreuses **basques**, comme les **ceintures**, — barres idéales de l'**A** qui symbolise la Collection — ont toutes les proportions, de la plus longue à la plus courte.

Christian Dior, original sketch
for the *Astarté* cocktail dress.
Paris, Dior Héritage.

First page of the press release
for Christian Dior's Spring–Summer 1955
haute couture collection, *A* line.
Paris, Dior Héritage.

Christian Dior would write the press
releases for his collections himself,
to explain the fundamental principles of
each collection and highlight their various
elements (lines, categories, fabrics,
colors, accessories).

Christian Dior
Astarté

Cocktail dress in taffeta,
Spring–Summer 1955
haute couture collection, *A* line.
Paris, Fondation Azzedine Alaïa.

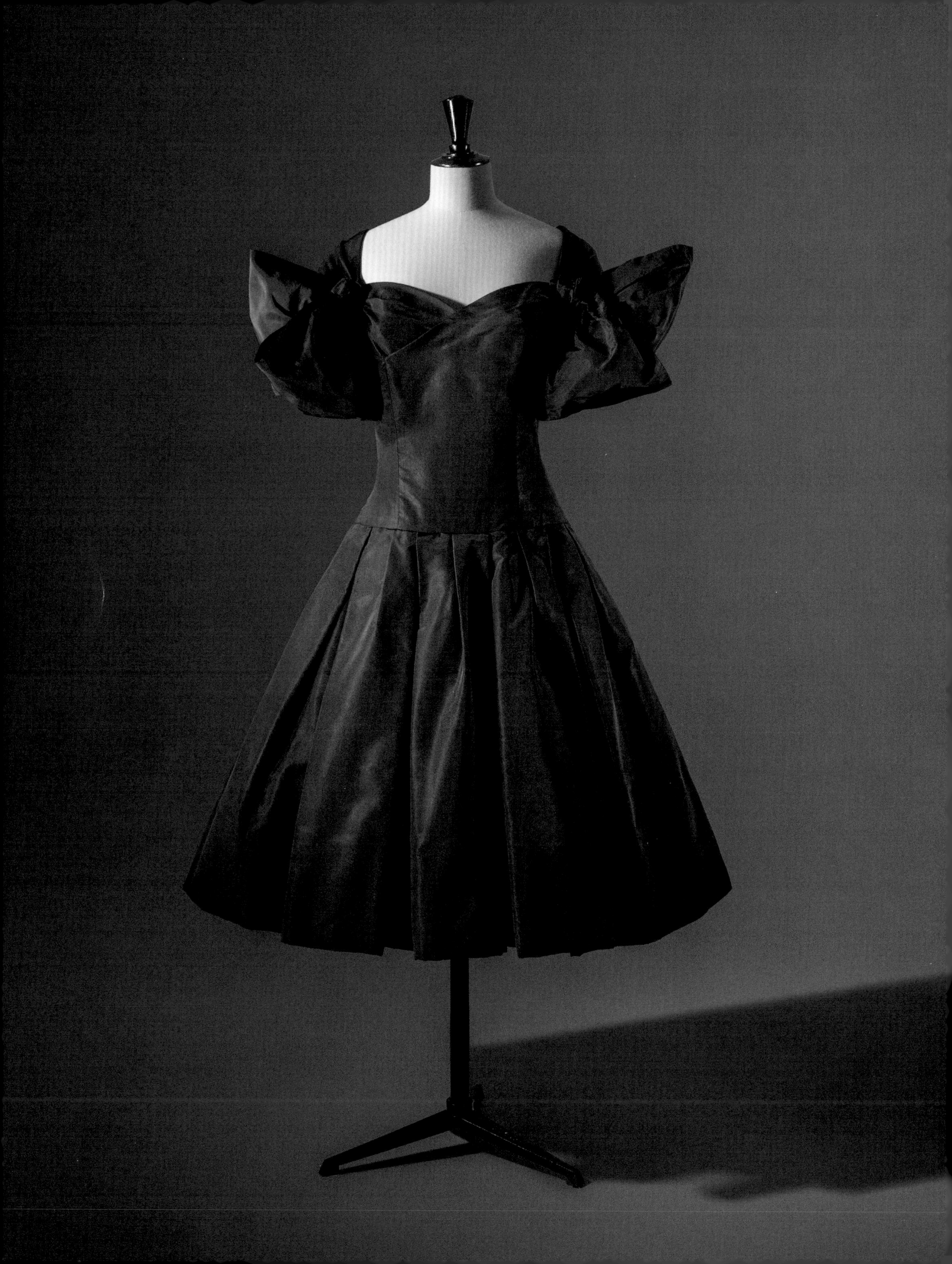

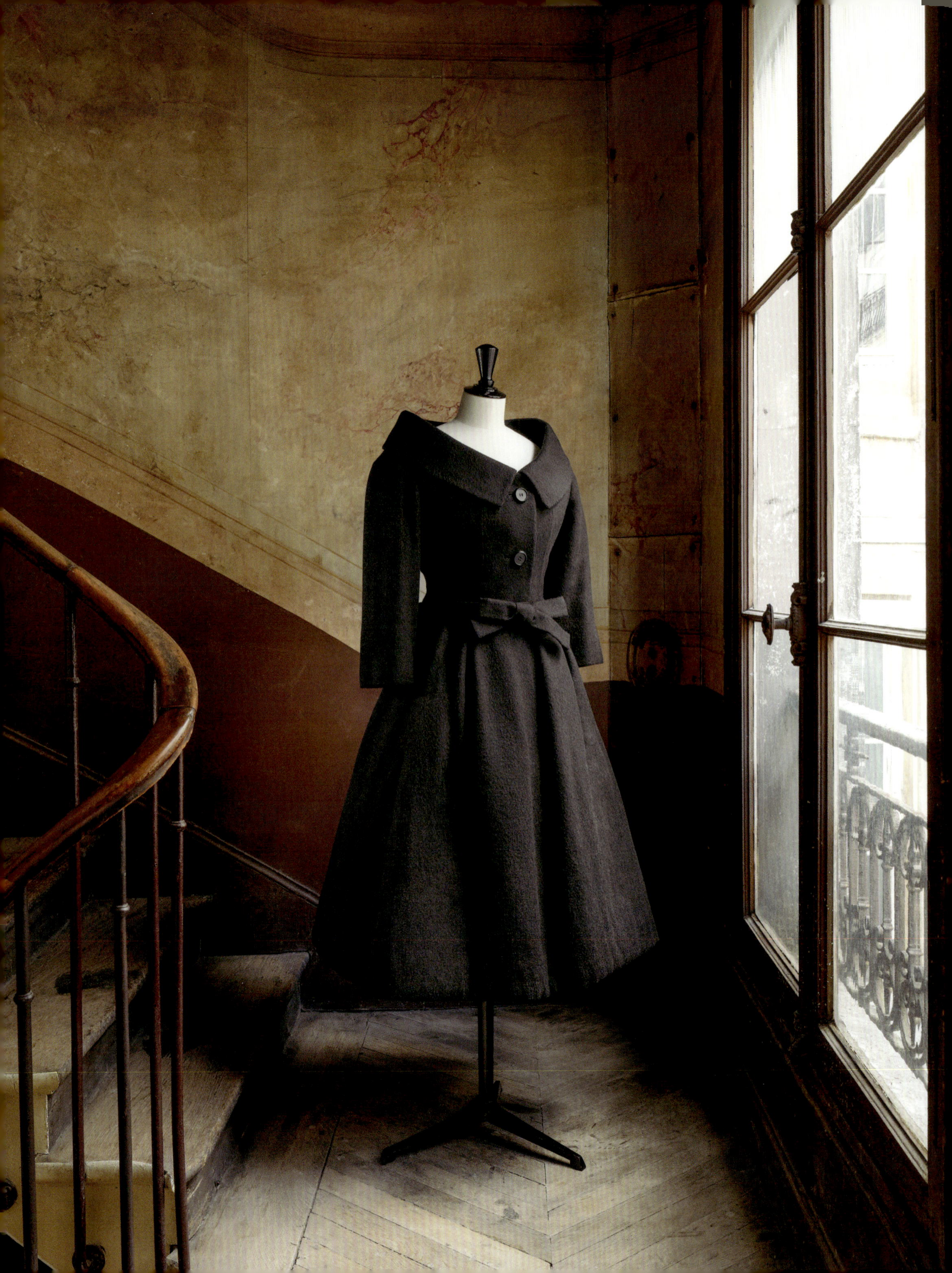

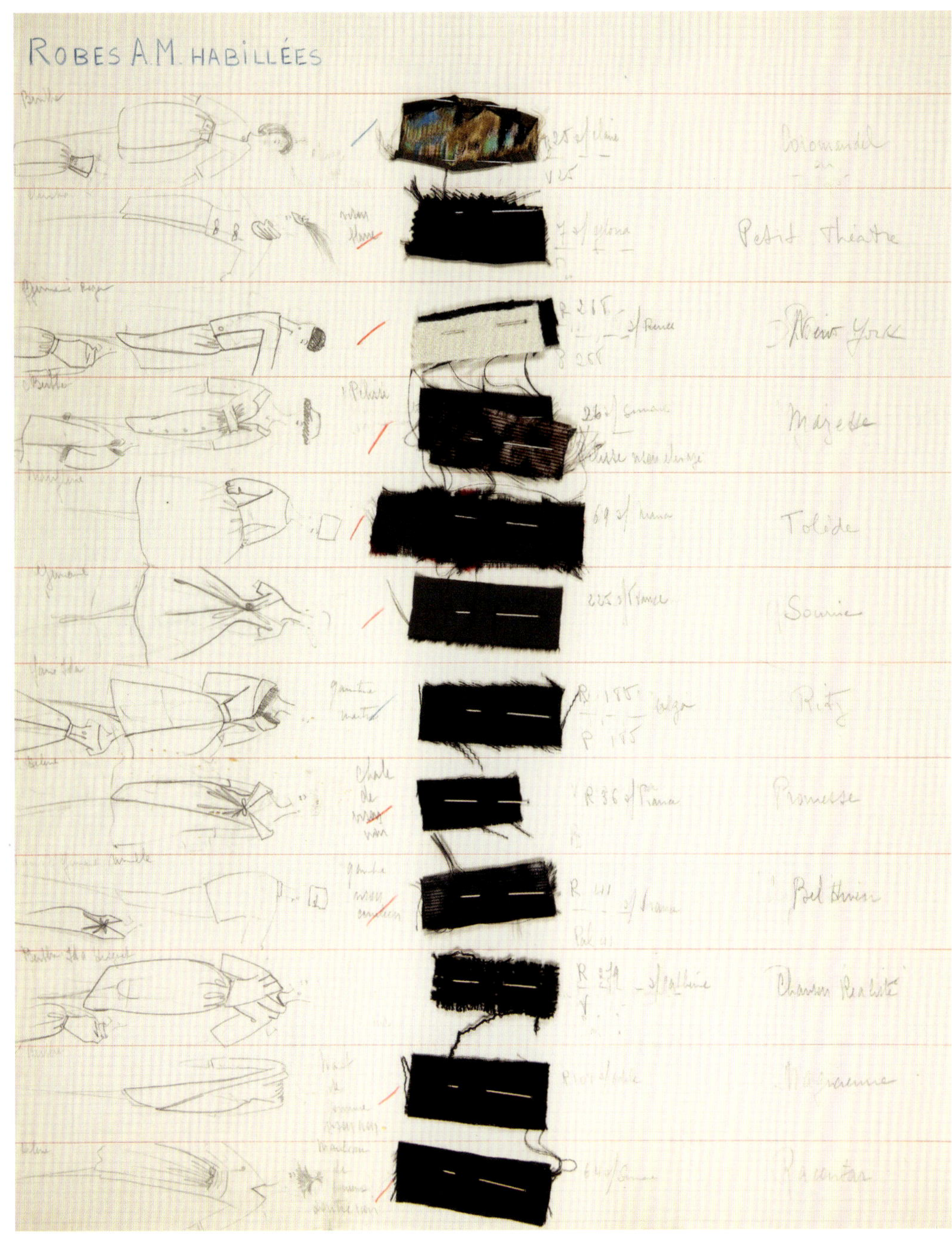

Christian Dior
Ritz

Afternoon ensemble in frieze,
Autumn–Winter 1956
haute couture collection,
Aimant line. Paris,
Fondation Azzedine Alaïa.

"Formal afternoon dresses" page
from the chart for Christian Dior's
Autumn–Winter 1956 haute couture
collection, *Aimant* line.
Paris, Dior Héritage.

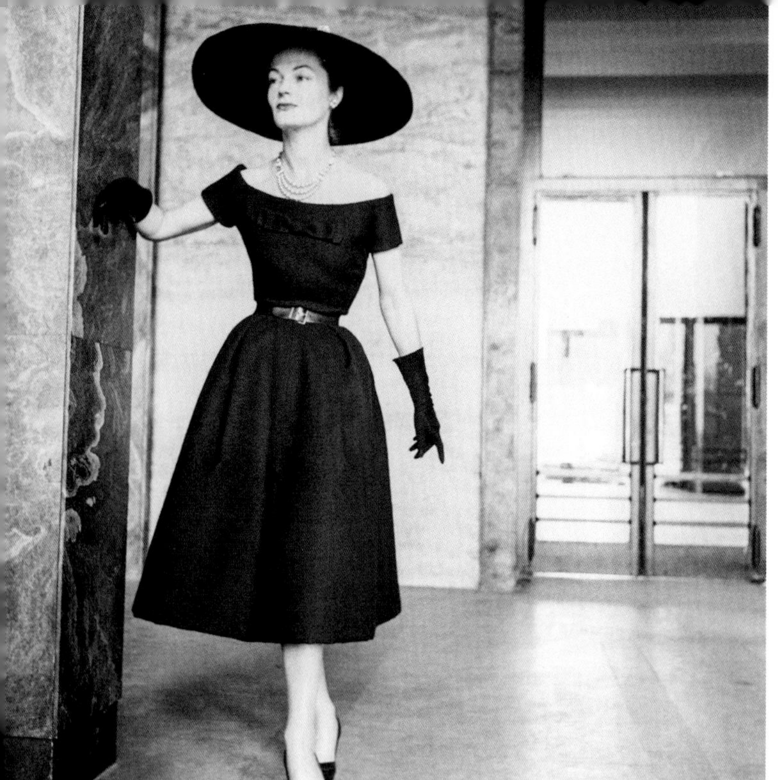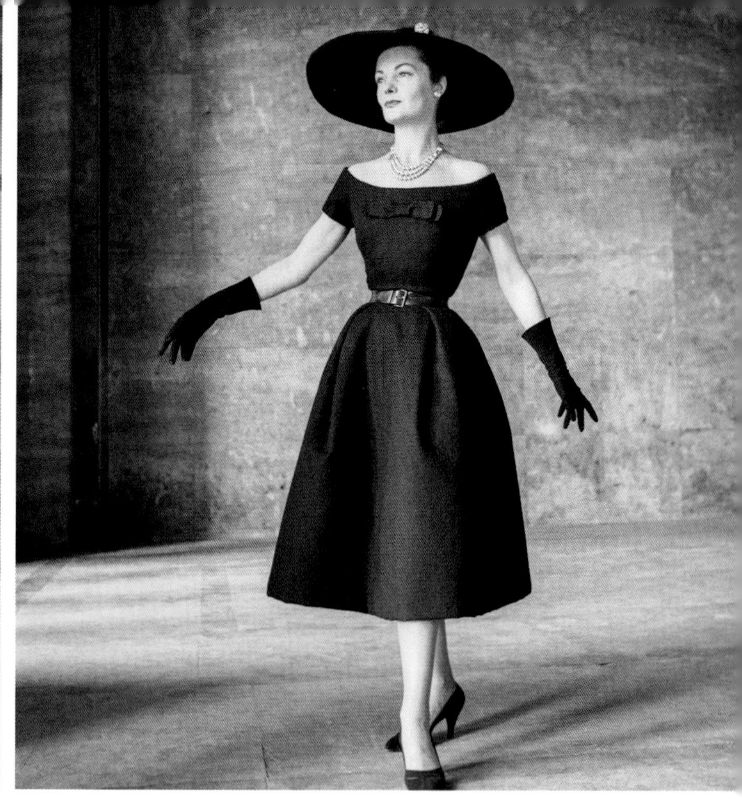

Model wearing the Christian Dior
Ritz afternoon ensemble,
Autumn–Winter 1956
haute couture collection, *Aimant* line.
Photographs by André Ostier.

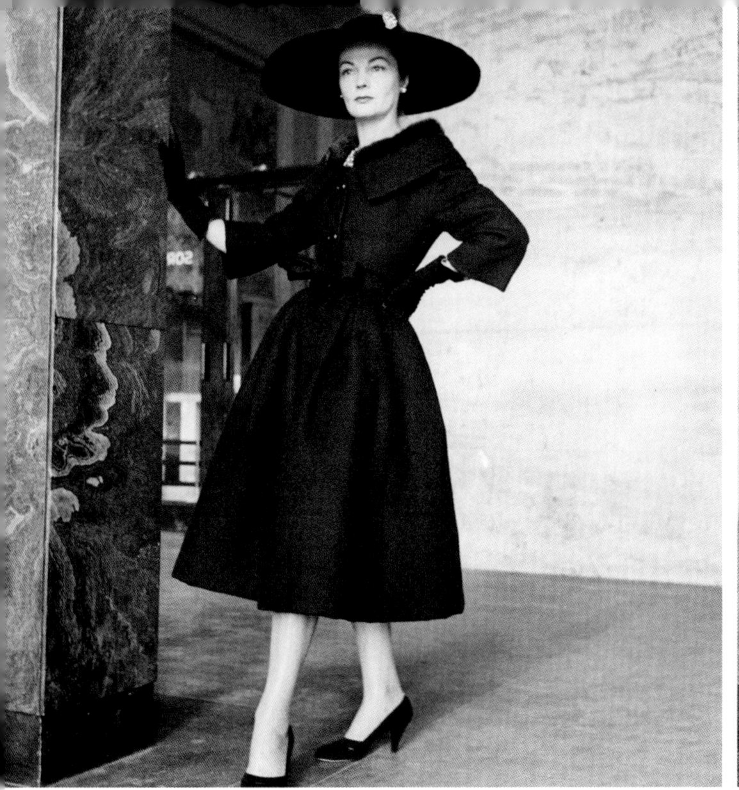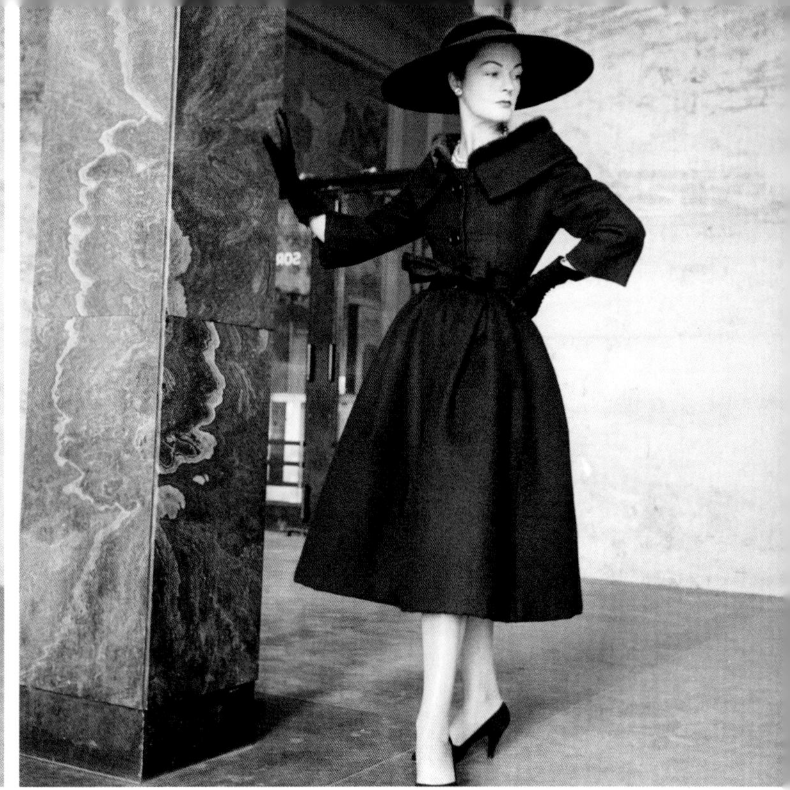

"BUSTS ARE ALSO ROUNDED,
WHEREAS THE WAIST IS RATHER
MORE FITTED. SKIRTS ARE FULL
AT THE HIPS AND BECOME NARROWER
FURTHER DOWN. THE MAGNET
IS IN EFFECT THE LEITMOTIF
WHICH REAPPEARS THROUGHOUT
THE COLLECTION." **CHRISTIAN DIOR**

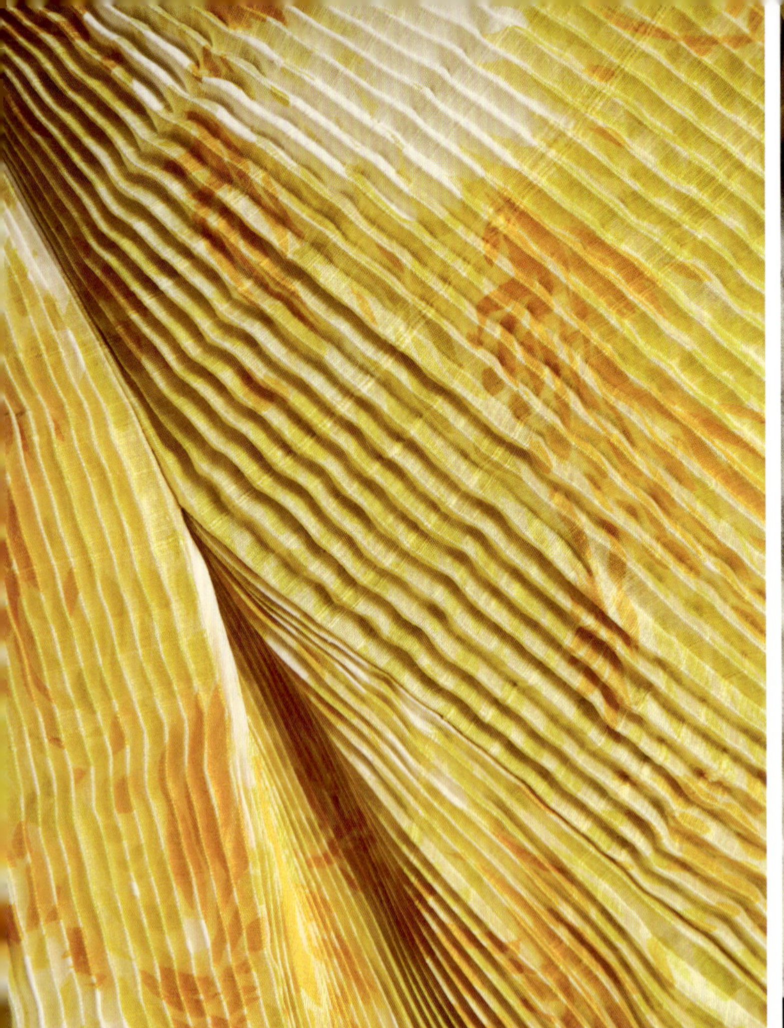

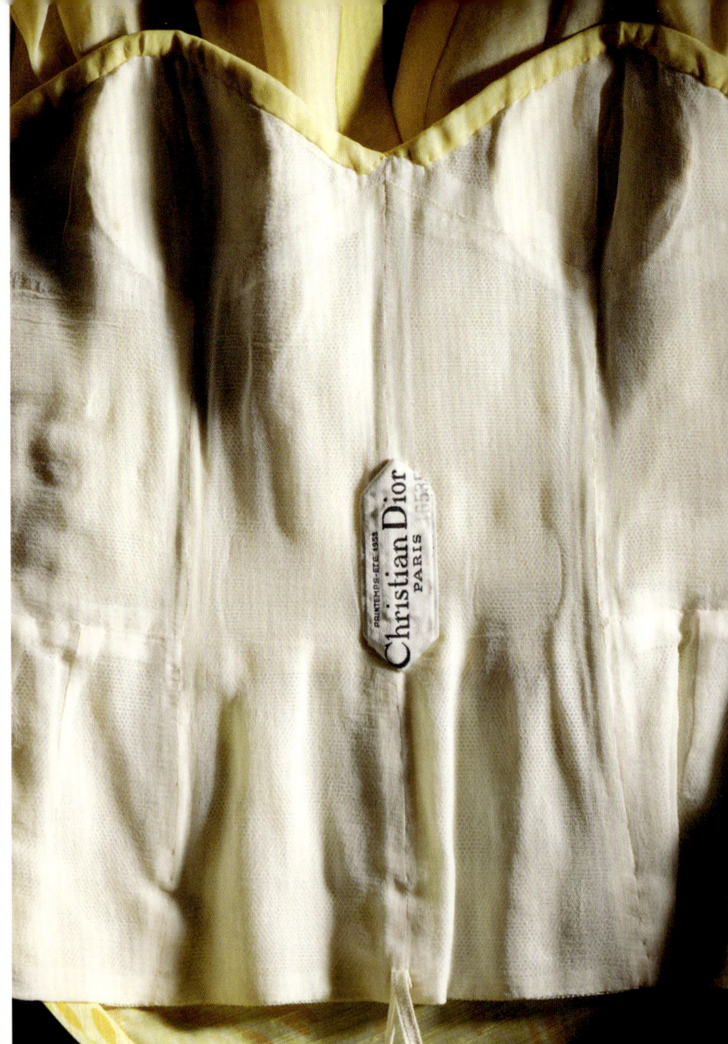

Christian Dior
Marcel Pagnol

Evening dress with bolero in silk
(with details), Spring–Summer 1952
haute couture collection, *Sinueuse* line.
Paris, Fondation Azzedine Alaïa.

This ensemble, for a client, is a version
of the original model in the *Crommelynck*
evening dress fabric.

FOLLOWING PAGES
Double-page spread from
an article in *Harper's Bazaar* titled
"The Inside Story," describing
the technical principles of fashion
according to Christian Dior,
Spring–Summer 1947 haute couture
collection, *Corolle* line, July 1947.

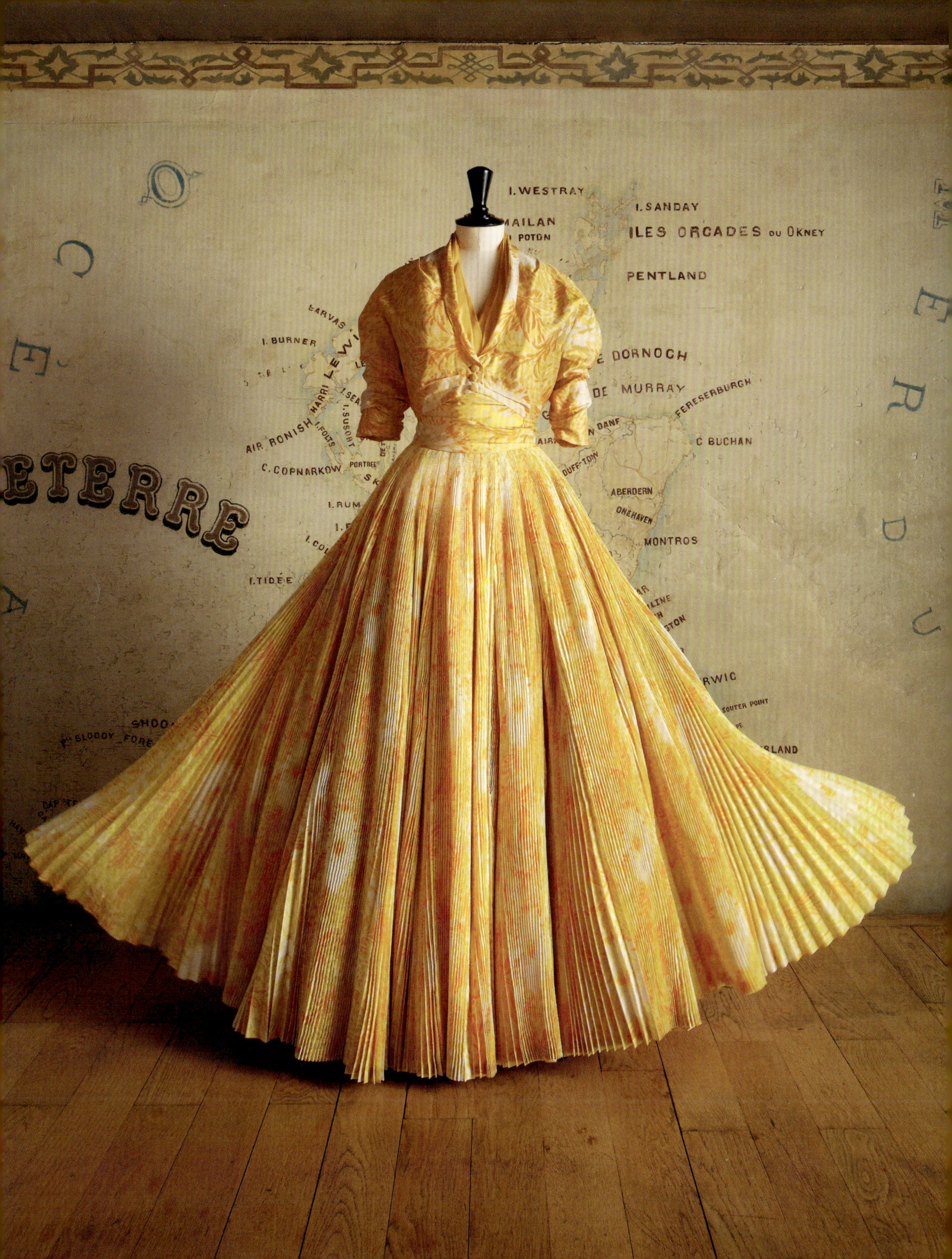
I. WESTRAY
I. SANDAY
MAILAN
POTON
ILES ORCADES du OKNEY
PENTLAND
LARVAS
I. BURNER
DORNOCH
DE MURRAY
FERESERBURGH
AIR RONISH HARRI LEWI
I. SUSONT
DANF
C BUCHAN
C. COPNARKOW
PORTREE
SK
DUFF-TON
ABERDERN
ONEHAVEN
I. RUM
MONTROS
ETERRE
I. COL
I. TIDÉE
RWIG
SOUTER POINT
RLAND
SHOO
BLODOY FORE
CAP TE

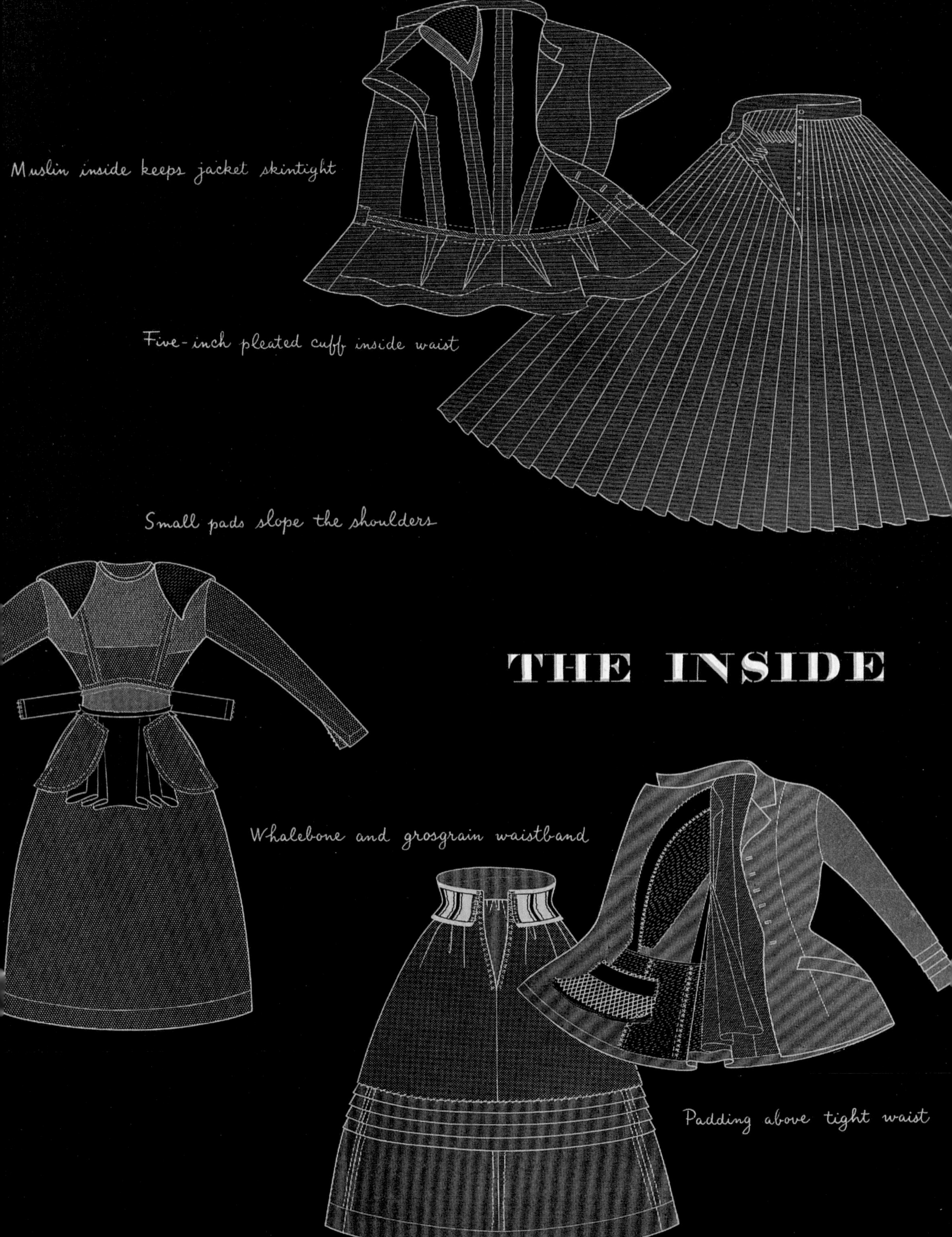

Muslin inside keeps jacket skintight
Five-inch pleated cuff inside waist
Small pads slope the shoulders
THE INSIDE
Whalebone and grosgrain waistband
Padding above tight waist

• An antique and entirely feminine principle in women's clothes is being revived. For the first time since the nineteenth century, dresses and suits are being made that are equipped for the kind of hips, breasts, shoulders, and waistlines that a designer thinks a woman should have. This is the return of dressmaking in the Grand Tradition. Look now in your closet, and if you have a strapless evening dress turn it inside out and you'll undoubtedly see "bones" (even though you may not have felt them when you were wearing the dress). Actually, many American designers have for several seasons lined their clothes, put in extra taffeta and buckram underpinnings . . . and have taken certain liberties with shoulder padding and "false bosoms."

• The most advanced examples to date are the clothes of Christian Dior. And since no reader of Harper's Bazaar has ever worn a dress with such elaborate foundations, we have selected six from his last collection and turned them inside out for a better look.

• On this page: One of Dior's great skirts. Each panel is reinforced with muslin and the hemline is faced with calico, for greater body. The total result: A skirt which stands stiffly away, as though it were covering ten petticoats.

STORY

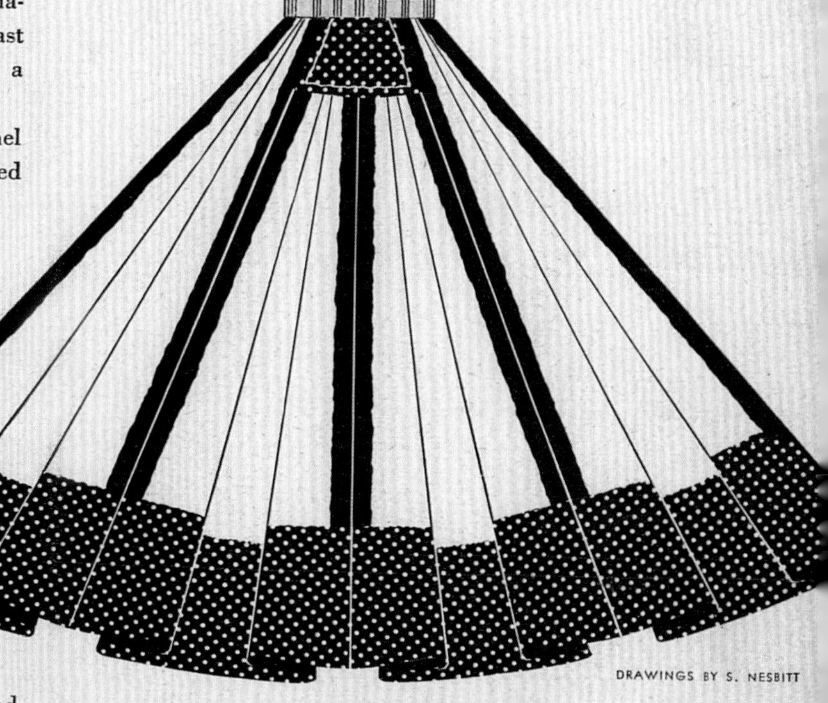

DRAWINGS BY S. NESBITT

• Opposite *(top)*: The accordion-pleated skirt fans sharply from the waist because there is an inner pleated ruffle in the waistband. Dior lines the jacket *(top left)* of a green taffeta suit-dress with muslin before it is gored, then works lining and fabric together. Result: The taffeta can stretch only as far as the muslin—which is not at all. The famous "Daisy" suit *(bottom)* is copied from an eighteenth century riding habit. The jacket is padded just above the waist, to give an hourglass curve, and rounded out with muslin below the waist, in back. The skirt of "Daisy" has a tight-waisted, bell-hipped look because it is fitted inside with a little corselet of whaleboned grosgrain. Carefully shaped pads give an oval line to the shoulders of a wool jersey dress *(far left)*. Muslin keeps the bodice tightly fitted and a muslin belt pulls the cloth flat at the waist while a chiffon flounce over the stomach puffs the cloth out. You see, even the simplest dress may lead the most elaborate inner life, in this year of graceful dressmaking—1947.

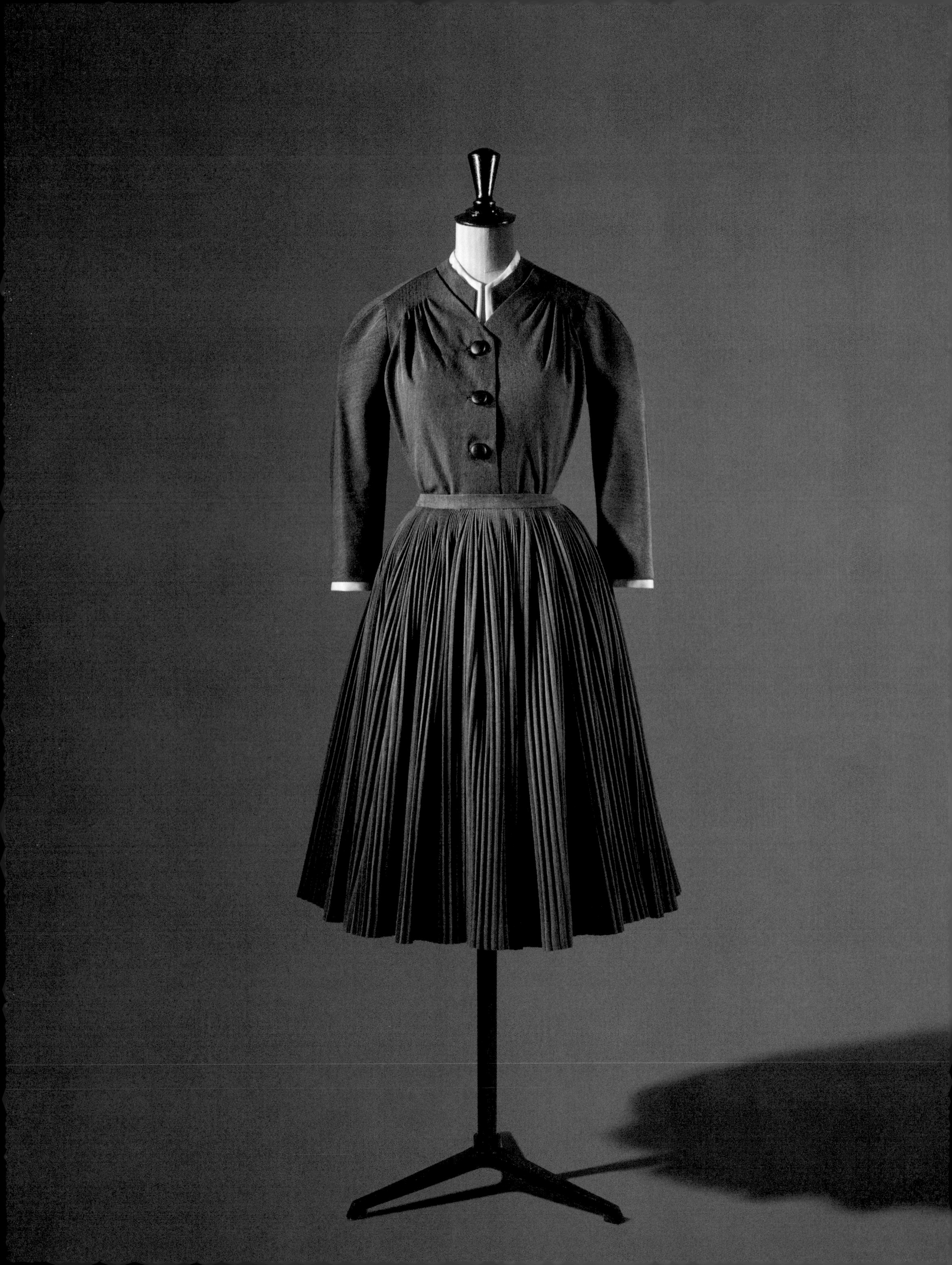

Christian Dior

Ovale du visage, ovale du buste, ovale des hanches; ces trois ovales superposés expriment le mieux la ligne 1951 dont la coupe a dû entièrement se renouveler pour suivre les courbes **naturelles** du corps féminin. Tout s'y modèle sur ses courbes subtiles. Subtiles, en effet, les inflexions de la coupe qui profile le buste, moule les basques et donne aux emmanchures une ligne radicalement nouvelle.

Souple sans être flottante, simple sans être sèche, la mode 1951 est toute en nuances.

OVALE

Le sens des tissus s'infléchit pour mouler doucement le buste qui va s'amenuisant vers la taille. Celle-ci, à sa place **naturelle**, reste fine mais jamais étranglée. Le buste forme donc un **ovale** qu'accentue la **rondeur** des épaules

La coupe souligne également la **rondeur naturelle** des hanches qui évoquent, elles aussi, le sommet d'un **ovale** que soulignent ou suggèrent les jupes larges ou étroites

Nous avons intentionnellement répété le mot **rondeur** car, dans cette coupe toute en finesse, il n'est pas une couture qui soit rigoureusement droite.

TAILLEURS

Leur silhouette est radicalement changée. Ils suivent scrupuleusement l'anatomie du buste.

Manches. — Les emmanchures viennent creuser les épaules à l'attache du bras qu'elles soulignent. Cette nouvelle monture des manches a une grande importance pour la ligne. Elle vient donner à la carrure de la largeur, au bras du rond, sans cependant donner à la manche trop d'importance. Celle-ci bombée du haut se rétrécit vers le bas. Nous l'avons baptisée : manche en « cuisse de poulet » car c'est vraiment la forme naturelle dont elle se rapproche le plus.

Dos. — Ces manches toutes montées devant sont à même dans le dos. Elles donnent à celui-ci un intérêt nouveau par la largeur qu'elles lui confèrent.

Buste. — Revenant au buste, nous voyons, à partir du cou, le tissu s'arrondir puis se rétrécir pour donner à la poitrine son volume idéal et à la taille une souple minceur.

Basques. — Assez courtes, elles moulent doucement les hanches et tendent ensuite à se resserrer pour amorcer la ligne de la jupe.

Christian Dior

Afternoon dress in wool, Spring–Summer 1951
haute couture collection, *Naturelle* line.
Paris, Fondation Azzedine Alaïa.

This model, for a client, could be a specially adapted version of the *Mine de rien* town dress or of the *En catimini* afternoon dress from the Spring–Summer 1951 haute couture collection.

ABOVE
First page of the press release
for Christian Dior's Spring–Summer 1951
haute couture collection, *Naturelle* line.
Paris, Dior Héritage.

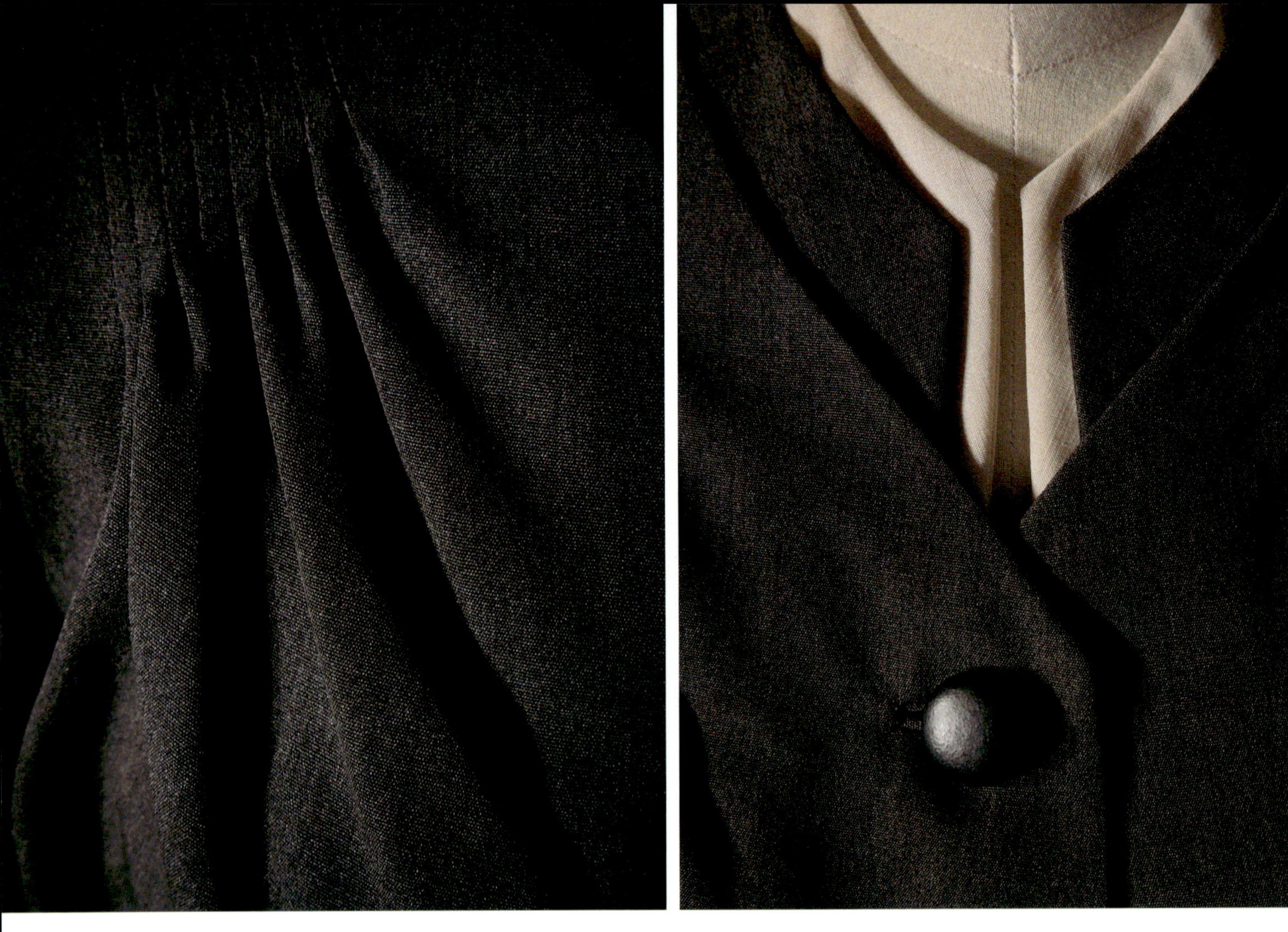

Christian Dior

Afternoon dress in wool
(details), Spring–Summer 1951
haute couture collection,
Naturelle line. Paris,
Fondation Azzedine Alaïa.

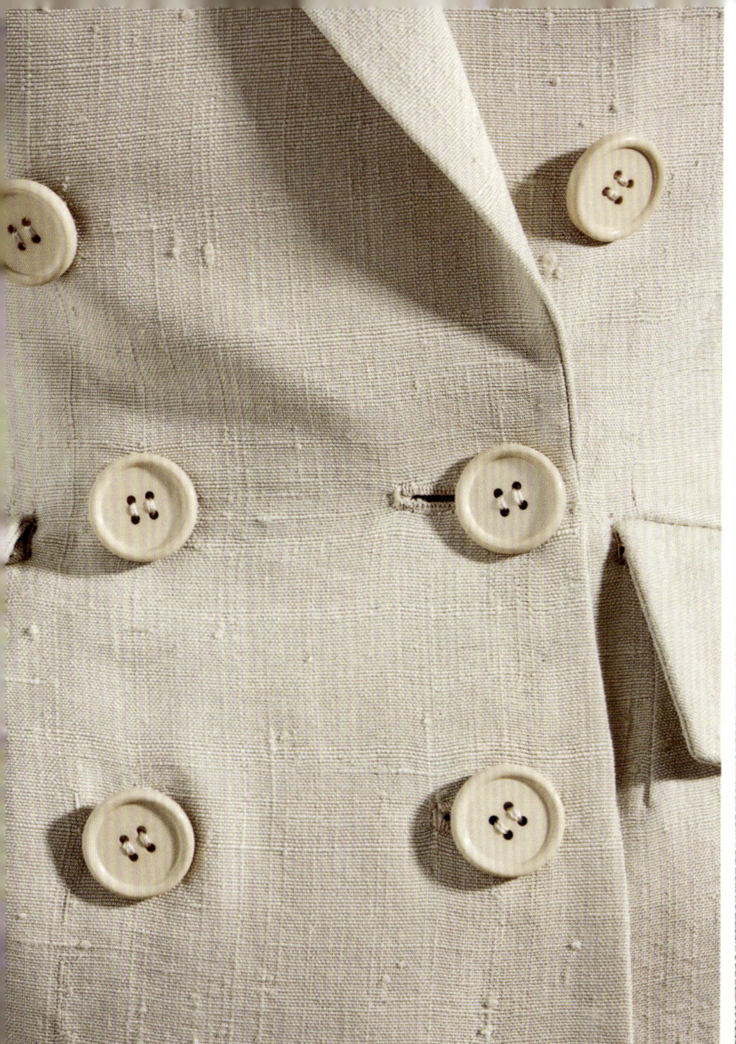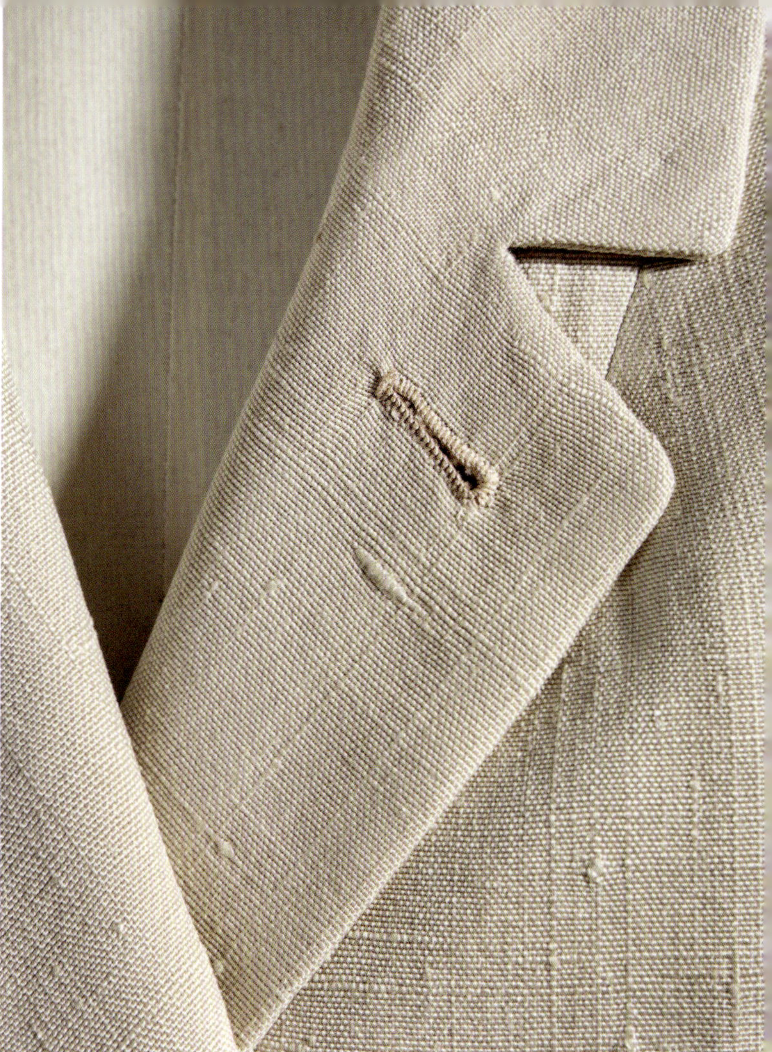

"IT IS THROUGH THE CUT THAT
DRESSES TODAY AVOID THE INSIPID
OVERABUNDANCE OF SEAMS,
AND IN THIS WAY ARE AKIN
TO THE GARMENTS OF ANTIQUITY,
POSSESSING THE SAME APPARENT
SIMPLICITY." **CHRISTIAN DIOR**

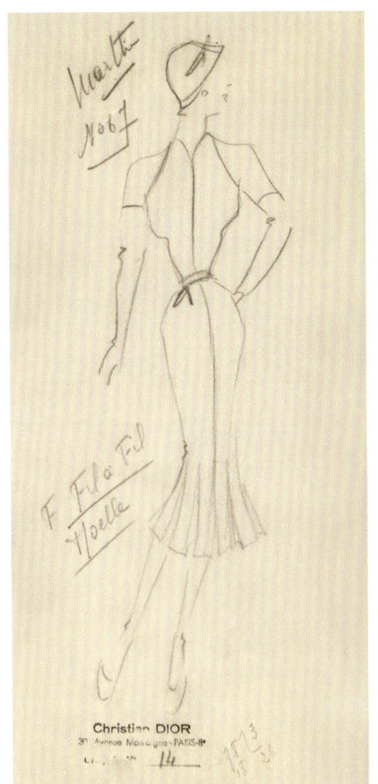

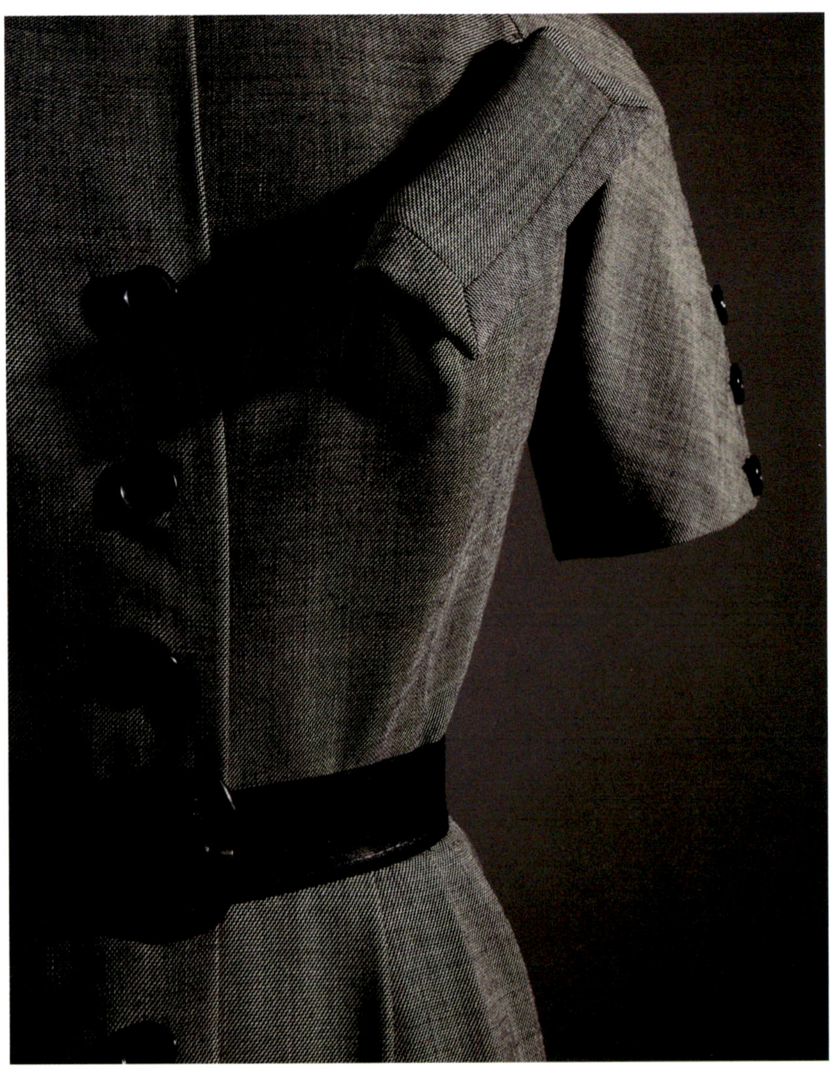

Christian Dior
Fil à fil

Day dress in end-on-end (with detail),
Spring–Summer 1950 haute couture
collection, *Verticale* line. Paris,
Fondation Azzedine Alaïa.

Christian Dior, original sketch
for the *Fil à fil* day dress.
Paris, Dior Héritage.

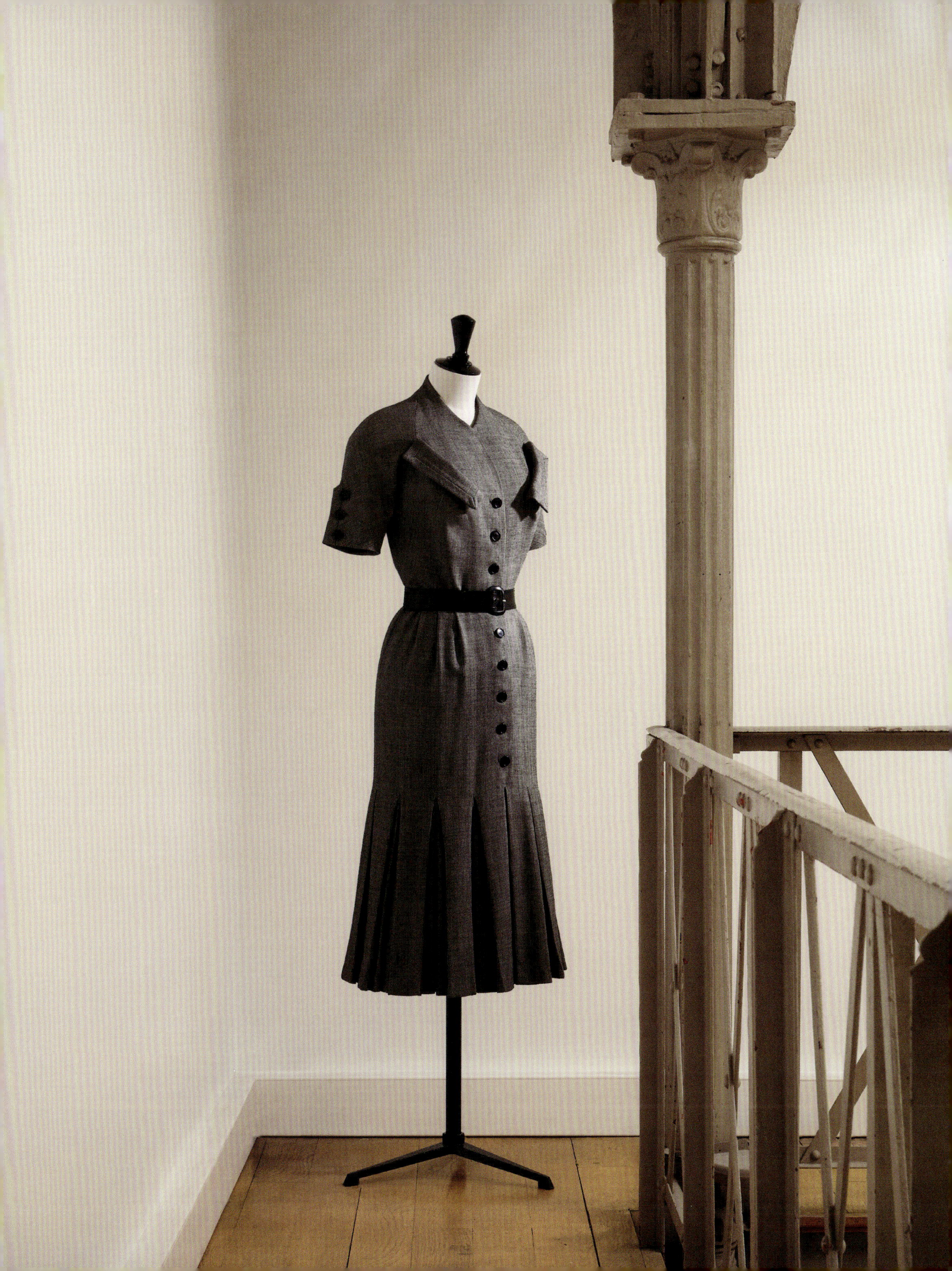

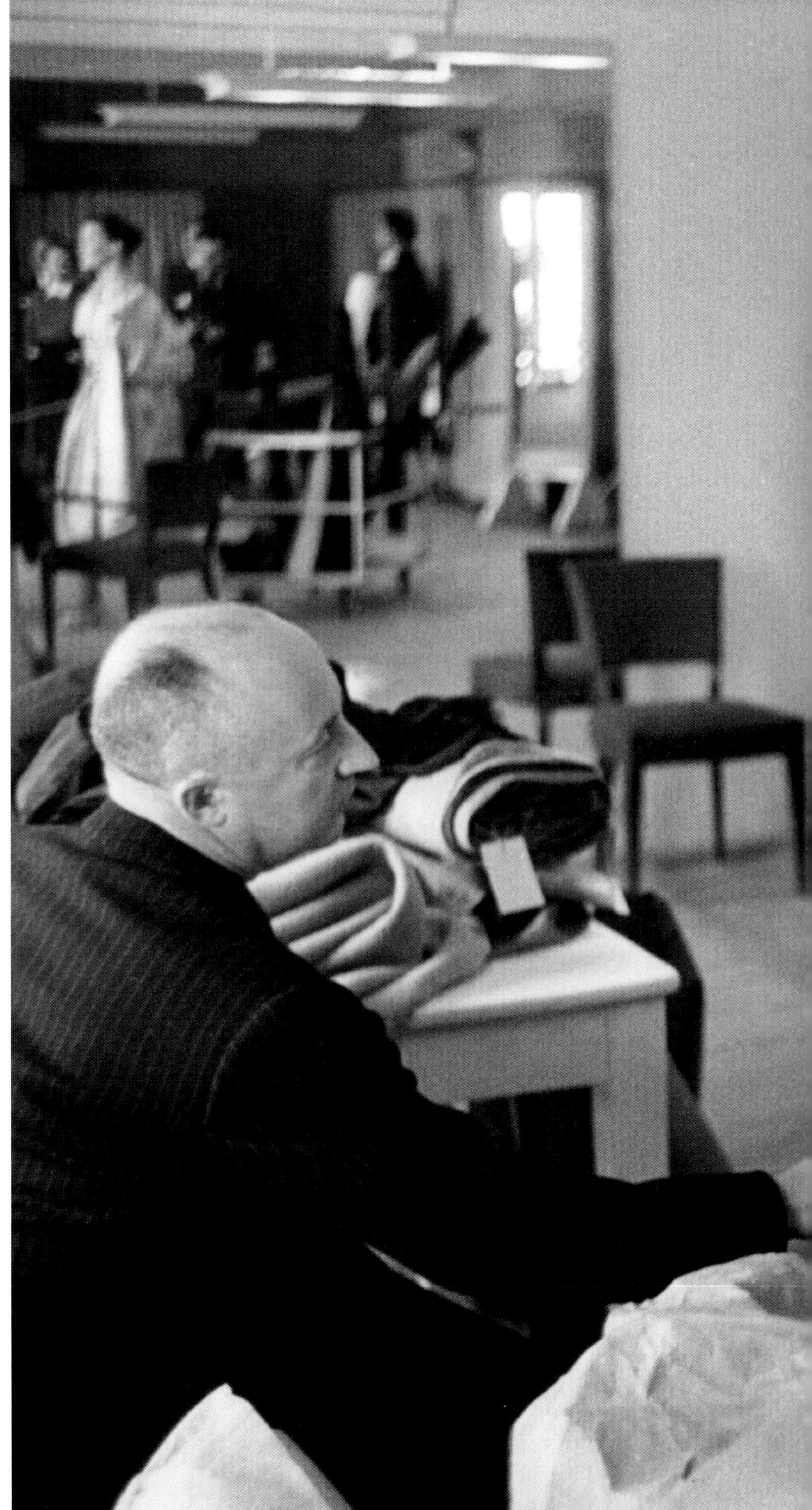

Christian Dior examining
the *Tournesol* afternoon
ensemble, Spring–Summer 1952
haute couture collection,
Sinueuse line, worn by
the model Lucky in the studio
at 30 Avenue Montaigne, Paris.
Photograph by Roger Wood.

The Fondation Azzedine Alaïa
has an example of this ensemble
in its collections.

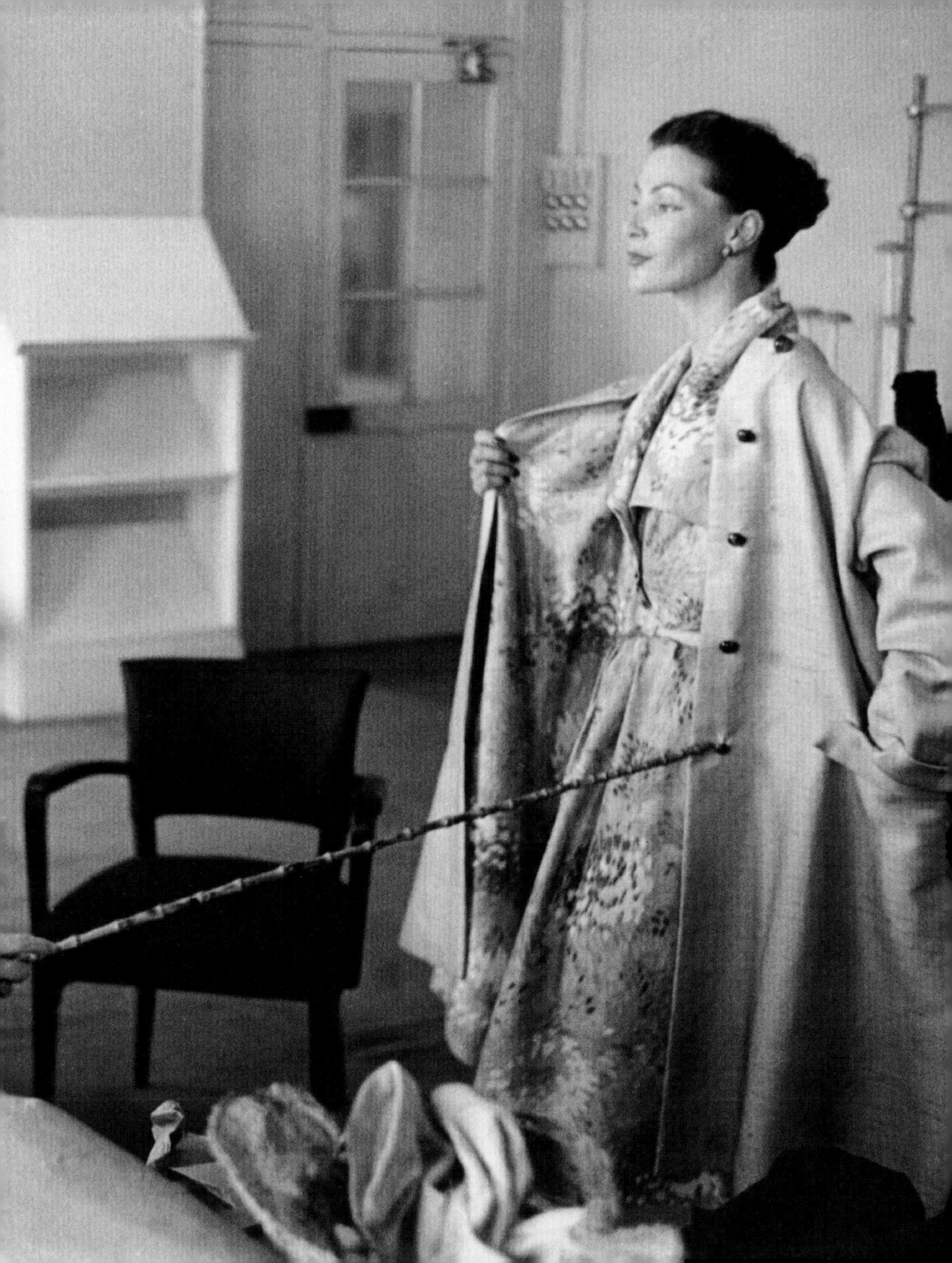

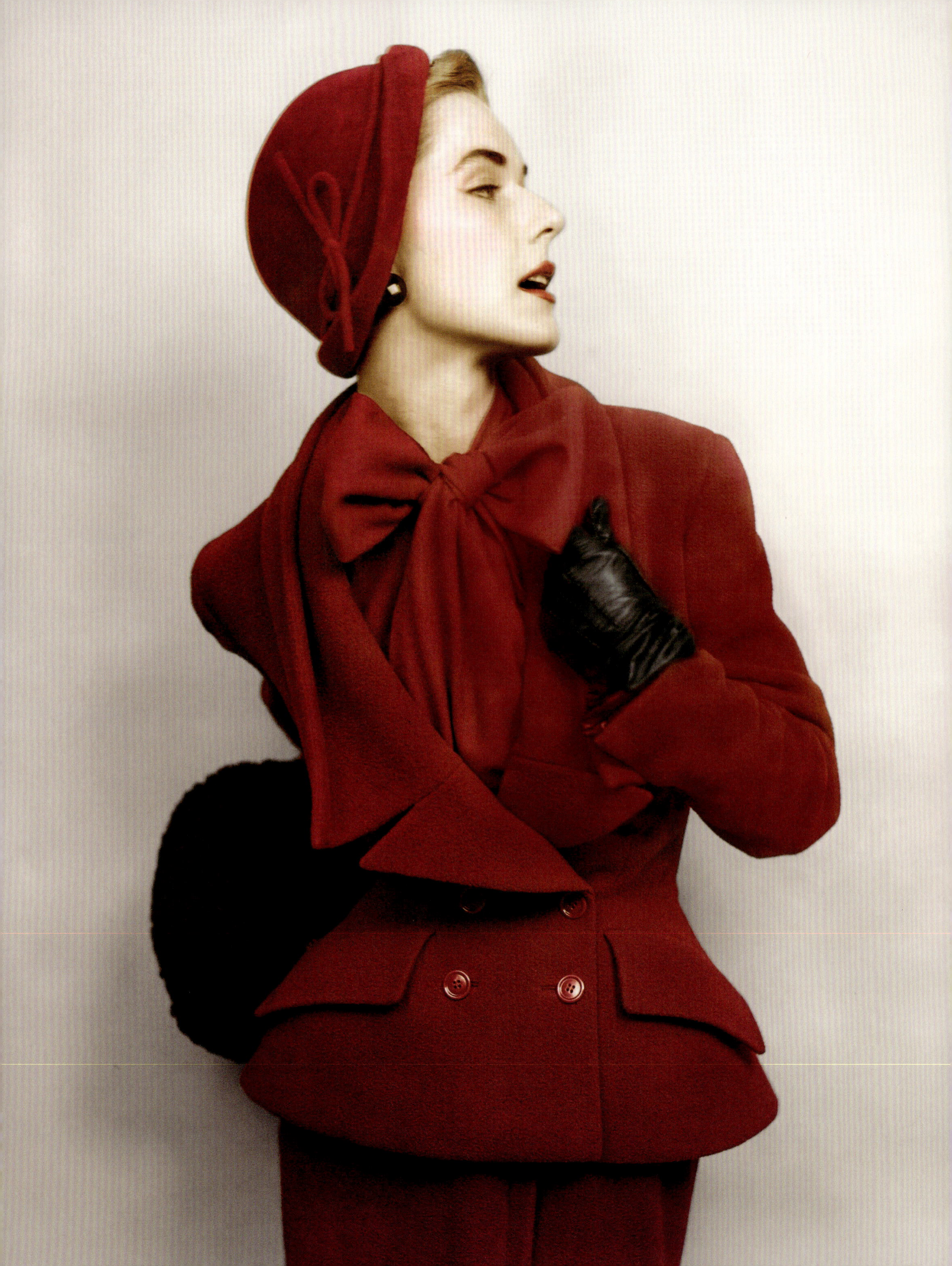

CHRISTIAN DIOR AND THE CULTURE OF COLOR

ALESSANDRA RONETTI

COLOR AND VISUAL IMAGINARIES IN THE MEDIA

The first decade of the House of Dior (1947–1957) marked a major turning point in the visual culture of color. The media—press, advertising, cinema—all moved toward color, deeply influencing perceptions of fashion.[1] The transition manifested itself by a rise in color photography, which gradually replaced illustration in specialist journals.[2] It was made possible by the increased availability of Kodachrome film, first produced in 1935, and Ektachrome, introduced in the early 1940s.[3] Offering different renderings, the two processes were used extensively to photograph vividly colored clothes: Kodachrome, appreciated for its tonal saturation and durability, was mainly reserved for prestigious reports and magazine covers, while Ektachrome, quicker to develop and with a more neutral chromatic quality, was used primarily for fashion shoots, lookbooks, and advertisements. The magazine *Claudine* immortalized some of Christian Dior's creations for Autumn–Winter 1947 thanks to these two technologies (pp. 86–87, 95). This shifting visual context shaped the couturier's ideas: "I am assisted by the photographs or drawings published in the papers which often present me with an entirely new light on my creations."[4] Although he does not mention color explicitly, it is fair to assume that this "new light" included the influence of printed imagery on how his models were perceived chromatically.

Dior recognized that color possesses strong and almost essential powers of attraction. This seductiveness was at the core of commercial theories at the time, as witnessed by the book *Selling with Color* (1945) by Faber Birren, an established American expert who considered color a key means of persuasion. Still, despite this recognition

Model wearing a suit from the Christian Dior–New York Autumn–Winter 1949 collection. Photograph by Clifford Coffin, published in *Vogue*, September 1, 1949.

1   Federico Pierotti, *La Couleur: Une passion cinématographique* (Paris: Classiques Garnier, 2020), 103–134.
2   Alexander Liberman (ed.), *The Art and Technique of Color Photography* (New York: Simon and Schuster, 1951).
3   Brian Coe, *Colour Photography: The First Hundred Years 1840–1940* (London: Ash & Grant, 1978).
4   Christian Dior, *Dior by Dior: The Autobiography of Christian Dior* (London: V&A Publishing, 2025; orig. published in 1957), 81.

of the impact of chromatics, Dior upheld black and white as an aesthetic basis, as though returning to the essentials of line and silhouette: "I have no wish to deprive fashion (and the ladies) of the added allure and charm of color, but I could perfectly well design a whole collection simply in black or white and express all my ideas to my complete satisfaction."[5] When he spoke of color, it would usually be in reference to bright ones, which he contrasted with the neutral tones—white, gray, black—that were his preference. Regardless, his collections were adapted for international markets in accordance with a well-judged strategy. From 1948, with the foundation of Christian Dior–New York, and then with CD Models, in London, in 1952, his designs responded to the tastes of the English-speaking world. Sometimes the clients' color preferences were taken into consideration, as witnessed by annotated sale sketches that display various color options for the same piece. The *Cuba* ensemble, for instance, was initially presented in pink, but also offered in blue (p. 104).

"I HAVE NO WISH TO DEPRIVE FASHION (AND THE LADIES) OF THE ADDED ALLURE AND CHARM OF COLOR, BUT I COULD PERFECTLY WELL DESIGN A WHOLE COLLECTION SIMPLY IN BLACK OR WHITE."

CHRISTIAN DIOR

Dior's visual culture was rich and multilayered. It drew both from his childhood memories, marked by a bourgeois aesthetic, and from the arts—notably Cubism and Surrealism, which he supported through the gallery he set up in 1928 with Jacques Bonjean. In his autobiography, he describes his deep attachment to the colors of his youth, which laid the foundations for his emotional perspective. He writes of the façade of his childhood home in Granville, Normandy, painted "a very soft pink, mixed with grey gravelling"—two tones that, he notes, "remained my favorite colors in *couture*."[6] White and gray were predominant in the domestic setting in the Passy district where he spent the Parisian part of his formative years—neo–Louis XVI (Seize) interiors, all the rage between 1900 and 1914, that

---

5   *Ibid.*, 94.
6   *Ibid.*, 229.

he describes as having "white woodwork, white lacquered furniture, grey hangings, doors with square panes of beveled glass and bronze light brackets with small lampshades."[7] This chromatic repertoire became a tool for designing his silhouettes. When he opened his couture house, Dior drew inspiration from these ambiences to define the very place where he would present his creations: a restrained, neutral décor of white woodwork, gray hangings, and soft light, conceived so as never to detract attention from the dresses. Here, color is memory, moderation, and harmony. For Dior, these silent tones embodied an idea of enduring elegance that was both Parisian and resolutely modern.

Alongside the artistic and decorative influences was another element that helped shape Dior's sensibilities: the flower-cultivation manuals that he would leaf through as a child, and especially the color plates published by the Vilmorin-Andrieux seed company.[8] From these, he learned flowers' names, descriptions, and color palettes, developing a refined taste for organic motifs as well as chromatic scales. At the time, the spread of photomechanical techniques such as chromolithography was enabling wide circulation of color images, helping to frame a visual culture that was on the lookout for intense shades. This naturalistic inspiration was reflected in the way that fashion magazines paid homage to Dior. In the fall of 1947, *Vogue Paris* published a plate depicting a bouquet of flowers to illustrate the colors of several couturiers' collections, including Dior's, which was associated with a range of greens, ambers, russets, and pinks (p. 88).[9] *Claudine* magazine went even further, transforming the then-fashionable shades into a painter's palette: an Ektachrome photograph shows Dior's *Vénitienne* afternoon dress in russet-colored satin (Autumn–Winter 1947 haute couture collection, *Corolle* line), detailing the season's colors with evocative names such as "ambre blond" (blond amber), "gris soupir" (sigh gray), and "abricot cendré" (dusty apricot) (pp. 86–87).[10] Dior called the color of the *Vénitienne* dress "barbe de Bébé" (Bébé's beard),[11] in tribute to his friend, the artist Christian Bérard. The "sigh gray" mentioned in the magazine appeared on the *Aladin* early-evening dress, in satin, and on the *Grisette* luncheon ensemble, in wool.[12] Dior specified a "color range" for every season, using poetic names inspired by the world of paintings ("Titien" [Titian] brown); nature ("gris phalène" [geometrid

---

7 *Ibid.*, 21.
8 *Ibid.*, 229.
9 "La Botanique des Modes de Paris: Ces bouquets donnent automatiquement la gamme des coloris préférés cet hiver," *Vogue Paris*, October 1, 1947, 94–95.
10 "La palette de la mode," *Claudine*, no. 116, September 25, 1947, 12.
11 Press release, Autumn–Winter 1947 haute couture collection, *Corolle* line.
12 *Ibid.*

gray], "lichen" [lichen] and "algue" [seaweed] greens);[13] natural dyes ("garance" [madder] red); and atmospheric phenomena ("altitude" [altitude] and "orage" [storm] blues, "nuage pâle" [pale cloud] pink, "aube" [dawn] and "crépuscule" [dusk] greens).[14] His keenness to name colors seems to be linked to his predilection for in-between shades: this nuanced vocabulary allowed him to convey subtleties that would be impossible through a simple designation of pure hues.

NEUTRAL COLORS: AN AESTHETIC OF HARMONY

Christian Dior's *The Little Dictionary of Fashion*, which was published—in English—in 1954, was aimed first and foremost at middle-class women around the world to whom he offered an education in good taste, which in his view meant adhering to French standards.[15] The book follows in a tradition of aesthetic democratization that was already well-established in the English-speaking world, notably through numerous treatises on the application of chromatic harmony to fashion. It took up various principles from manuals that were in circulation from the late nineteenth century, one of the best-known being *Colour Harmony in Dress* by George Ashdown Audsley, a follower of John Ruskin, which was released in 1912 and 1922. These books offered color recommendations to suit different occasions and/ or the tones of the wearer's skin, eyes, and hair. Dior updated this advice using a vocabulary that better fitted the aspirations of women in the 1950s. Two years later, in his autobiography *Christian Dior et moi* (the English edition of which, *Dior by Dior*, followed in 1957), he noted that American women often lacked the subtle discernment of what he considered European taste, highlighting their liking for chromatic excess. In 1953, the year before his dictionary was published, Howard Hawks's film *Gentlemen Prefer Blondes* came out, with its costumes in shades of red, fuchsia, and sparkle, and worn by Marilyn Monroe, illustrating this American exuberance.

Dior wanted to show how vivid colors could be made harmonious; hence his insistence on the role of neutrals. These had been popular since the 1920s as a reaction to the color revolution of artificial dyes that had taken place in the second half of the nineteenth century, and to the avant-garde's influence on fashion.[16] Christian Dior's

---

13 *Ibid.*

14 Press release, Spring–Summer 1948 haute couture collections, *Zig-Zag* and *Envol* lines.

15 Christian Dior, *The Little Dictionary of Fashion: A Guide to Dress Sense for Every Woman* (London: V&A Publishing, 2008; orig. published in 1954). On Dior as an international arbiter of taste, see Alexandra Palmer, *Dior: A New Look, A New Enterprise, 1947–57* (London: V&A Publishing, 2019), 115–129.

16 Alessandra Ronetti, "Back to Black: A Fashionable Colour from Worth to Chanel," *Technè*, no. 56, 2023, 62–71.

62

preference for these tones, which he shared with couturiers such as Cristóbal Balenciaga, was born of a rejection of prewar decorative excess, as characterized by the orientalism and flamboyant colors of the Ballets Russes, embodied by Paul Poiret and Elsa Schiaparelli.[17] After World War I, black returned as an expression of formal rigor: "Besides, black was in vogue. The influence of the war—mourning and black-out—combined with cubist severity, had banished from houses jade and gold cushions, and violet and orange blinds, in short the whole orgy of oriental colors, the short-lived conquerors of 1910 Louis Seize white."[18] Dior interpreted the return of black as an act of visual purification, a classicism revisited, paradoxically more expressive than many bright colors. Black became the symbol of aesthetic radicalism and synonymous with modernity.

"BLACK WAS IN VOGUE. THE INFLUENCE OF THE WAR—COMBINED WITH CUBIST SEVERITY, HAD BANISHED FROM HOUSES THE WHOLE ORGY OF ORIENTAL COLORS, THE SHORT-LIVED CONQUERORS OF 1910 LOUIS SEIZE WHITE." CHRISTIAN DIOR

In his dictionary, Dior asserts his preference for black, as well as gray and white. There is an entry for neutral shades, which he judges appropriate for unlimited everyday use.[19] He considers gray, in particular, to be suitable for all occasions and for any complexion, unlike beige. Dark blue, although not strictly neutral, is viewed as such by Dior: a classic hue, easy to pair with other colors and restful on the eye. Conversely, bright colors need to be used discerningly: limited to a single element or accessory, varied over time, and worn with neutral tones to soften their visual impact.[20] This preoccupation was not new to studies of color harmony, the French tradition of which began with the chemist Michel-Eugène Chevreul's treatise *De la loi du contraste simultané des couleurs* (*On the Law of Simultaneous Contrast of Colors*, 1839). Chevreul discusses ways of minimizing "*bariolage*,"

17   Dior, *Dior by Dior*, 15–16 and 28.
18   *Ibid.*, 235.
19   Dior, *The Little Dictionary of Fashion*, 79–80.
20   *Ibid.*, 26–27.

instead favoring more harmonious contrasts. His thinking had a lasting impact on fashion, calling for visual balance in order to avoid overstimulation or sensory fatigue. Dior was part of this tradition, henceforth integral to color culture. He reassessed the role of neutrals—which the exuberance of the saturated artificial colors of the nineteenth century had relegated to the background—to develop a modern model of harmony, in tune with Parisian haute couture's predilection for these hues.

ENERGY-RED

Dior described red as an "energetic" and "beneficial" color. [21] Of all the intense shades, it was unquestionably the one he used the most, to the point of making it his signature from 1953 onward, featured on everything from dresses to lipsticks produced under the moniker *Rouge Dior*. This vision was in line with a tradition that had been well established since the late nineteenth century, which attributed physiological and psychological effects to colors. The physician Charles Féré had already considered red as the ultimate color of energy, because of its strong capacity for sensory stimulation.[22] This discourse from treatises on chromatic harmony was relayed in the popular press in the form of advice purportedly offered by experts—or even by doctors—proclaiming the "therapeutic" virtues of colors applied to clothing.

Emblematic of this was an article published in *Ici Paris* in 1948—a year after Christian Dior established his couture house—titled "La chromothérapie au service de notre santé" (Chromotherapy at the service of our health). In it, we read that: "Red […] generates physical energy, creates strength and warmth […], it has genuine powers of stimulation. Red alone expresses passion, revolution, and ardent love. But when offset by a cold color, its fierceness falls away, while it retains its strength."[23] These ideas were circulating in fashion magazines, as was testified to in an article by Faber Birren in *Vogue* (1949), which cites the stimulating effects of red ("red packs more excitement") in relation to the theories of chromotherapy.[24] This essay provided a foretaste of reflections that Birren developed further in his book *Color Psychology and Color Therapy*, published shortly afterward, in 1950. It is illustrated with a sketch that aims to offer a visual representation of this red as simultaneously "energetic" and structural: a woman wearing a red

---

21 *Ibid.*, 95.
22 Charles Féré, *Sensation et mouvement: études expérimentales de psycho-mécanique* (Paris: Alcan, 1887).
23 Cécile Hauriac (recording statements by the dowser Hector Mellin), "La chromothérapie au service de notre santé: Le noir fait engraisser. Le blanc fait maigrir," *Ici Paris*, August 17–20, 1948, 7.
24 Faber Birren, "At the Mercy of Color," *Vogue*, April 15, 1949, 51 and 109.

64

"butterfly jacket" and a Dior hat (p. 80, left). The caption reinforces the idea of red as both classic and dependable: "Pure Red . . . Color that can live as long as black . . . Your red coat follows you season into season, day into night."[25] Here, red represents an enduring aesthetic while also being highly expressive. It was on this same dual basis, at the crossroads of reflections on color and fashion, that Dior established his use of red, absorbing its powerful psychological charge.

From his very first collection for Spring–Summer 1947, red features alongside other radiant tones such as "longchamp" green and "porcelaine" pink, notably on the *Saint James* fitted coat, made of red woolen cloth from England, as well as more restrained tones such as navy blue, grayish-beige, black, khaki, and "terre de Paris" ("Paris soil").[26] The Autumn–Winter 1947 collection introduced even more vibrant shades—"rouge éclatant" (dazzling red), "zinnia," and "rouge satan" (Satan red)—ranging from garnet to scarlet.[27] The second Christian Dior–New York collection, produced in 1949—the same year that Birren's article was published—features a "Red like Black," returning to the idea of a classic red as the symbolic equivalent of black.[28]

With the launch of *Rouge Dior* in 1953, the couture house formalized a whole palette of reds. The makeup, and especially the lipstick, was made available in shades that coordinated with the textile collections (pp. 102–103). *Rouge Dior* also appeared in haute couture, such as on the *Tourbillon* short evening dress from the *Aimant* line of Autumn–Winter 1956 (p. 85). The chart for this collection features the sketch for the dress with a sample of bright red fabric, dialoguing with other vibrant colors such as "electric" pinks and "magnetic" blues that were mostly destined for evening dresses.[29] The rest of the collection was dominated by all-over black, combinations of black and white, and "gris foncé de l'Aimant" (the dark gray of the magnet).[30]

Dior always made sure to establish a subtle balance in his collections. Neutrals formed the base, punctuated by vibrant colors such as red—heralding the "shocking models, those which are designed to draw attention to the new line," shown about halfway through the collection presentation and dubbed "Trafalgars"[31]—which were reserved for specific occasions and complemented by a range of more understated tones and some prints.[32] This chromatic structure followed

---

25 *Ibid.*, 51.
26 Press release, Spring–Summer 1947 haute couture collection, *Corolle* and *En 8* lines.
27 Press release, Autumn–Winter 1947 haute couture collection, *Corolle* line.
28 Press release, Christian Dior–New York, Autumn–Winter 1949 collection.
29 Press release, Autumn–Winter 1956 haute couture collection, *Aimant* line.
30 *Ibid.*
31 Dior, *Dior by Dior*, 122 and 131.
32 Christian Dior with Alice Chavane and Élie Rabourdin, *Talking About Fashion* (first published in 1951, as *Je suis couturier*), translated by Eugenia Sheppard (New York: G. P. Putnam's Sons, 1954), 62 and 68.

the same principle of harmony that was applied on the scale of a single outfit or when matching accessories to garments, where Dior recommended combining red with a neutral color, such as gray or black, in order to reinforce its visual impact.[33]

This aesthetic, based on the contrast between intense and neutral tones, was typical of the visual culture at the time, as found in fashion and images related to it. Bright red was often placed in contrast with gray or black on a white background, as in the illustration in Birren's article. One might consider the drawing of a red hat worn on the side of the head, designed by Dior with Maud Roser and published in *Vogue Paris* in 1947 (p. 80, right).[34] In his dictionary, Dior suggests donning a red hat with a black or gray ensemble, or combining a gray outfit with a red umbrella.[35] This contrast appeared again in 1958 in a photograph by Sabine Weiss of the model Svetlana Lloyd wearing the gray *Bonne conduite* dress designed by Yves Saint Laurent—then creative director of the House of Dior—with a valet holding a red umbrella over her (p. 81).

"RUST" VERSUS "PINK"

In the 1950s, the name Christian Dior became a symbol of stylistic authority that was frequently mentioned beyond the realms of couture. In the Stanley Donen film *Funny Face* (1957), a fictional fashion journalist called Maggie Prescott—inspired by Diana Vreeland and Carmel Snow—launches her slogan "Think Pink," in opposition to Dior's supposed preference for black and "rust" tones.[36] Symbolic rather than factual, this duality set two different models of aesthetics against each other: on the one hand, the restraint of the Parisian couturier, embodied by a subtle, autumnal shade; on the other, American exuberance, made of fuchsia pinks, vivid reds, and coral hues. The "rust" attributed to Dior is less a reflection of a genuine taste than an image of French fashion as contained and aristocratic, compared with the spectacular, consumerist vision of the United States. This sequence in *Funny Face* illustrates a shift: from a system based on the authority of European couturiers toward a paradigm dominated by the New York magazines and media.[37]

---

33 Dior, *The Little Dictionary of Fashion*, 96. See also "Le noir joue avec la couleur," *L'Officiel de la couture et de la mode de Paris*, nos. 343–344, October 1950, 134–135.
34 "Christian Dior avec Maud Roser crée le chapeau porté d'un côté de la tête," *Vogue Paris*, October 1, 1947, 74.
35 Dior, *The Little Dictionary of Fashion*, 96.
36 She says: "Think pink! Forget that Dior says black and rust."
37 Regina Lee Blaszczyk, *The Color Revolution* (Cambridge, MA: The MIT Press, 2012), 265–266.

Dior highlighted this difference of sensibilities himself: on his first trip to New York in 1947 he criticized the "bold essays of color which […] all appeared to be battling against each other," comparing the bright colors of the clothing to that of paintwork on cars, and noticing the tendency of American women toward exaggeration in their color choices.[38] This view aligns with a long-standing *topos*: already in 1872, Hippolyte Taine had noted English women's liking for garish colors, which he contrasted with French refinement.[39] In response to urban visual overload, Dior defended "the taste for subtle colors" as "the smartest of all tastes."[40] Color became a cultural battleground, a marker of ideologies that pitted commercial expressiveness against classical restraint. This contrast reveals a deep divergence in concepts of style: for Dior, subtle colors became a moral and aesthetic manifesto. It is essentially this aspect, which he highlighted in his autobiography, that the sequence from *Funny Face* illustrates. Ironically, in the "Think Pink" sequence, Maggie Prescott and her colleagues are all dressed in neutral tones, creating a visual contrast with the bright pink of the fabric that she brandishes—a color combination that Dior particularly recommended.[41]

"THE TASTE FOR SUBTLE COLORS, THE SMARTEST OF ALL TASTES, HAS DEVELOPED." CHRISTIAN DIOR

The fashion for pink that is visible in the film reflects a trend that was emerging in the 1950s—as witnessed by several issues of *Vogue* between 1956 and 1957 devoted to shades of pink, lilac, or fuchsia—and culminated in the United States with a dress worn by Mamie Eisenhower.[42] Dior, too, used "electric pinks," even though fuchsia seldom featured in his output; the *Opéra bouffe* short evening dress, designed for the *Aimant* line of Autumn–Winter 1956, is one of the rare examples of it.[43] In the "Think Pink" spirit, a photograph by Lionel Kazan immerses the *Rose, rose* model—a day ensemble

---

38 Dior, *Dior by Dior*, 71–72.
39 Hippolyte Taine, *Notes sur l'Angleterre* (Paris: Hachette, 1872), 25–26.
40 Dior, *Dior by Dior*, 72.
41 Dior, *The Little Dictionary of Fashion*, 26.
42 See, for example, *Vogue UK*, February 1956; *Vogue Paris*, October 1956; *Vogue UK*, August 1957. For a history of pink, see Valerie Steele (ed.), *Pink: The History of a Punk, Pretty, Powerful Color* (New York: Thames & Hudson, 2018).
43 Press release, Autumn–Winter 1956 haute couture collection, *Aimant* line. The *Bonne année* model, in the same collection, is another example.

from the *Flèche* line of Spring–Summer 1956—in an entirely pink atmosphere.[44] After Christian Dior's death in 1957, his couture house continued this exploration of bold pinks, as evidenced by the *Zaïre* evening dress designed by Yves Saint Laurent for the Autumn–Winter 1958 collection (pp. 96–97).[45] Still, the Dior signature remained more associated with soft tones, and this tendency had actually begun, in a sense, back in 1947 with the *Corolle* line. In the aftermath of the war, Dior expressed his wish to move from the utilitarian image of "female soldiers" to the more poetic one of "flower-like women"[46]— a new approach that translated into the return of soft fabrics (taffeta, percale) and gentler, more feminine hues. It marked a sudden shift away from the intense colors of the preceding decades, epitomized by the *Shocking Pink* that Elsa Schiaparelli launched in 1937— a highly fashionable shade, symbolic of the chromatic revolution that had begun in the nineteenth century and the craze for artificial colors such as fuchsia and magenta.

In the face of this, Dior restored a subtle, almost powdery-pink tone to favor. The *Bonbon* dress, in "rose soupir" (sigh pink) wool, its corolla cut created through an innovative technique, marked this turning point in the Autumn–Winter 1947 collection.[47] This delicate, almost childlike shade of pink was loaded with symbolism, both cultural and emotional: it testified to a sort of rediscovered joy that infused both the body and the garment. Seeing how enthusiastically the *Bonbon* dress was received in the United States, Dior quickly understood the color's strategic potential and showcased it the same year in the advertising campaign for the launch of his perfumes.[48] It was certainly not purely by chance that it was chosen a few years later for the *Cuba* ensemble dress and coat (Autumn–Winter 1954 collection, *H* line, p. 104). Aimed at international clients, this ensemble made its way into the era's visual imagination thanks to a cover that *Life* magazine dedicated to it in 1954.

These examples show the extent to which, with Dior, color had a function beyond pure decoration. A vehicle for memory, emotion, and strategy, it constituted a genuine language with the ability to convey the aesthetic, cultural, and commercial aspirations of his time. It was in this subtle coordination of tradition and modernity, moderation and expressiveness, that the uniqueness of Dior's chromatic culture took shape.

---

44 A variant was published as the cover of *Elle* magazine, no. 532, March 5, 1956. See Éric Pujalet-Plaà (ed.), *Dior and Roses* (New York: Rizzoli, 2021).
45 Press release, Autumn–Winter 1953 haute couture collection, *Vivante* line.
46 Dior, *Dior by Dior*, 24.
47 *Ibid.*, 52.
48 "Christian Dior présentera ses parfums pour Noël," *Vogue Paris*, October 1, 1947, 198.

Christian Dior draping the model Sylvie with gray silk in the studio at 30 Avenue Montaigne, Paris, 1948. Photograph by Bellini.

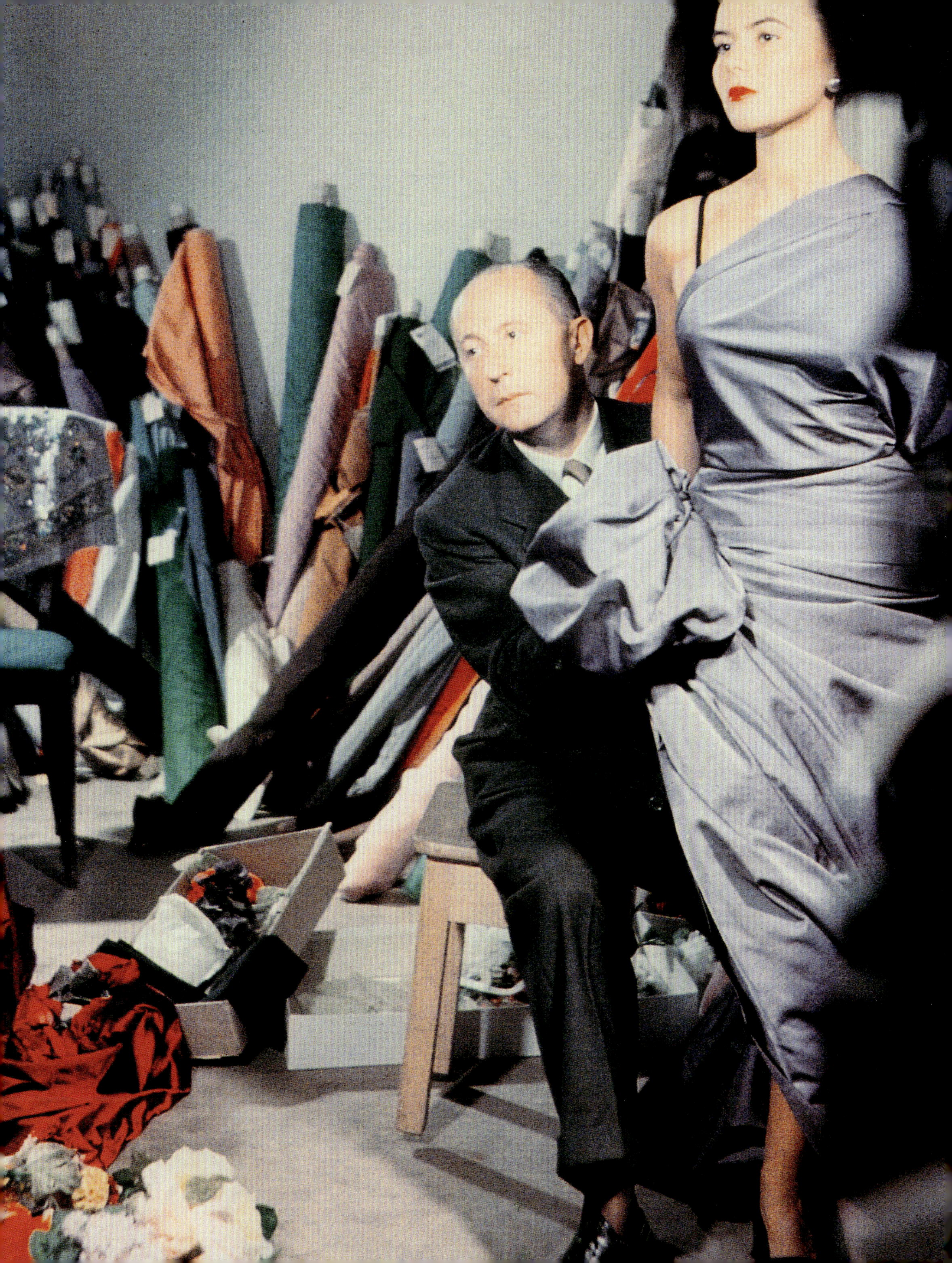

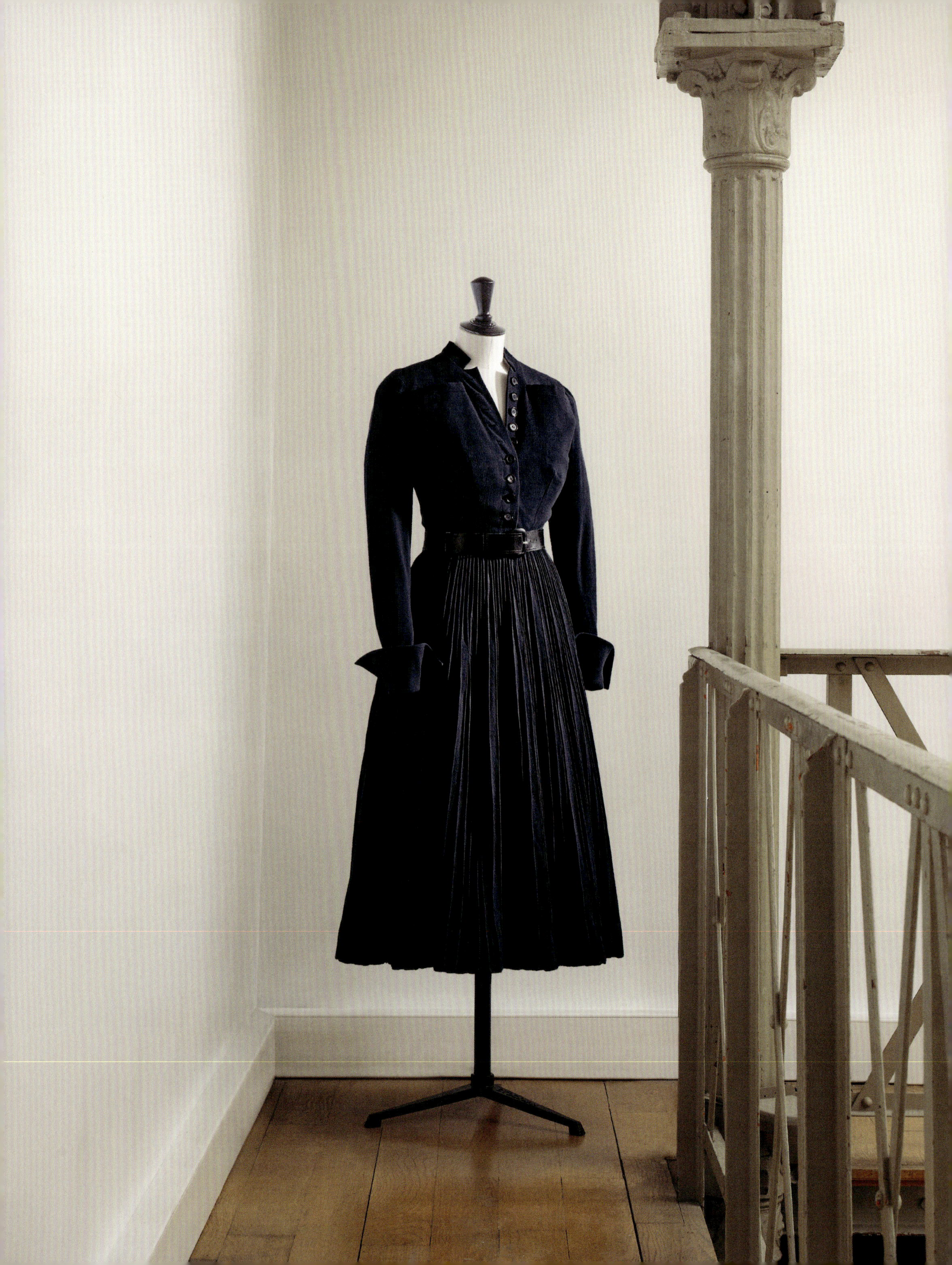

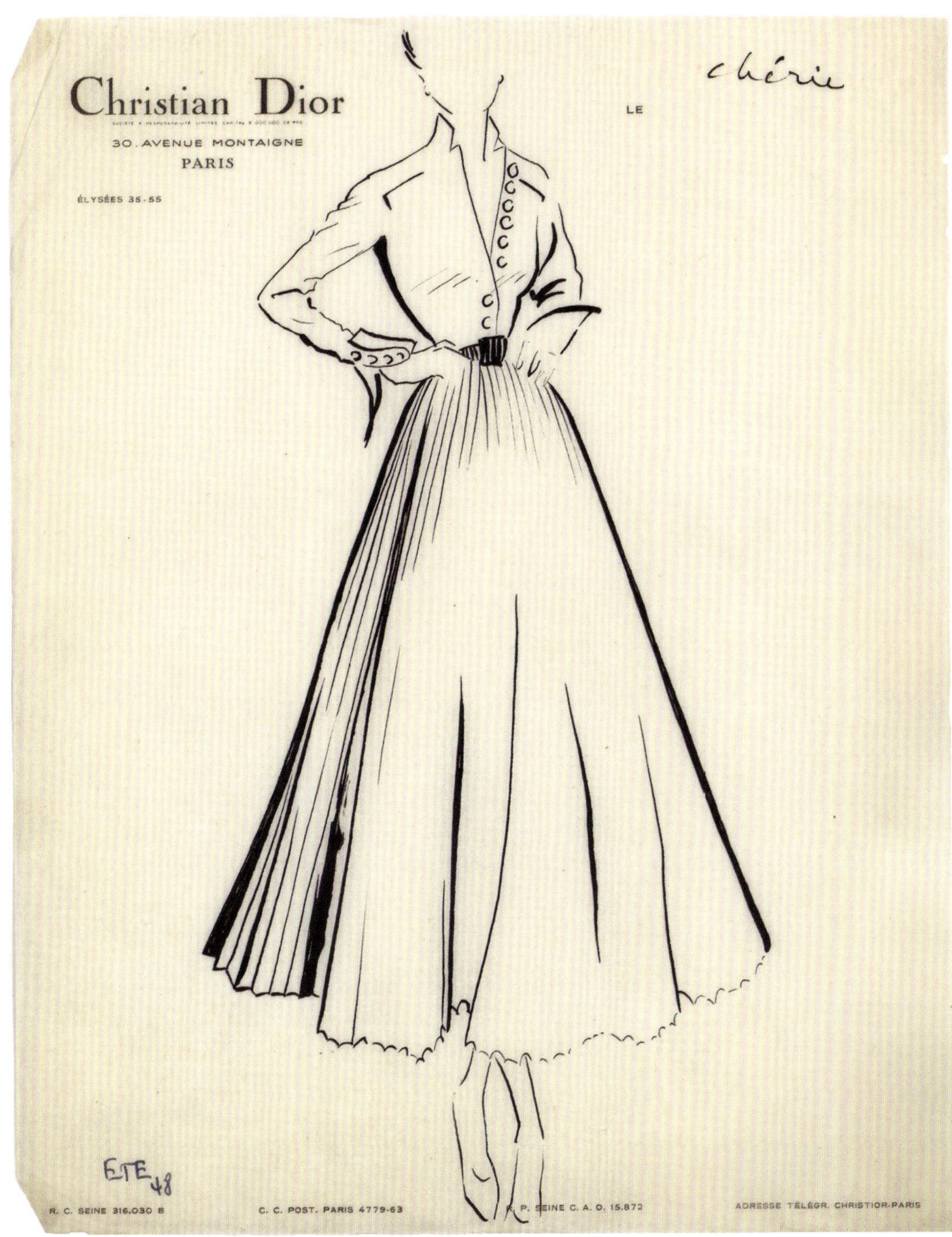

Christian Dior
Chérie

En taille dress in wool crêpe,
Spring–Summer 1948 haute couture
collection, *Envol* line. Paris,
Fondation Azzedine Alaïa.

Press sketch
for the Christian Dior
en taille dress *Chérie*.
Paris, Dior Héritage.

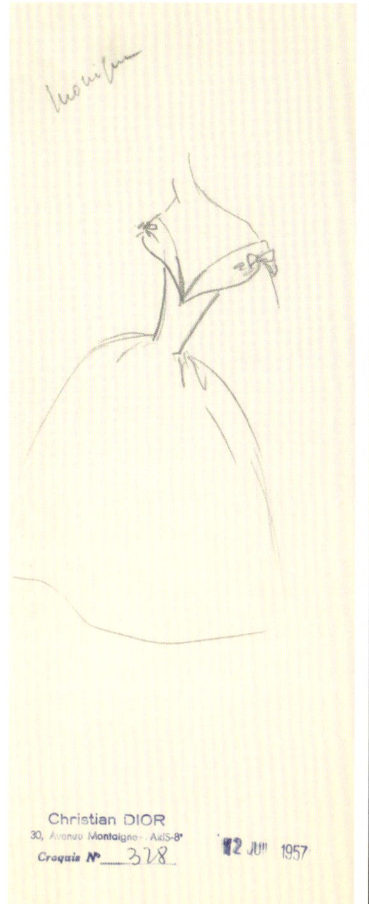

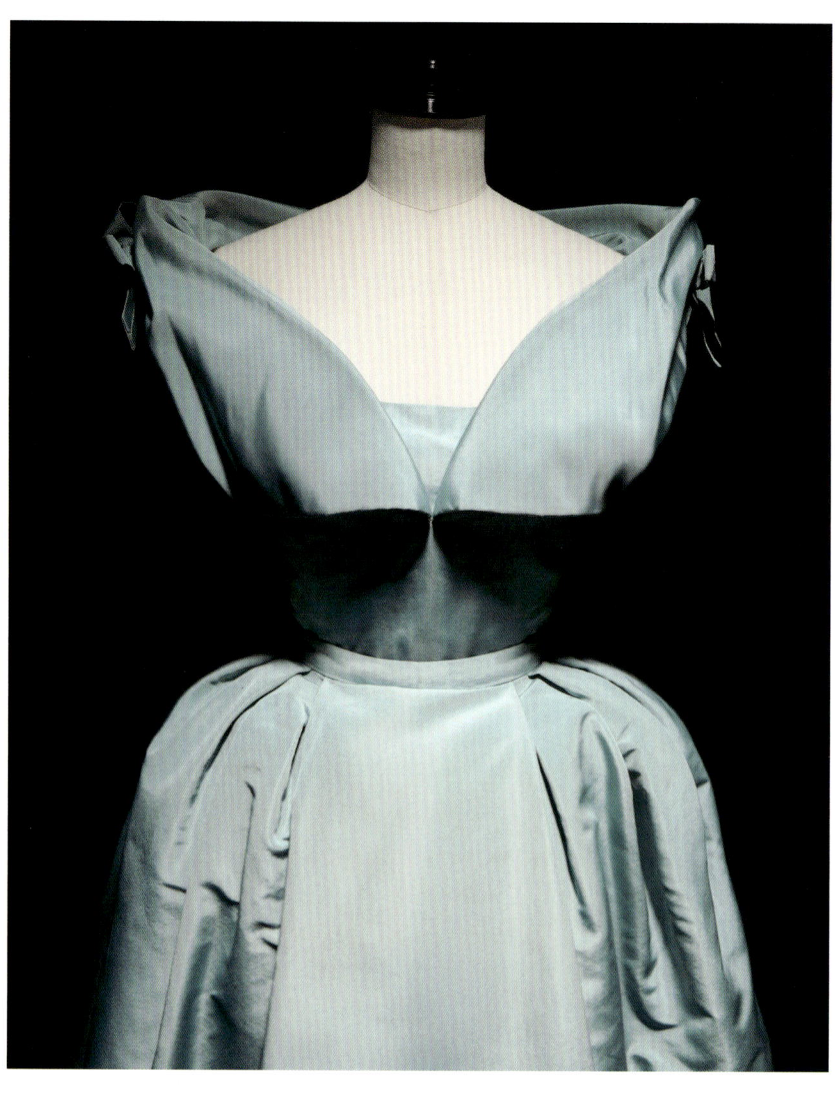

Christian Dior
Lancret
Reception dress in silk faille
(with detail), Autumn–Winter 1957
haute couture collection,
Fuseau line. Paris,
Fondation Azzedine Alaïa.

Christian Dior, original sketch
for the *Lancret* reception dress.
Paris, Dior Héritage.

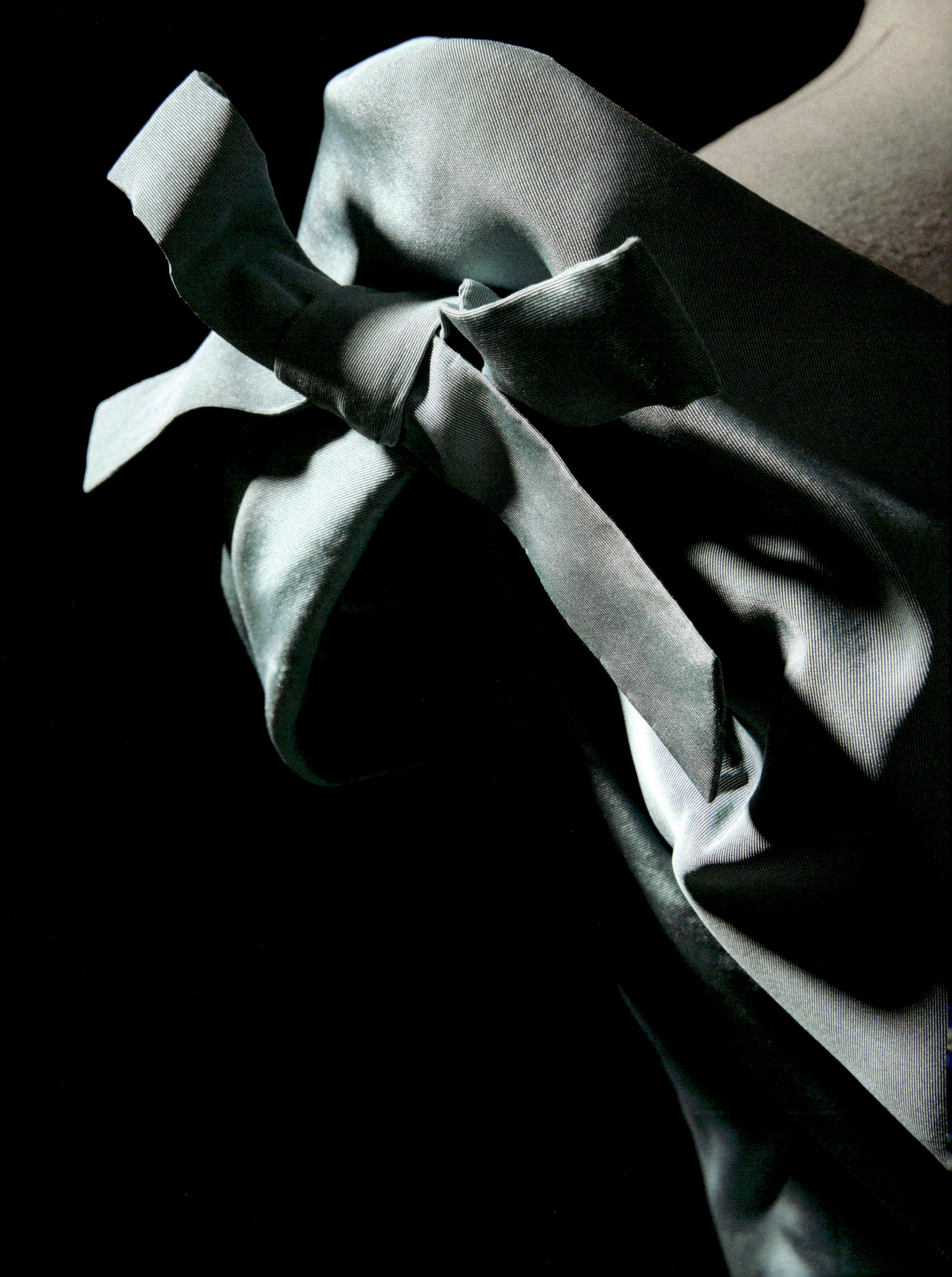

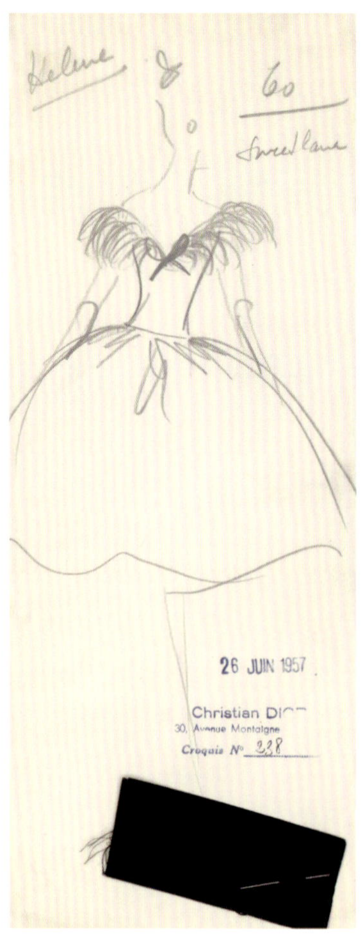

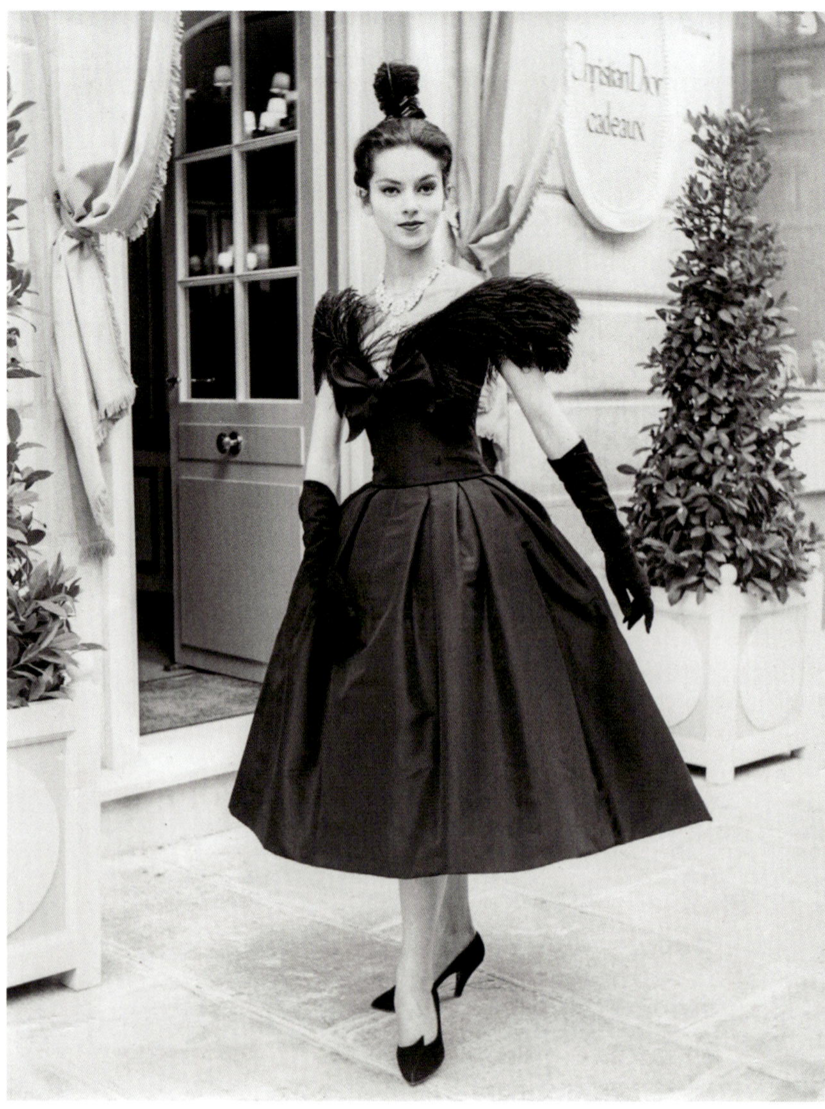

Christian Dior, original sketch,
with fabric sample, for the *Cygne noir*
reception dress. Paris, Dior Héritage.

The model Svetlana wearing the
Cygne noir reception dress outside
the entrance to the Christian Dior
boutique, Rue François Iᵉʳ, Paris, 1957.
Photograph by Willy Maywald.

Christian Dior
Cygne noir

Reception dress in silk faille,
Autumn–Winter 1957 haute couture
collection, *Fuseau* line. Paris,
Fondation Azzedine Alaïa.

This dress, for a client, is a specially
adapted version of the original model.

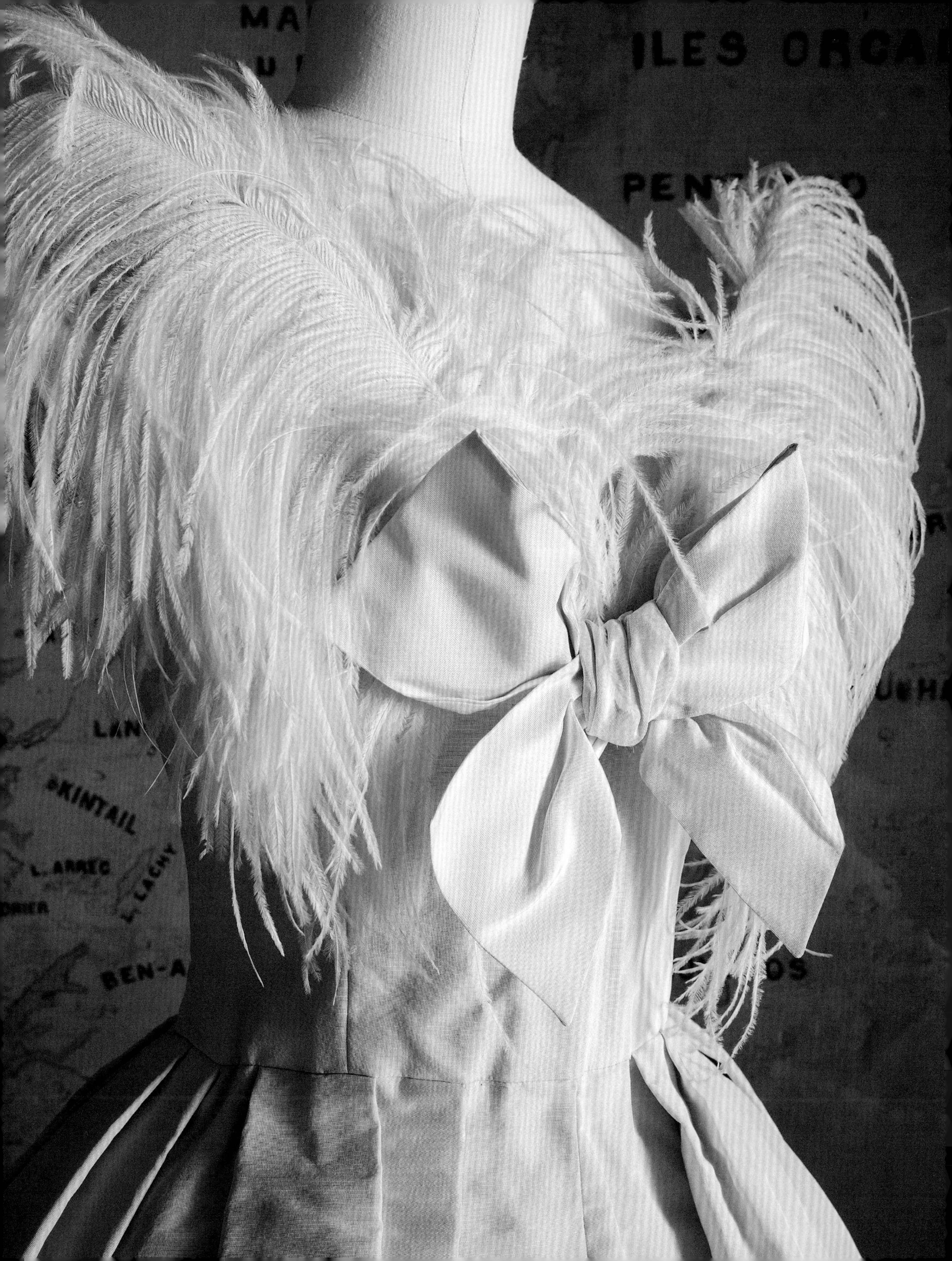

MA
ILES ORCA
PENT
SKINTAIL
LAN
L. ARREC
L. LAGNY
BEN-A

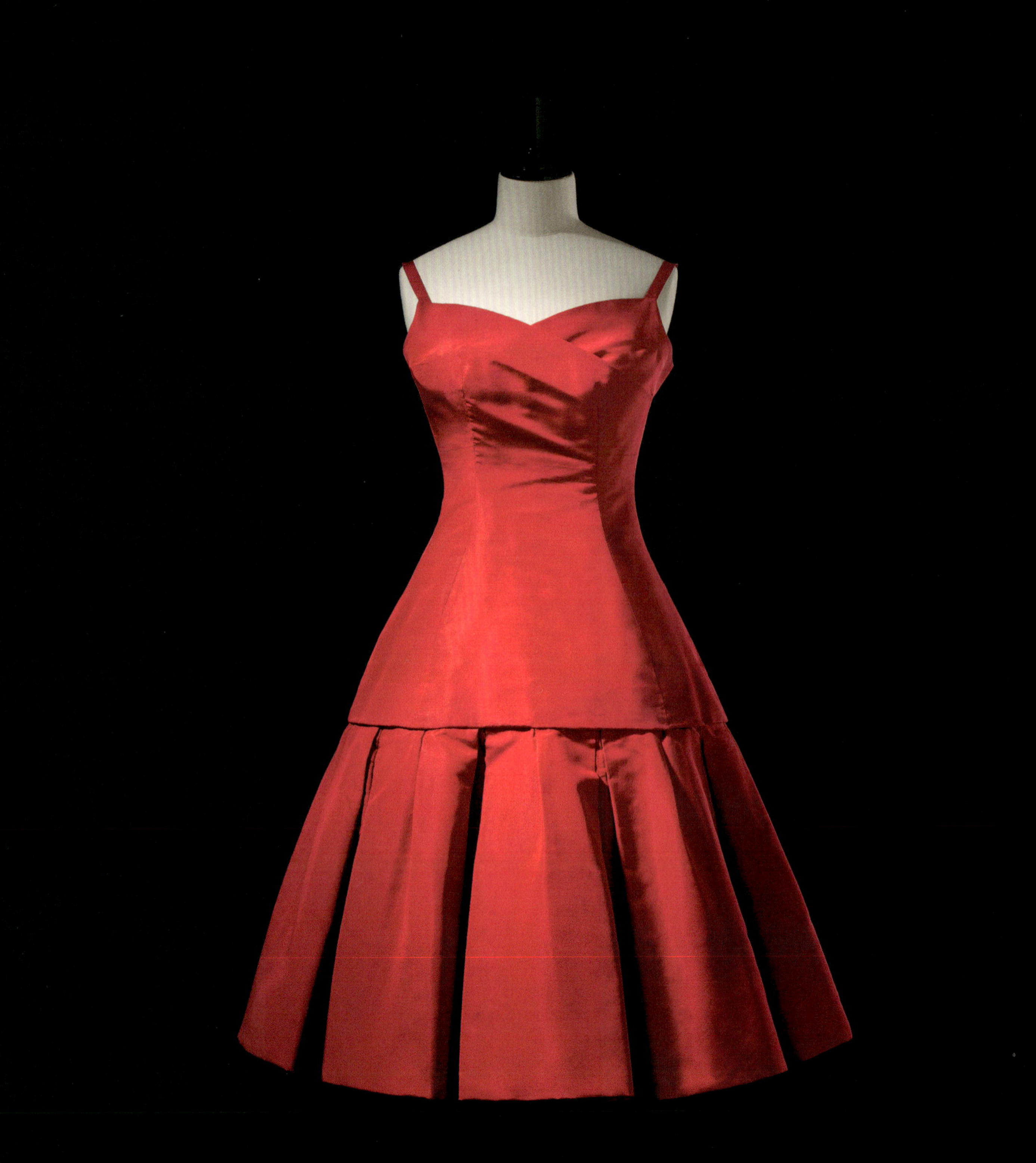

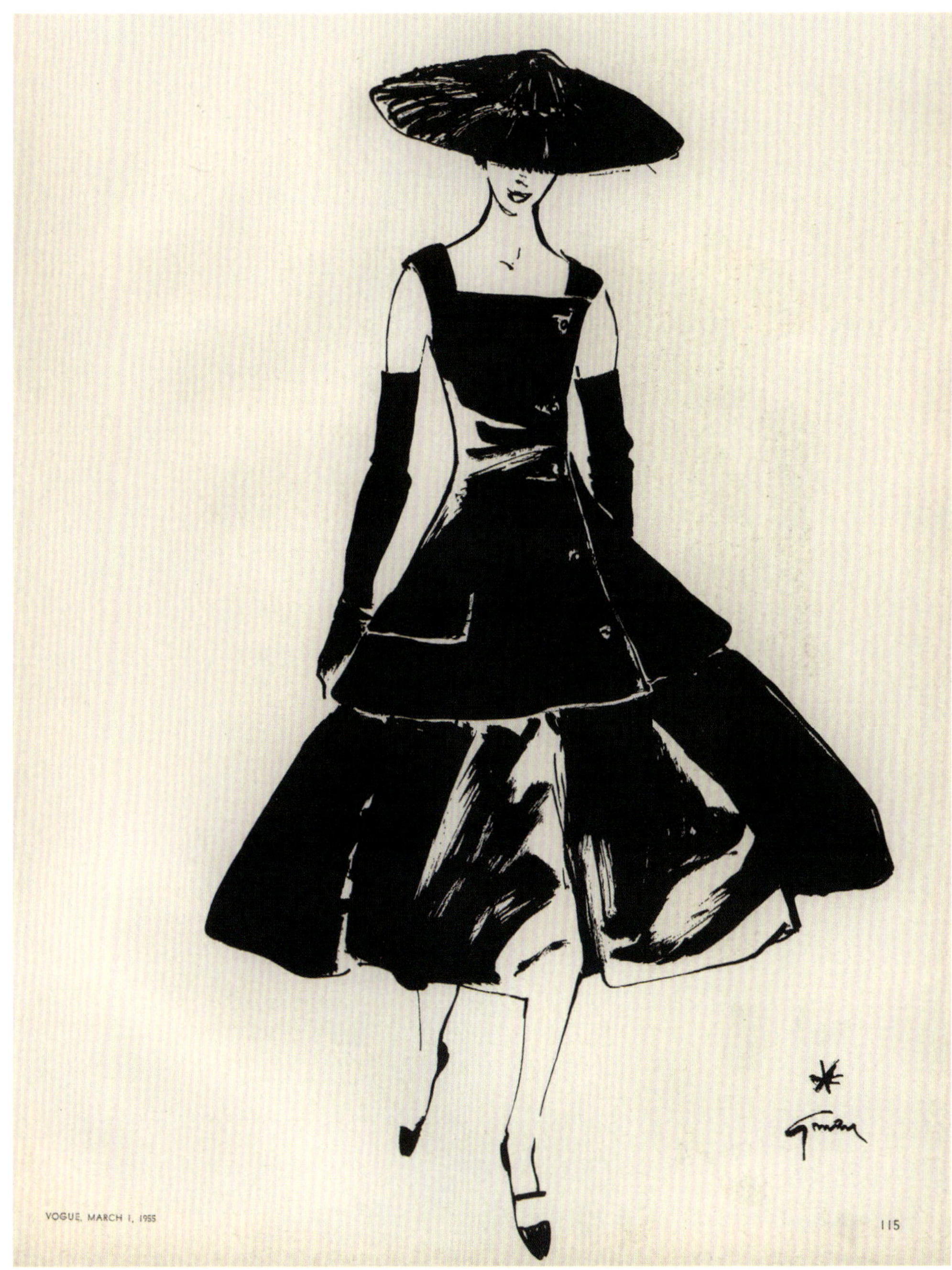

Christian Dior
Audacieuse

Dinner dress in silk satin,
Spring–Summer 1955
haute couture collection, *A* line.
Paris, Fondation Azzedine Alaïa.

René Gruau, illustration of
the Christian Dior *Audacieuse* dinner
ensemble comprising a dress and jacket,
published in *Vogue*, March 1, 1955.

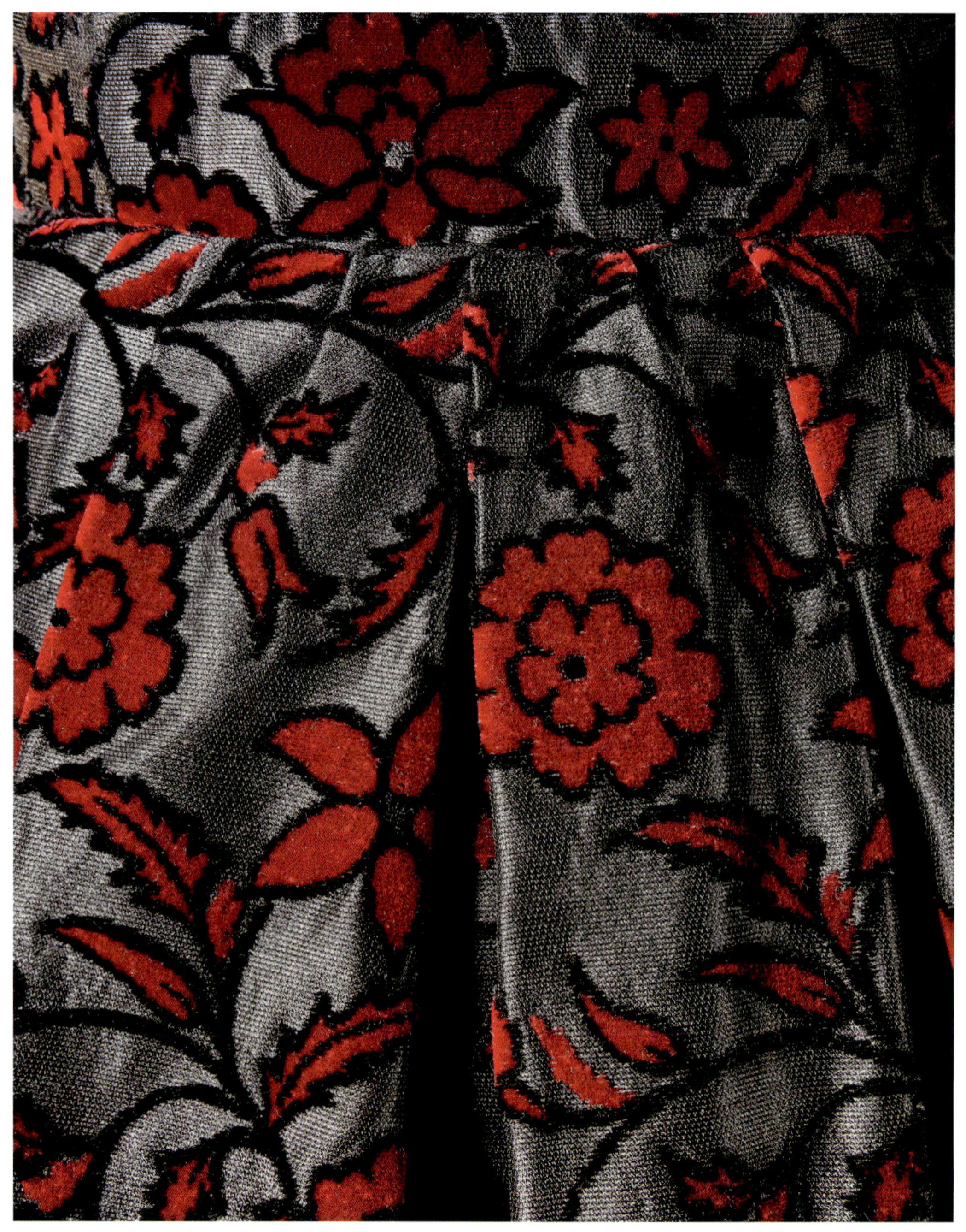

Christian Dior
Tolède

Afternoon dress in embossed silk velvet
(with detail), Autumn–Winter 1956
haute couture collection, *Aimant* line.
Paris, Fondation Azzedine Alaïa.

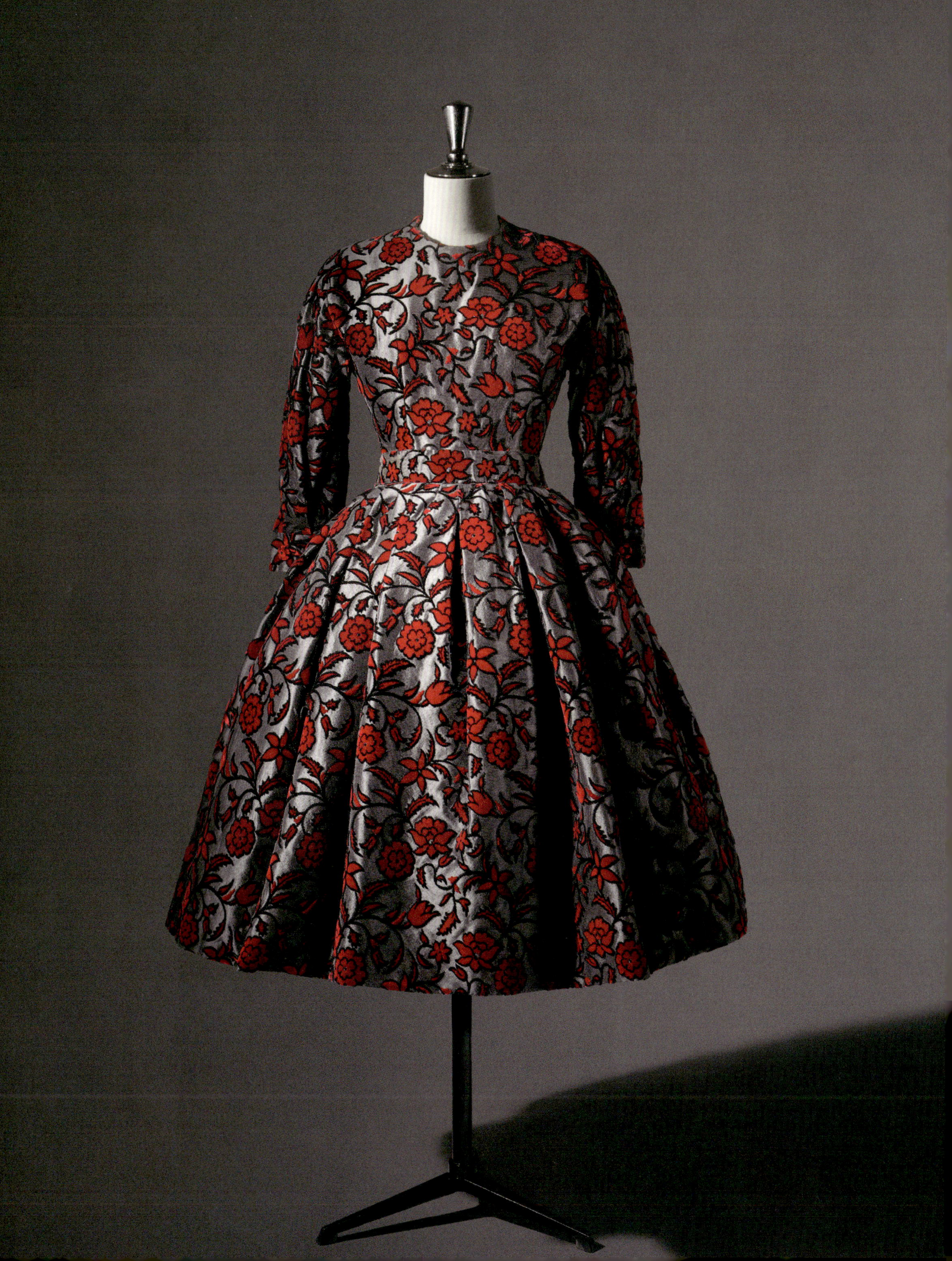

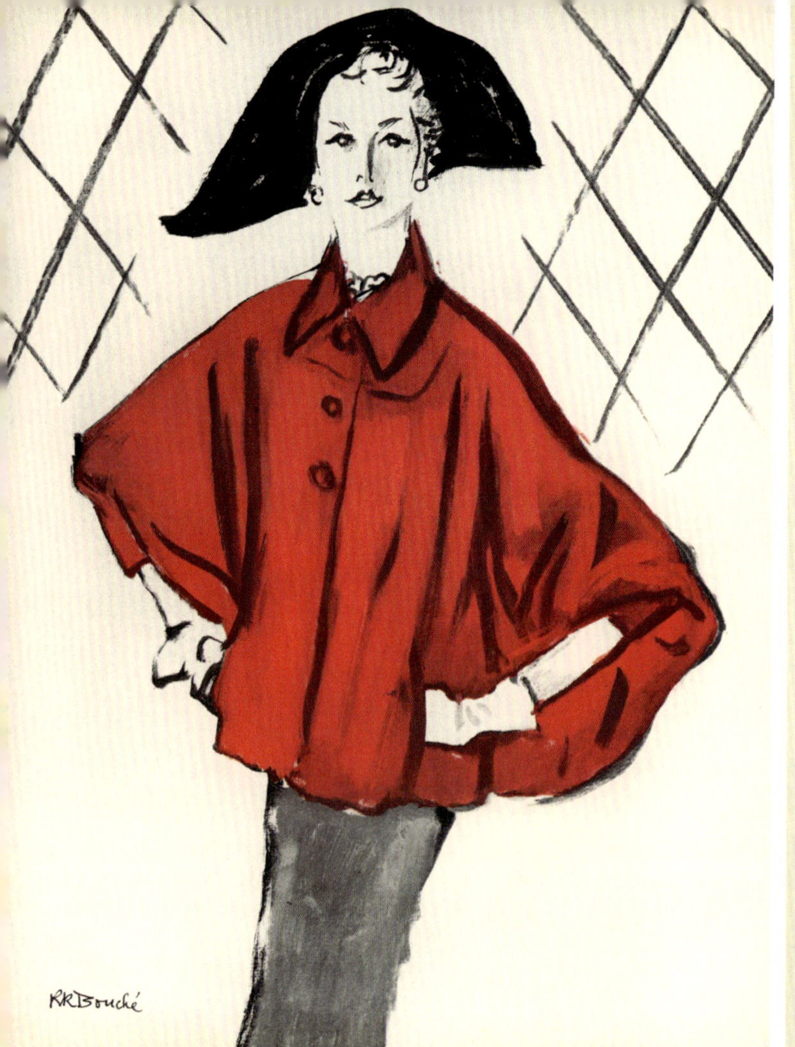

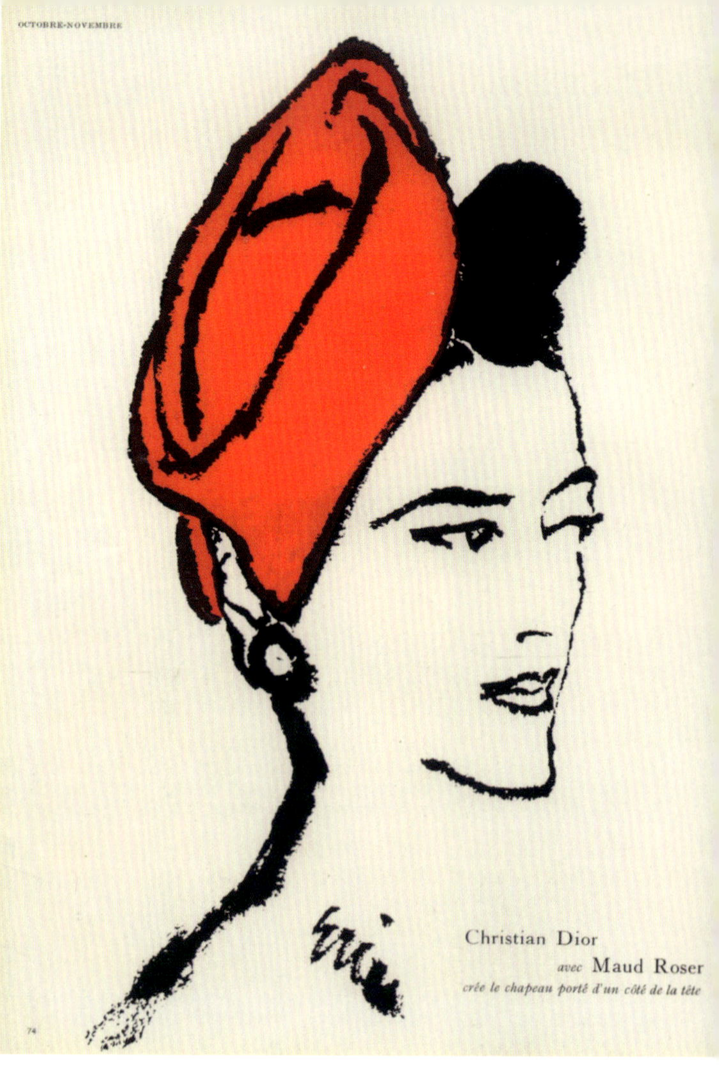

"RED. A VERY ENERGETIC AND BENEFICIAL COLOR. IT IS THE COLOR OF LIFE. I LOVE RED AND I THINK IT SUITS ALMOST EVERY COMPLEXION. IT IS GOOD **CHRISTIAN DIOR** FOR ANY TIME, TOO."

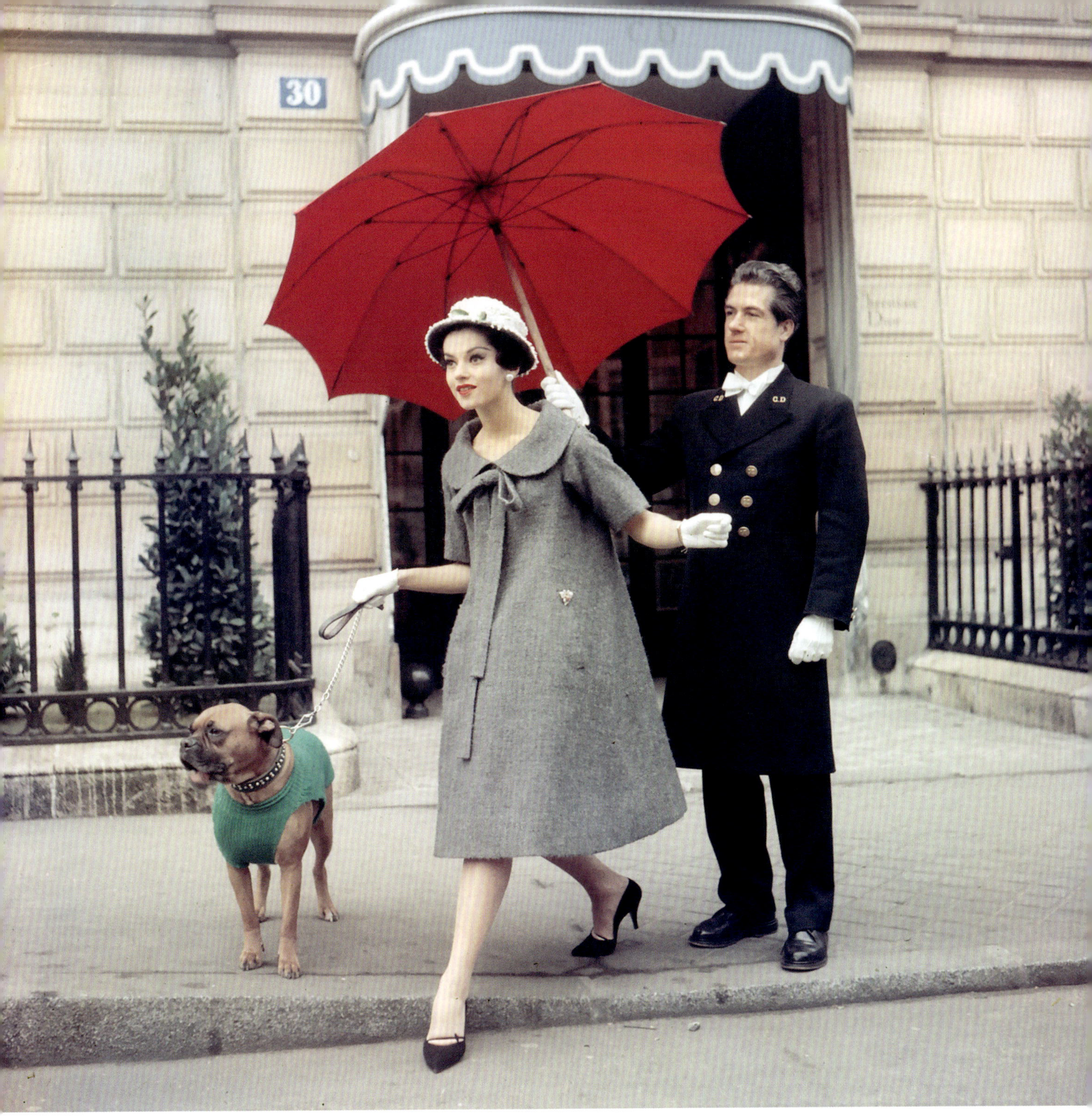

ABOVE
The model Svetlana wearing
the *Bonne conduite* dress, by Yves Saint Laurent
for Christian Dior, Spring–Summer 1958
haute couture collection, *Trapèze* line,
outside the Dior headquarters at
30 Avenue Montaigne, Paris.
Photograph by Sabine Weiss.

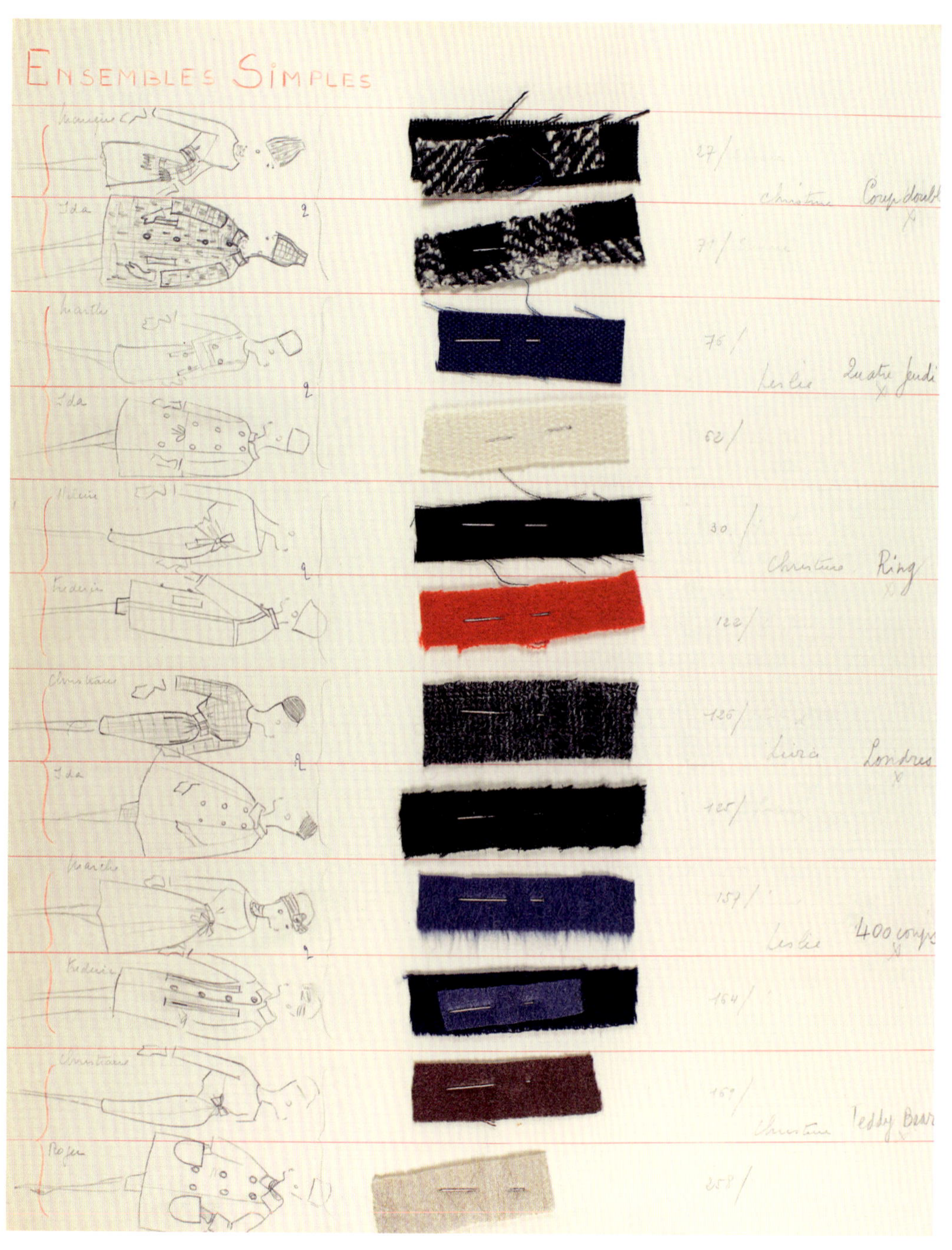

"Simple ensembles" page from the chart
for the Autumn–Winter 1959 haute couture
collection, *1960* line, by Yves Saint Laurent
for Christian Dior. Paris, Dior Héritage.

Yves Saint Laurent for Christian Dior
Londres

Afternoon ensemble in wool,
Autumn–Winter 1959 haute couture collection,
1960 line. Paris, Fondation Azzedine Alaïa.

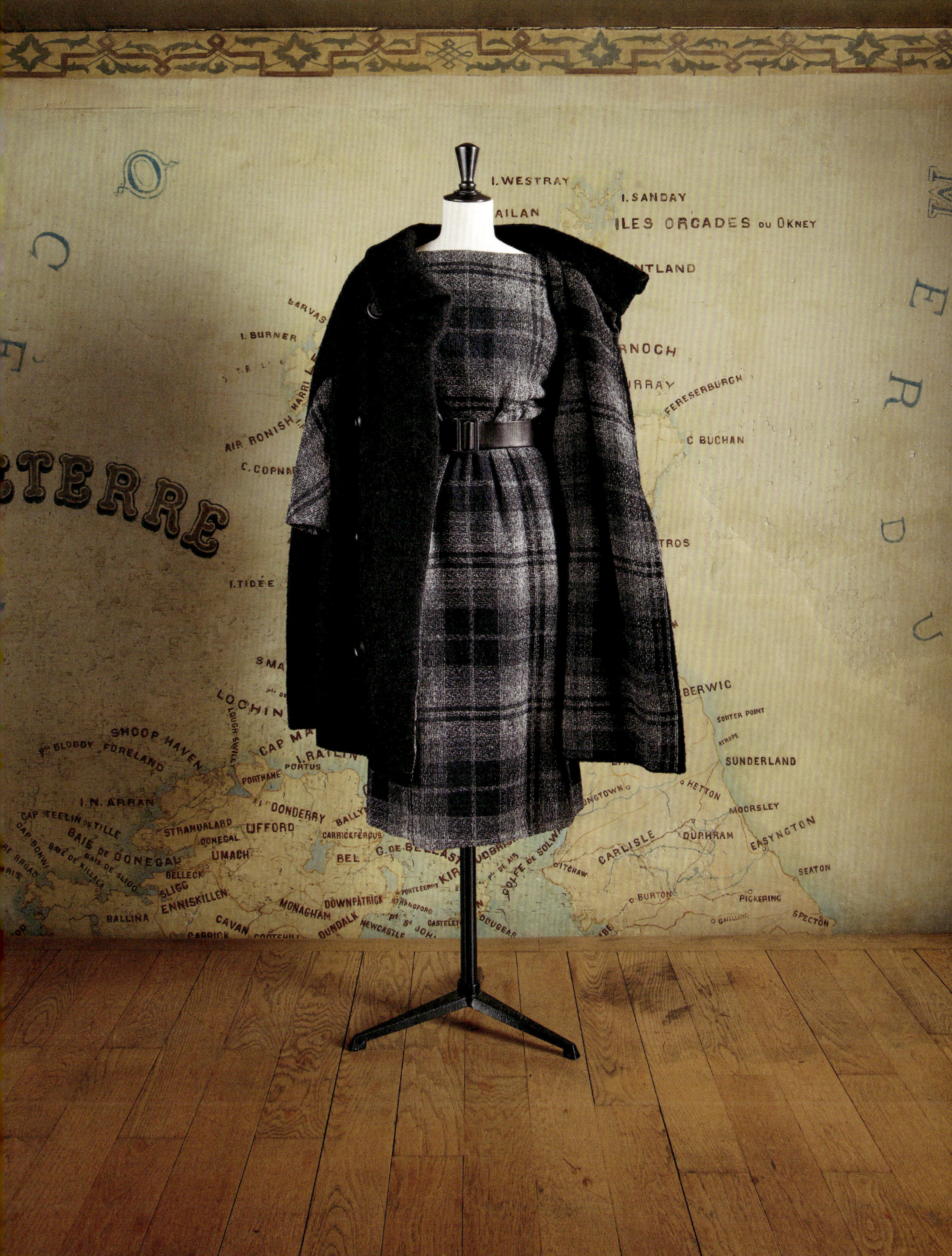

I. WESTRAY
I. SANDAY
AILAN
ILES ORCADES du OKNEY
 NTLAND
GARVAS
I. BURNER
RNOCH
URRAY
FERESERBURGH
AIR. RONISH HARRI
C BUCHAN
C. COPNA
TERRE
I. TIDÉE
TROS
SMA
BERWIC
LOCHIN
SOUTER POINT
SHOOP HAVEN
STROPE
P. BLODDY FORELAND
CAP MA
SUNDERLAND
I. RATLIN
I.N. ARRAN
HETTON
PORTHANE
PORTUS
MOORSLEY
DONDERRY
BALLY
NGTOWN
UFFORD
DURHRAM
EASYNCTON
CAP TEELIN DU TILLE
STRANUALARD
CARRICKFERGUS
CARLISLE
BAIS DE DONEGAL
OONEGAL
SEATON
CAP BONRI
UMACH
BEL
G. DE BEL FAST
KIR
ITCHAW
BURTON
PICKERING
BELLECK
GOLFE DE SOLWA
BROAD
SLIGG
SPECTON
BAIE DE KILLALA
ENNISKILLEN
MONAGHAM
DOWNPATRICK
STRANGFORD
GNILLING
BALLINA
CAVAN
COOTEHILL
OUNDALK
NEWCASTLE
DOUGEAR
CARRICK
JOH.
ETERRE
OCE
E
R
D
U
MER
O
M

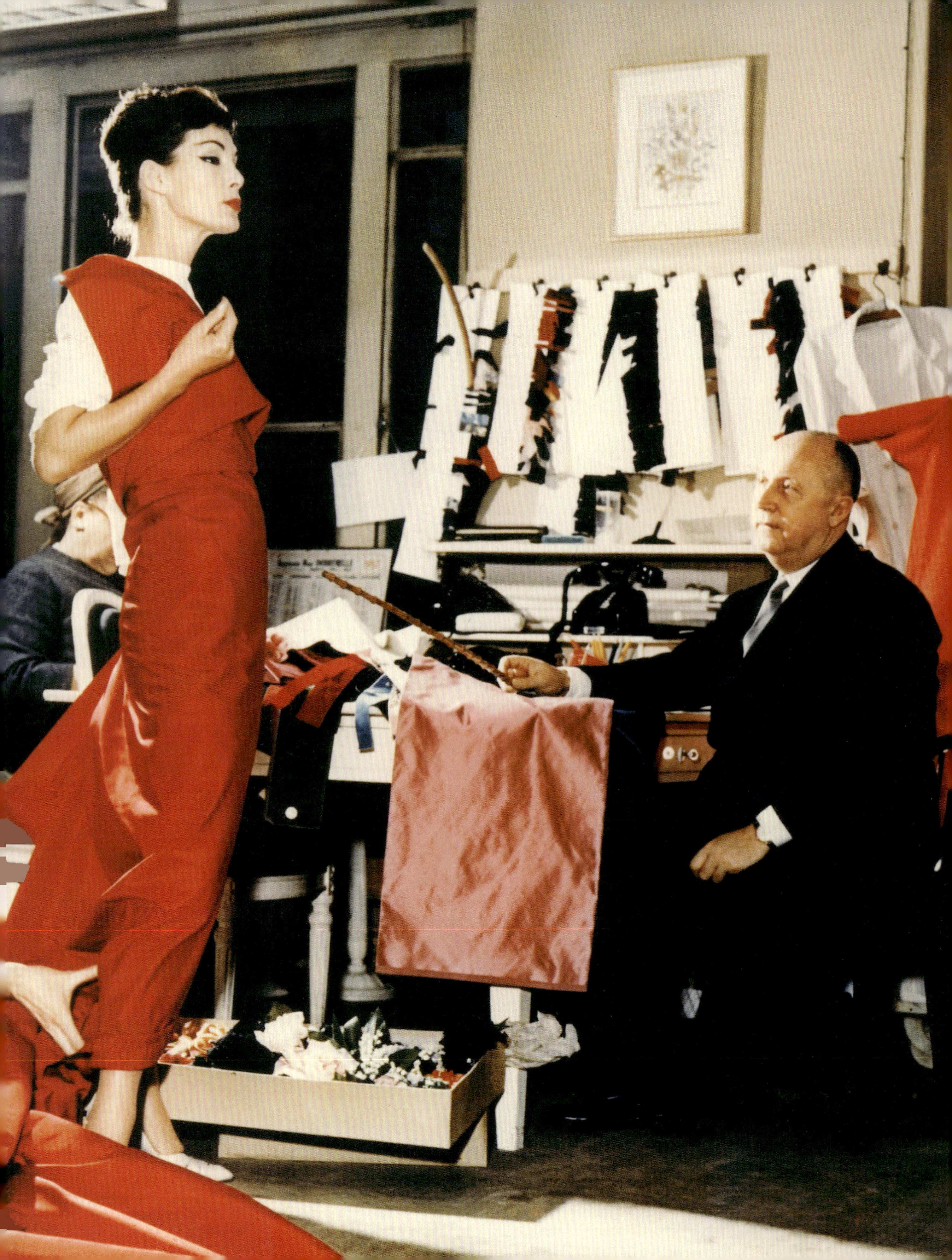

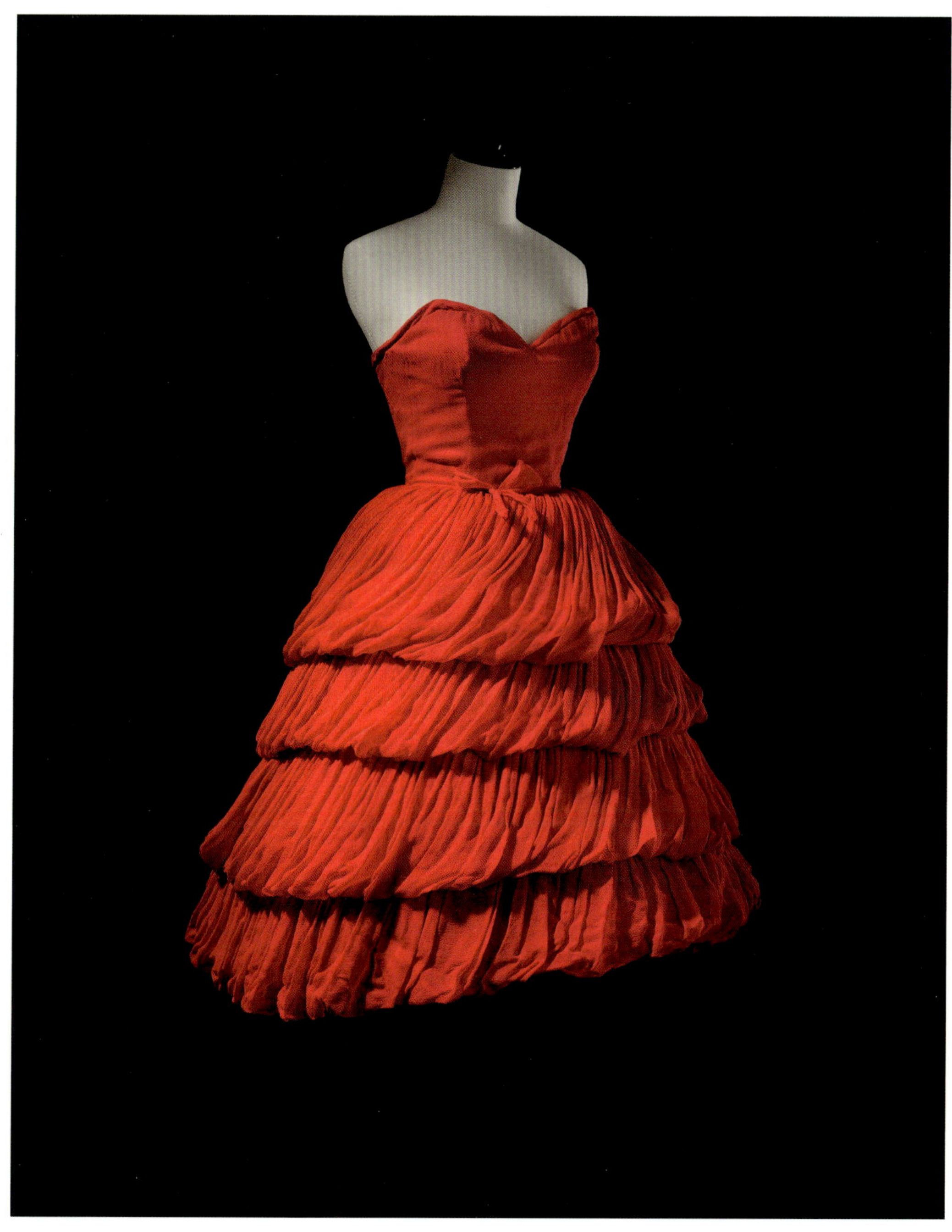

Christian Dior
Tourbillon

Short evening dress in silk chiffon,
Autumn–Winter 1956 haute couture
collection, *Aimant* line. Paris,
Fondation Azzedine Alaïa.

The model Lucky during a fitting
session with Christian Dior in
the studio at 30 Avenue Montaigne,
Paris, circa 1956. Photograph by Bellini.

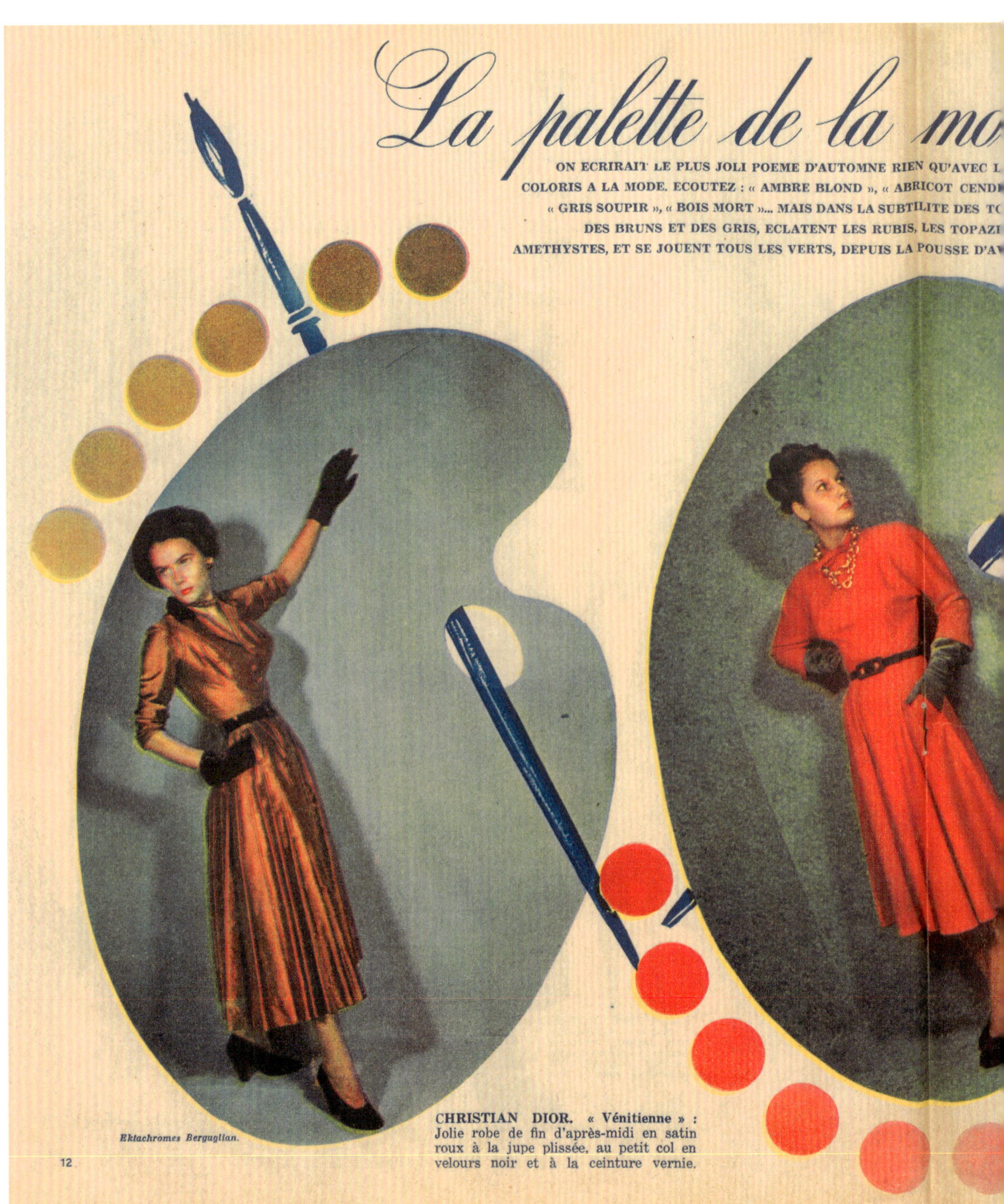

ON ECRIRAIT LE PLUS JOLI POEME D'AUTOMNE RIEN QU'AVEC L
COLORIS A LA MODE. ECOUTEZ : « AMBRE BLOND », « ABRICOT CEND
« GRIS SOUPIR », « BOIS MORT »... MAIS DANS LA SUBTILITE DES TO
DES BRUNS ET DES GRIS, ECLATENT LES RUBIS, LES TOPAZE
AMETHYSTES, ET SE JOUENT TOUS LES VERTS, DEPUIS LA POUSSE D'A

Ektachromes Berguglian.

CHRISTIAN DIOR. « Vénitienne » :
Jolie robe de fin d'après-midi en satin
roux à la jupe plissée, au petit col en
velours noir et à la ceinture vernie.

12

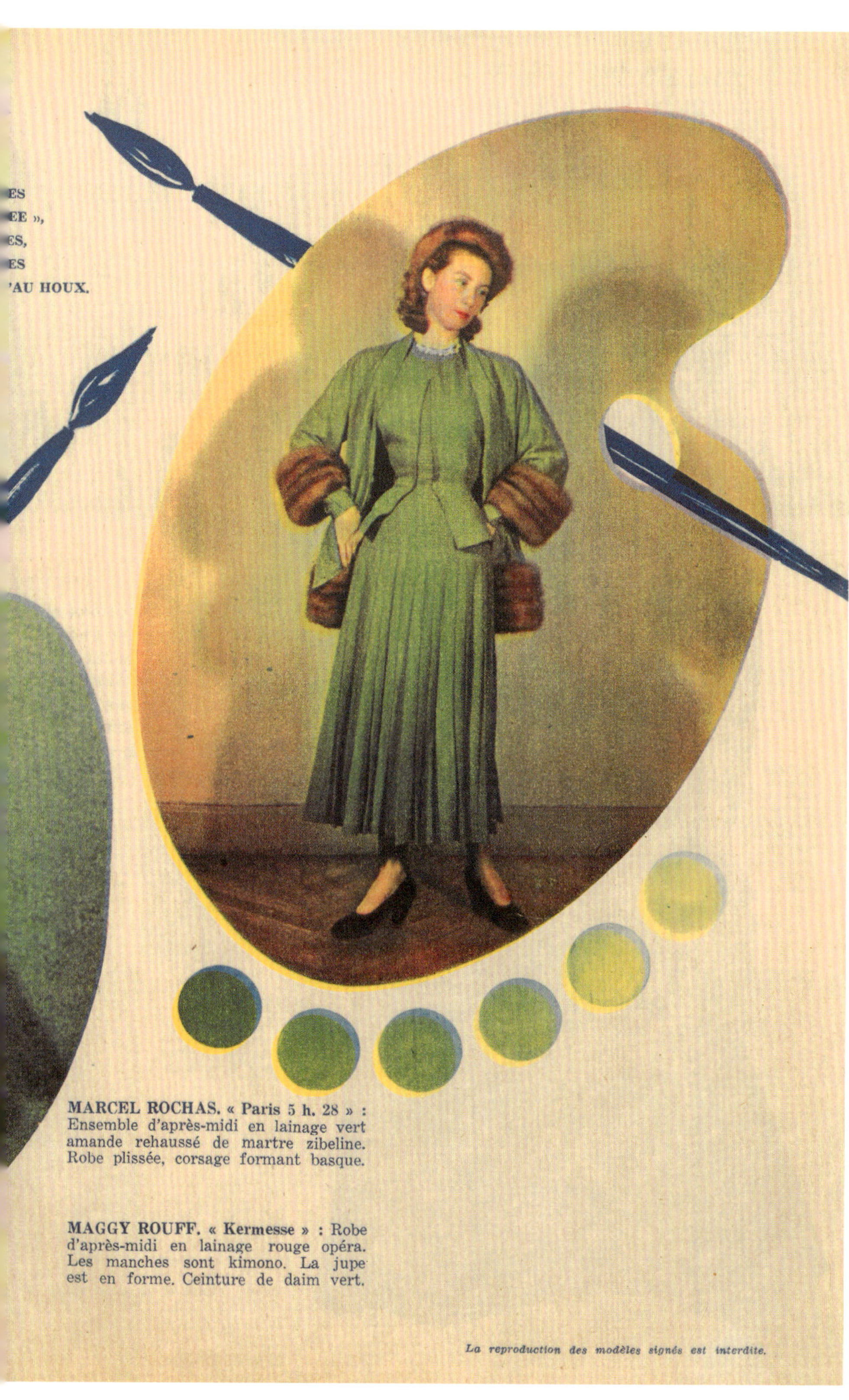

Spread from *Claudine* magazine
on "The palette of fashion."
Photographs by Alfred Berguglian,
published in the issue from
September 25, 1947.

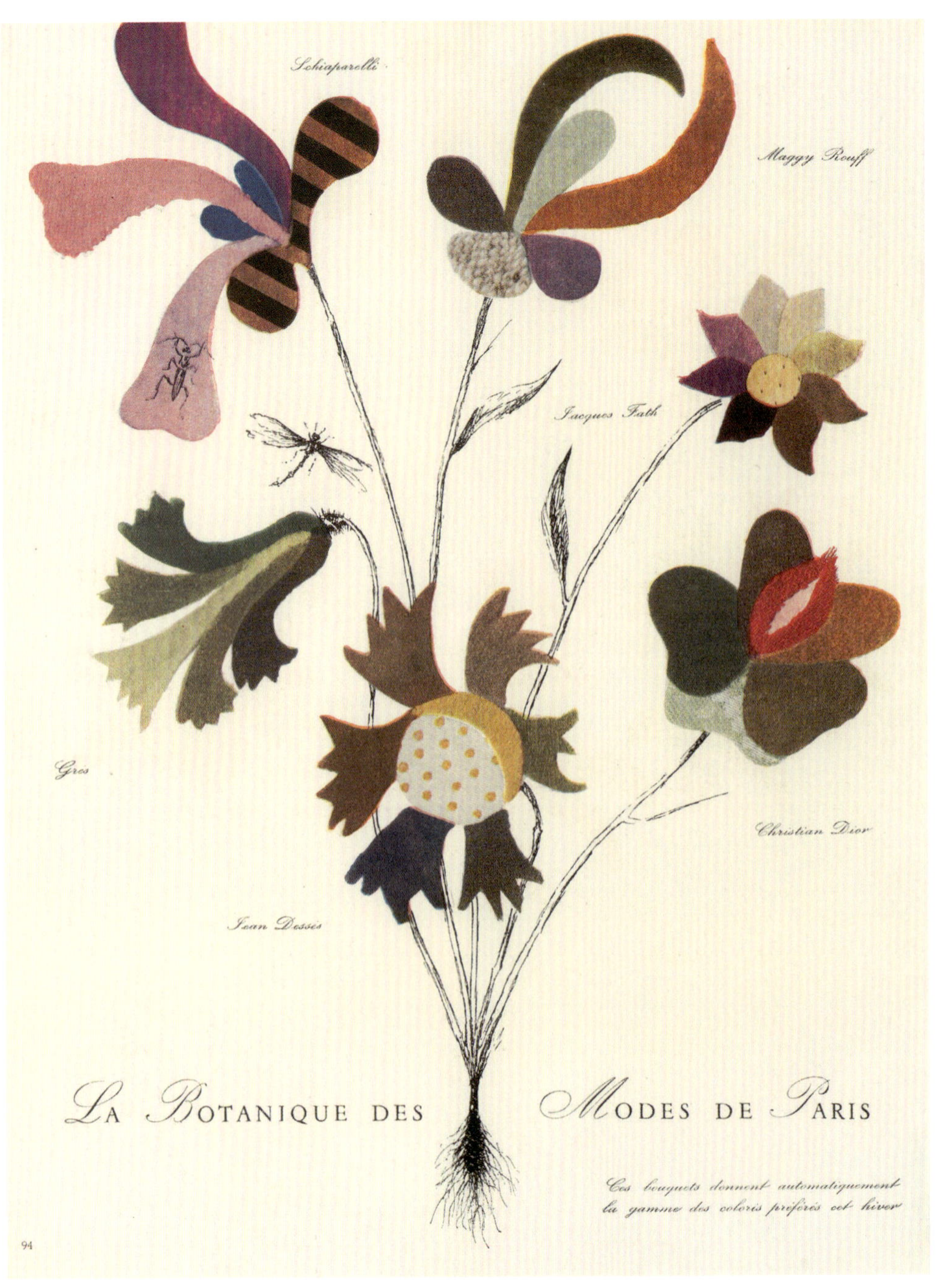

"The Botany of Paris Fashions,"
illustration, published in *Vogue Paris*,
October 1, 1947.

The model Ghislaine Arsac wearing
the Christian Dior *Jardin anglais*
afternoon dress, Spring–Summer 1954
haute couture collection, *Muguet* line.
Photograph by the Frères Séeberger,
published in *La Femme chic*, April 1954.

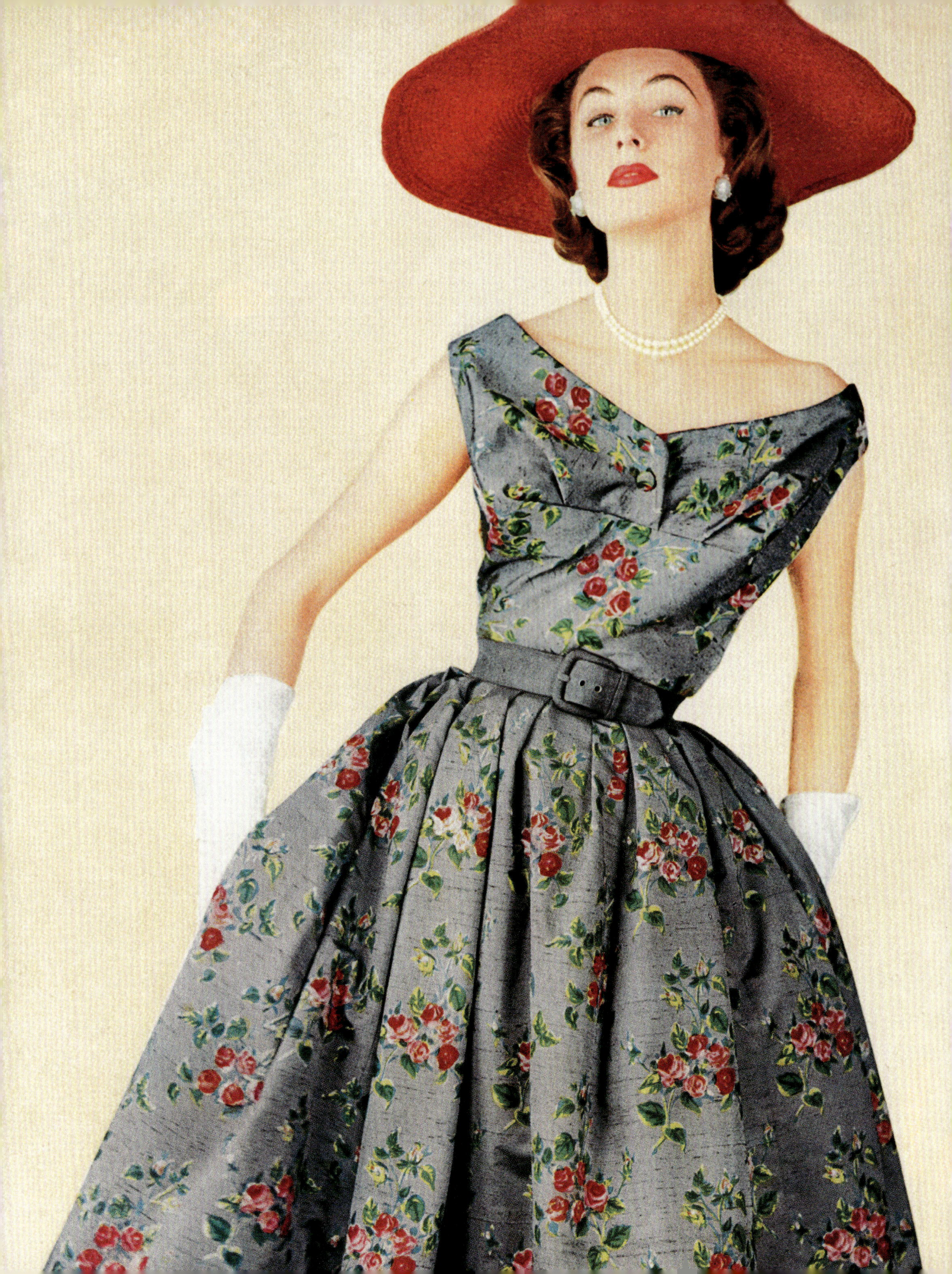

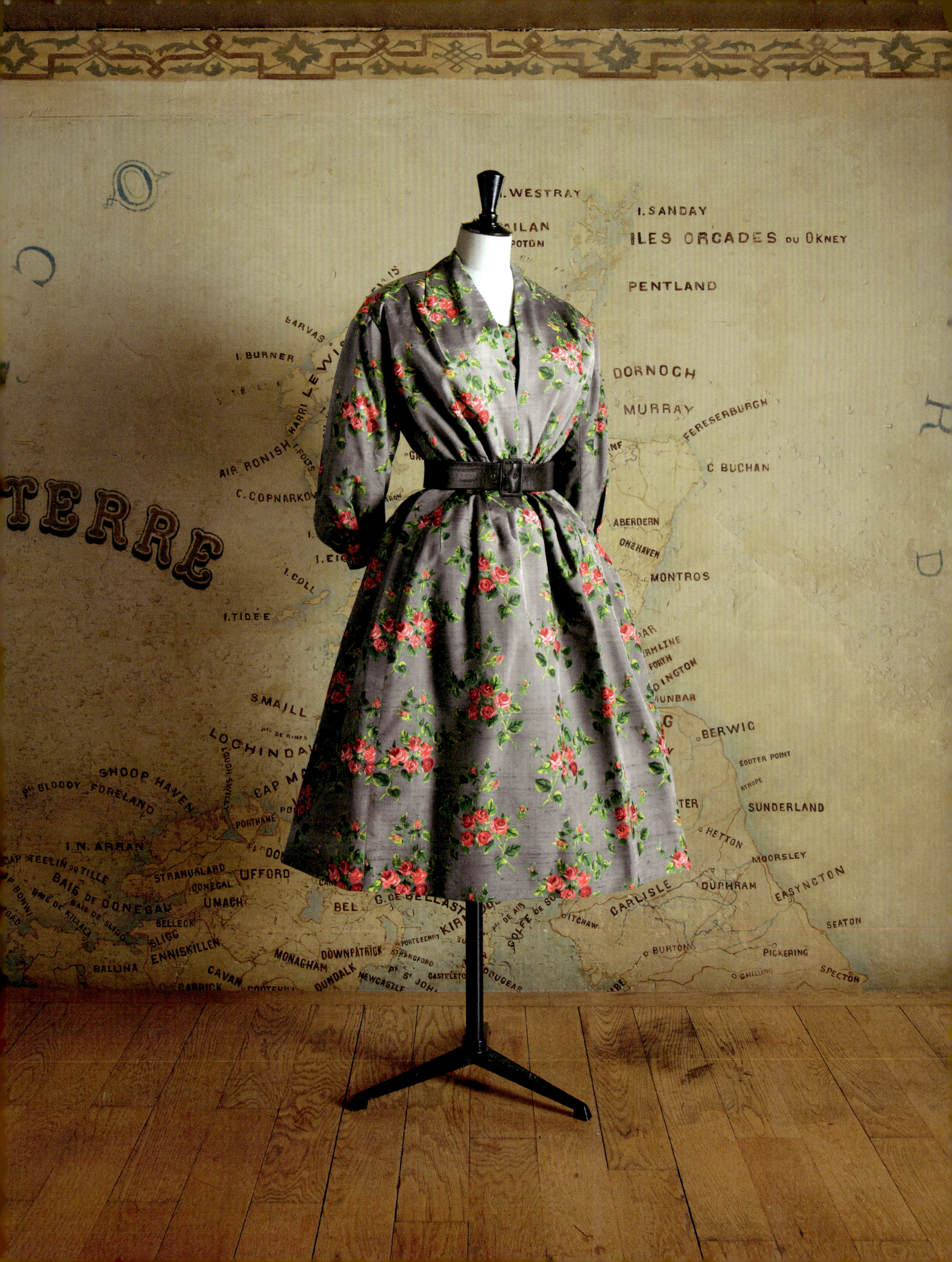

I. WESTRAY
I. SANDAY
ILES ORCADES du OKNEY
PENTLAND
DORNOCH
MURRAY
FERESERBURGH
C BUCHAN
ABERDERN
ONEHAVEN
MONTROS
TERRE
BARVAS
I. BURNER
LEWIS
AIR. RONISH HARRI I.FOITS
C. COPNARKOW
I. EIG
I. COLL
I.TIDEE
SMAILL
LOCHINDAL
CAP M
SHOOP HAVEN
Pit. BLODDY FORELAND
I. N. ARRAN
CAP TEELIN du TILLE
BAIS de DONEGAL
UMACH
STRANUALARD
DONEGAL
BELLECK
SLIGG
BALLINA
ENNISKILLEN
CAVAN
CARRICK
MONAGHAM
DOWNPATRICK
OUNDALK
NEWCASTLE
UFFORD
BEL
G. de BELLAST
KIR
BERWIC
SOUTER POINT
RYHOPE
SUNDERLAND
HETTON
MOORSLEY
DUPHRAM
EASYNGTON
CARLISLE
SEATON
PICKERING
SPECTON
O BURTON
DUNBAR
FORTH

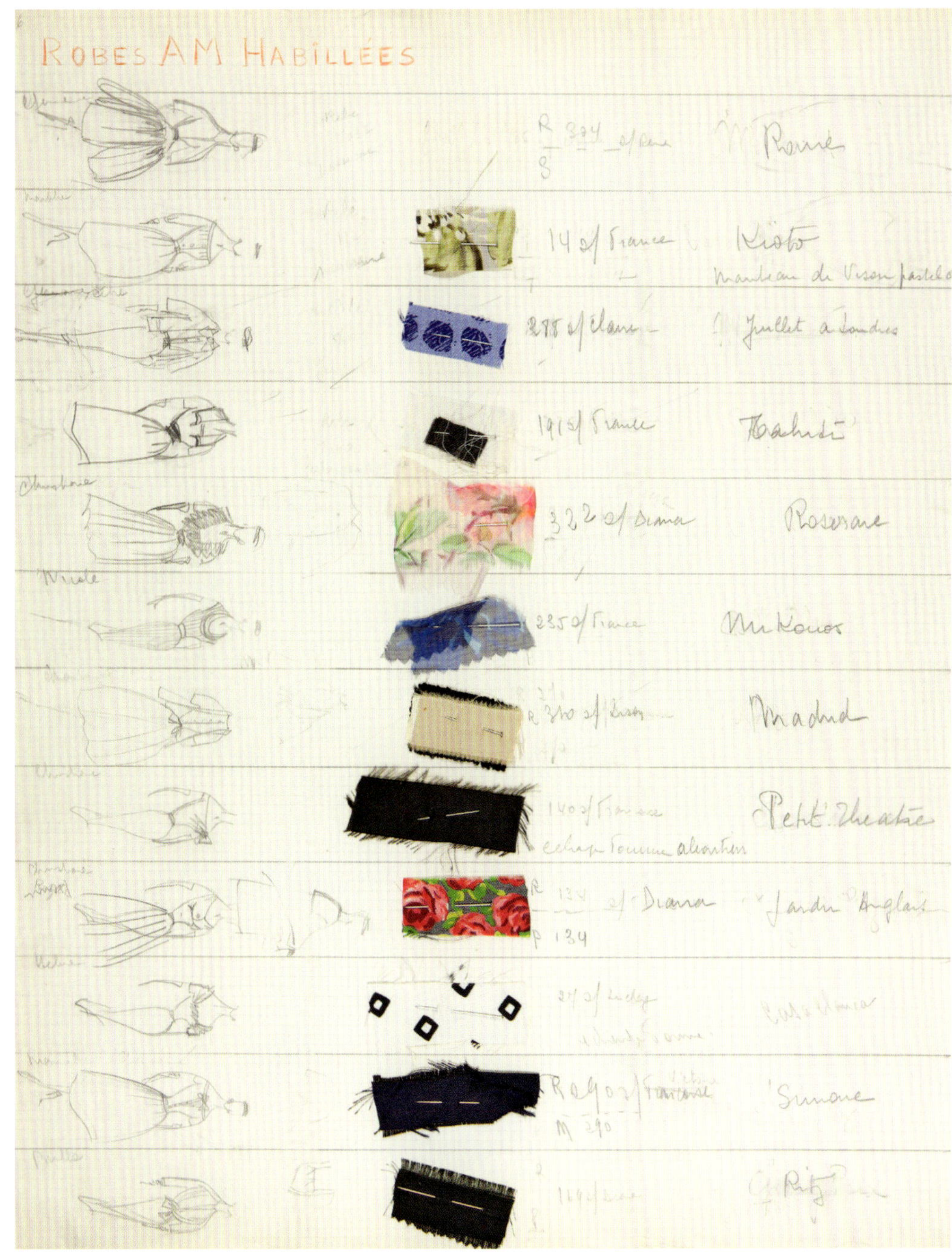

Christian Dior
Jardin anglais

Afternoon ensemble in printed silk shantung,
Spring–Summer 1954 haute couture collection,
Muguet line. Paris, Fondation Azzedine Alaïa.

"Formal afternoon dresses" page
from the chart for Christian Dior's
Spring–Summer 1954 haute couture collection,
Muguet line. Paris, Dior Héritage.

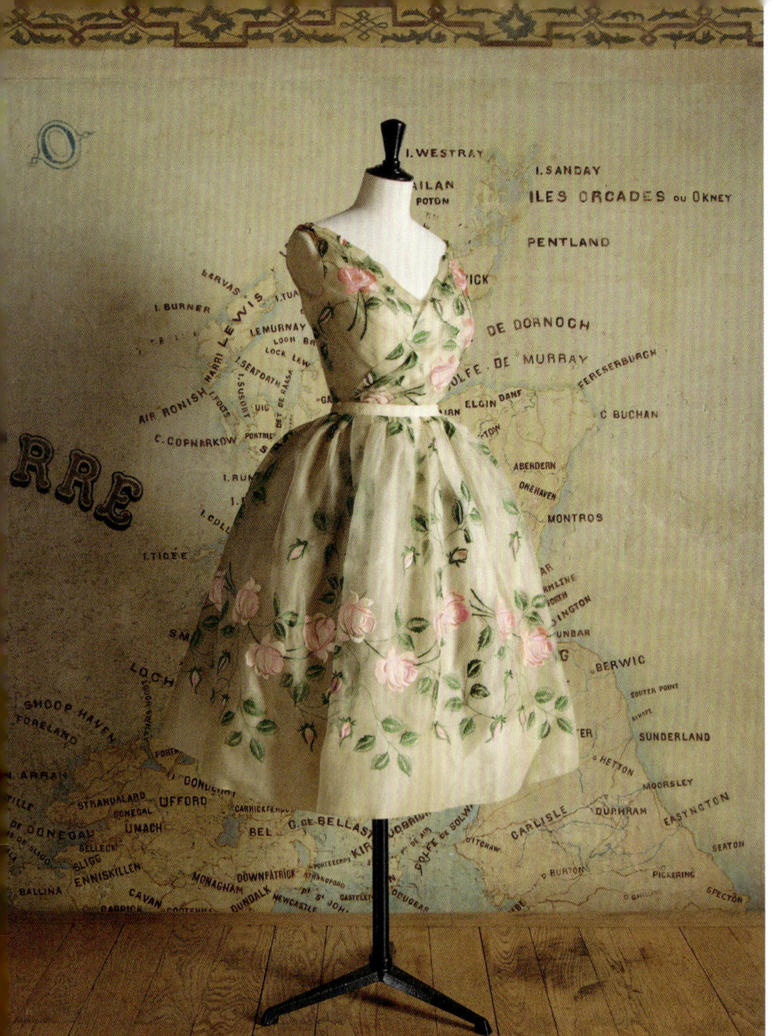
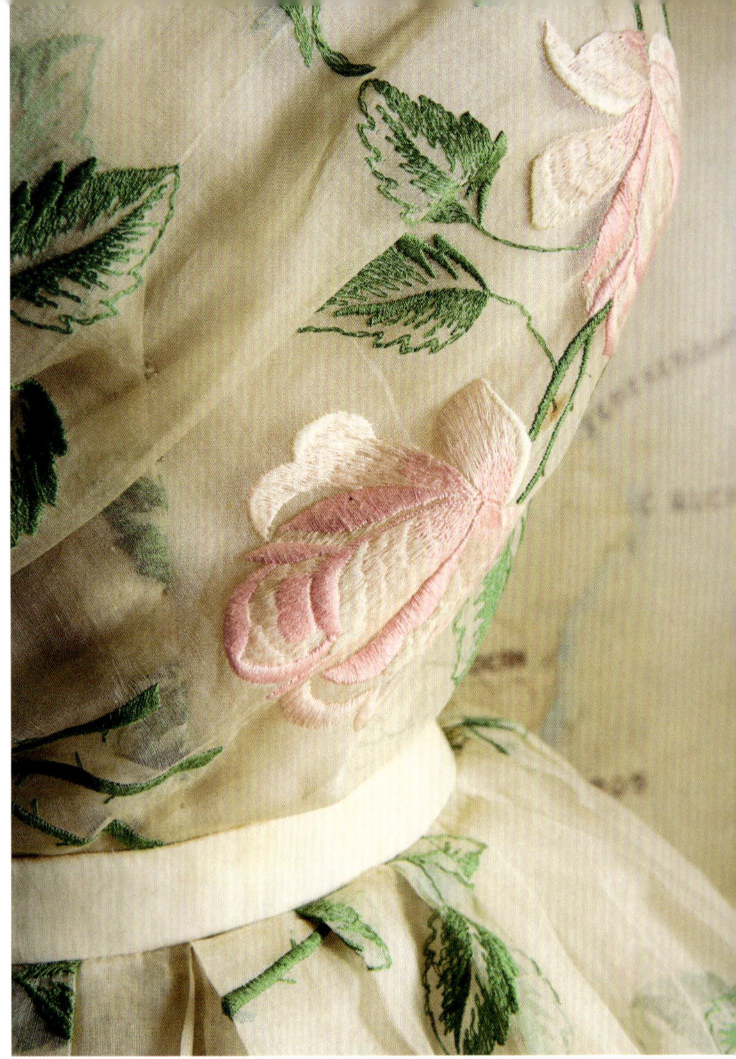

Christian Dior

Dress in embroidered organdy
from a boutique collection
(with detail), circa 1955.
Paris, Fondation Azzedine Alaïa.

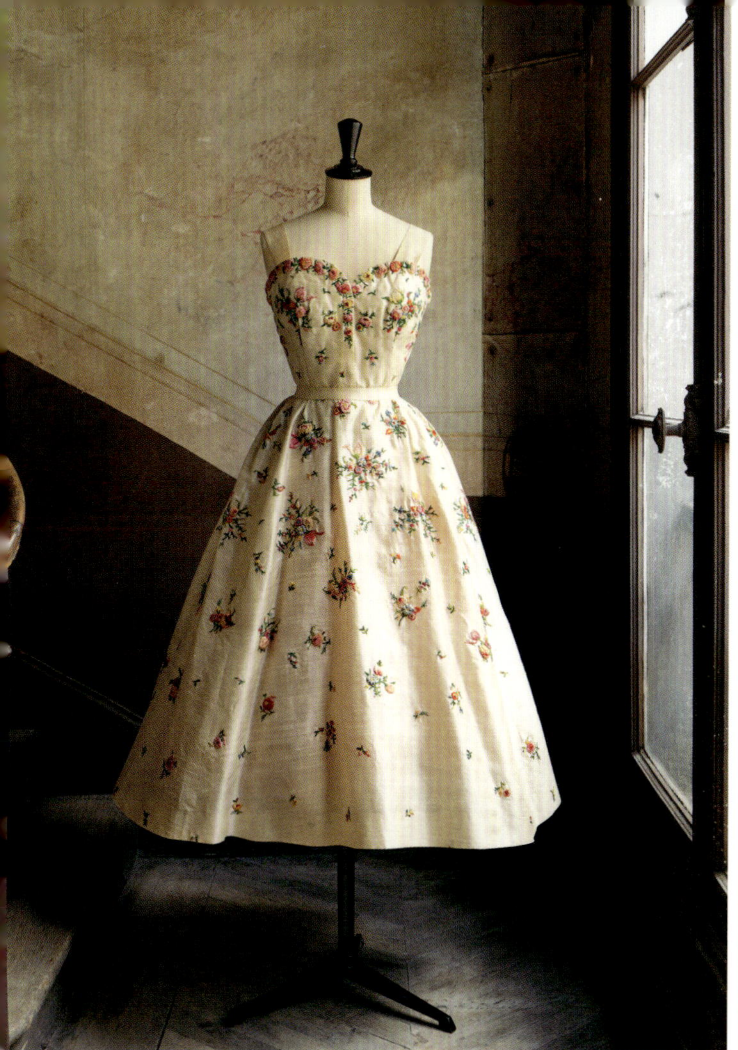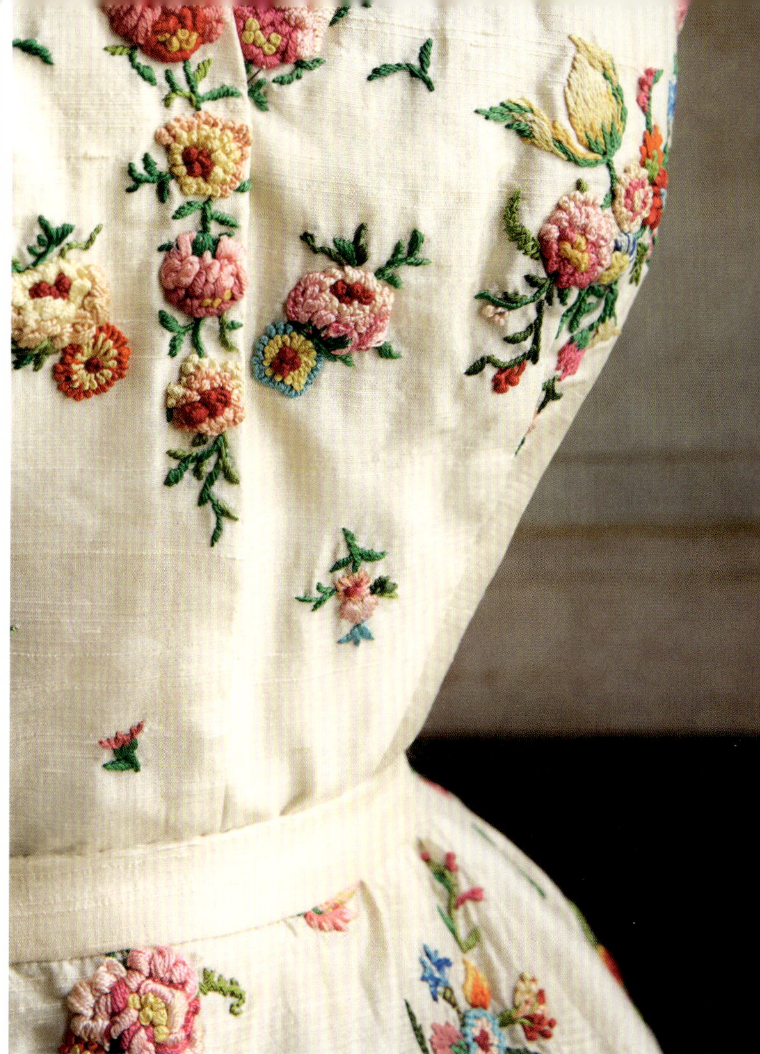

> "FOR LATE SPRING AND SUMMER, WE WANTED BOTH THE MELLOWEST AND THE MOST DAZZLING TONES. ALONGSIDE CLASSIC *ROUGE DIOR*, WE HAVE A FLOURISHING OF *BEGONIA* PINK, *AZALEA* MAUVE, *HYDRANGEA* BLUE, *DAFFODIL* YELLOW, AND *SOFT GRASS* GREEN."

CHRISTIAN DIOR

Evening dress in embroidered raw silk, (with detail), Spring–Summer 1952 haute couture collection, *Sinueuse* line. Paris, Fondation Azzedine Alaïa.

This dress, for a client, is a shorter version of the original model.

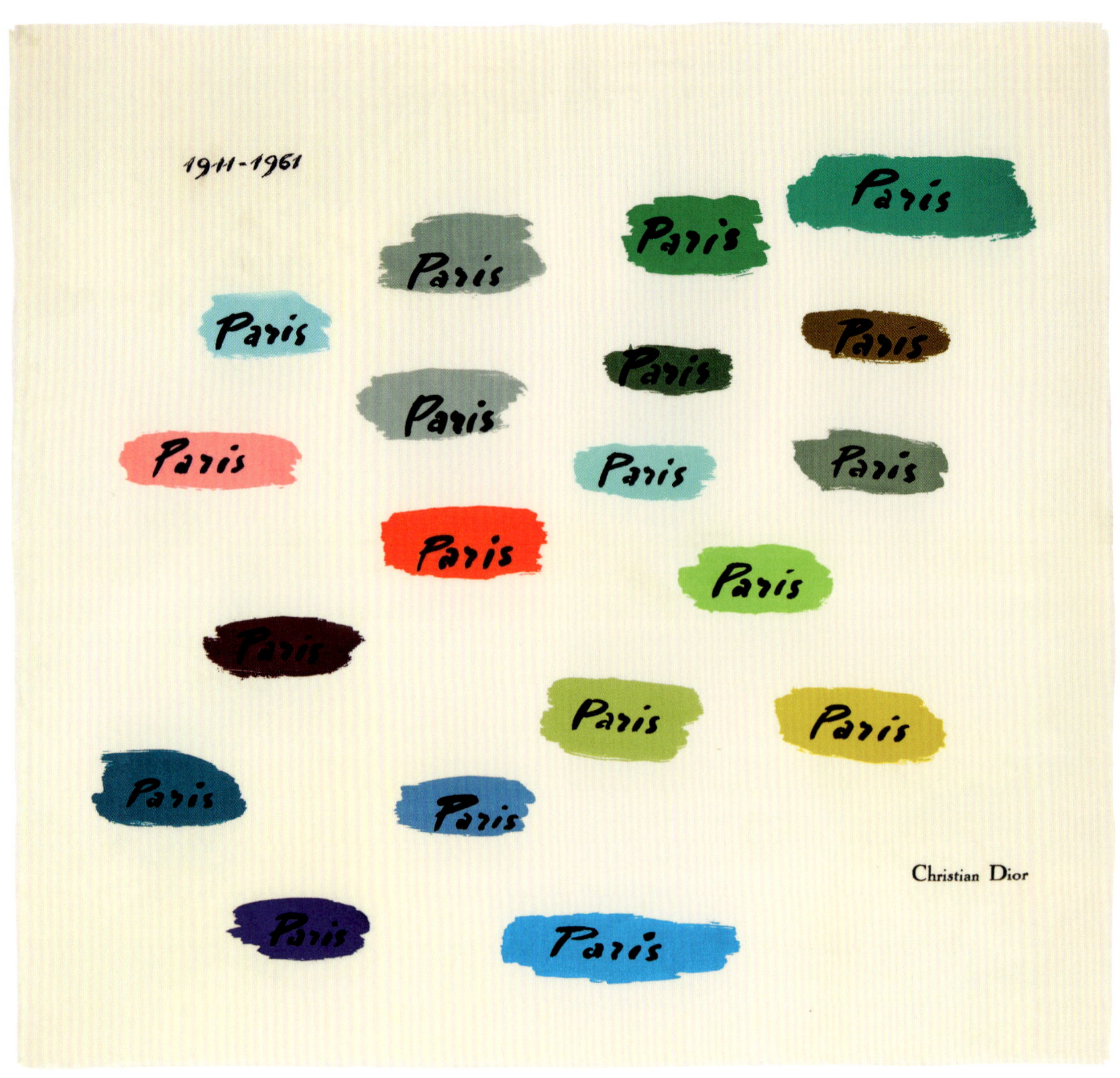

1911–1961
Paris
Christian Dior

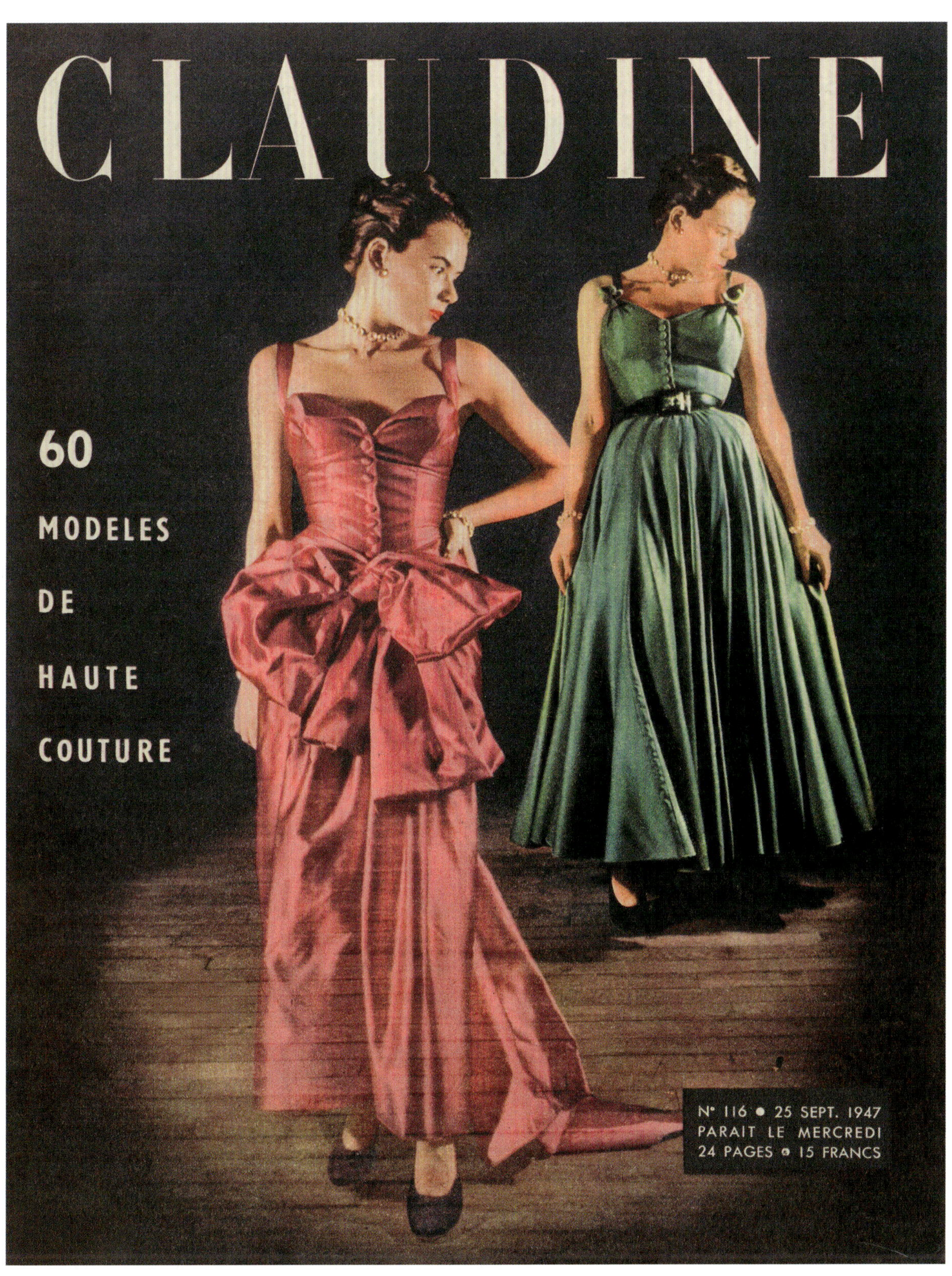

CLAUDINE
60
MODELES
DE
HAUTE
COUTURE
N° 116 ● 25 SEPT. 1947
PARAIT LE MERCREDI
24 PAGES ● 15 FRANCS

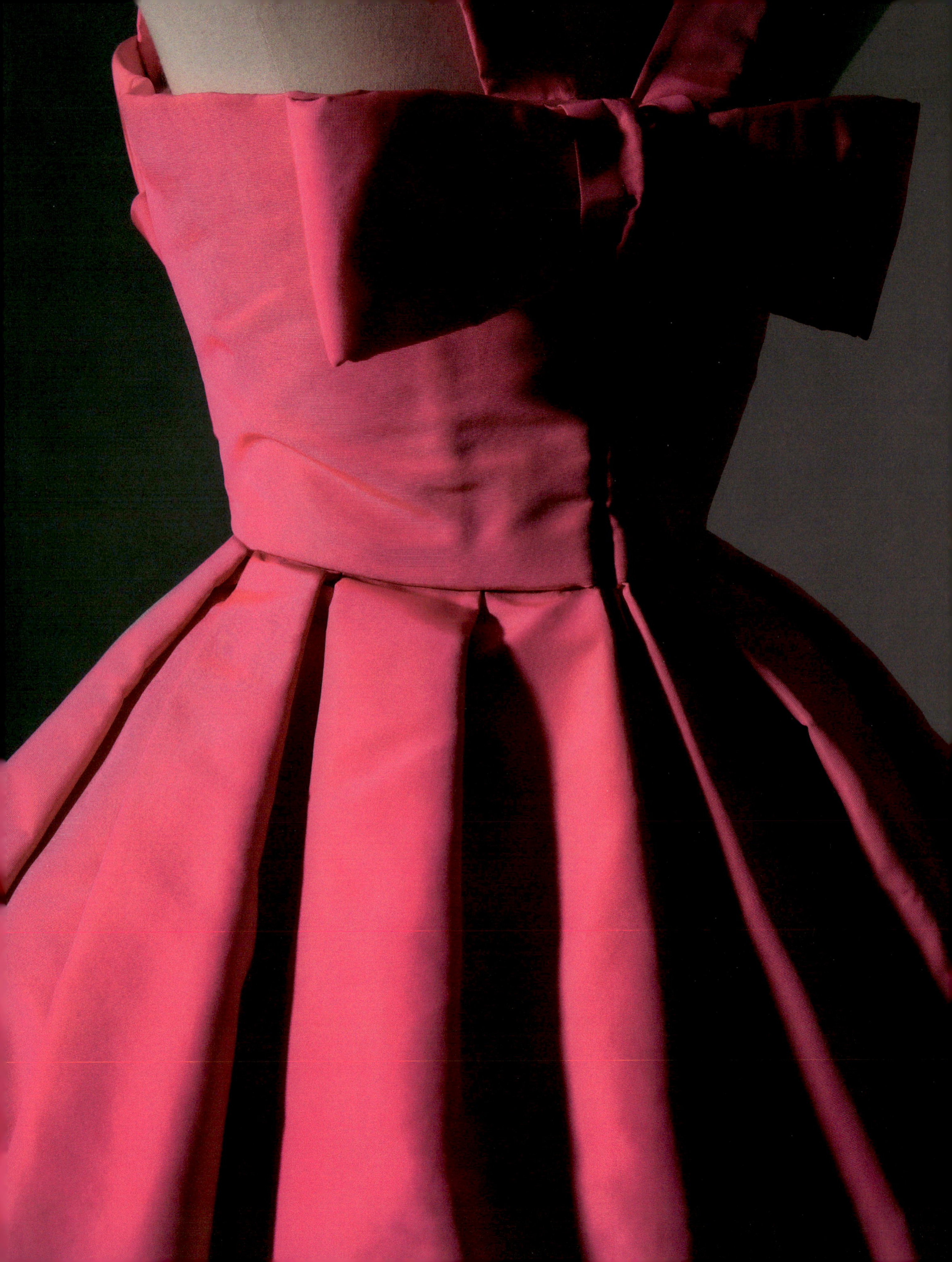

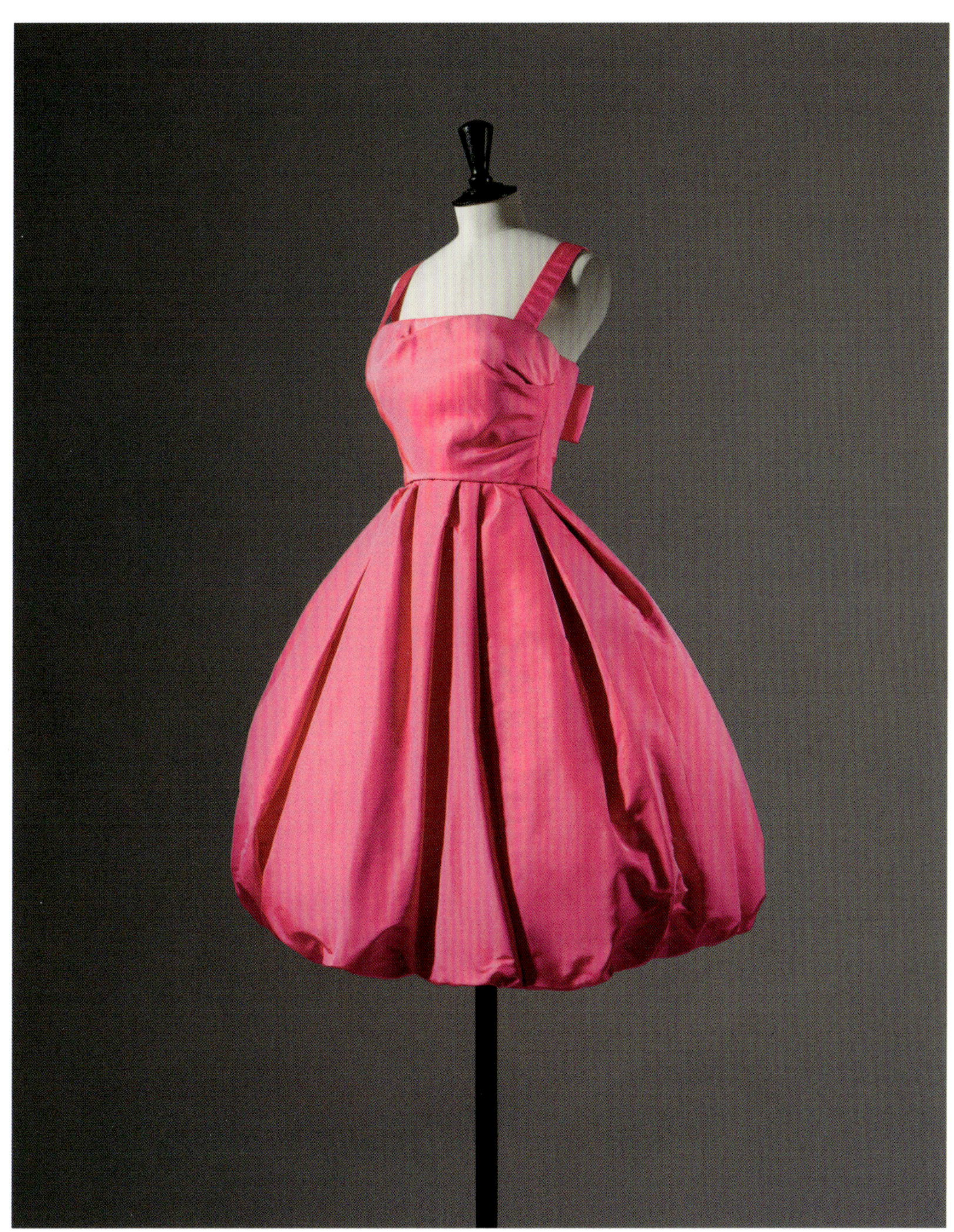

Yves Saint Laurent for Christian Dior

Evening dress in silk faille (with detail),
Autumn–Winter 1958 haute couture collection,
Courbe line. Paris, Fondation Azzedine Alaïa.

This dress is in the same fabric as the *Zaïre* evening dress
from the Autumn–Winter 1958 haute couture collection.

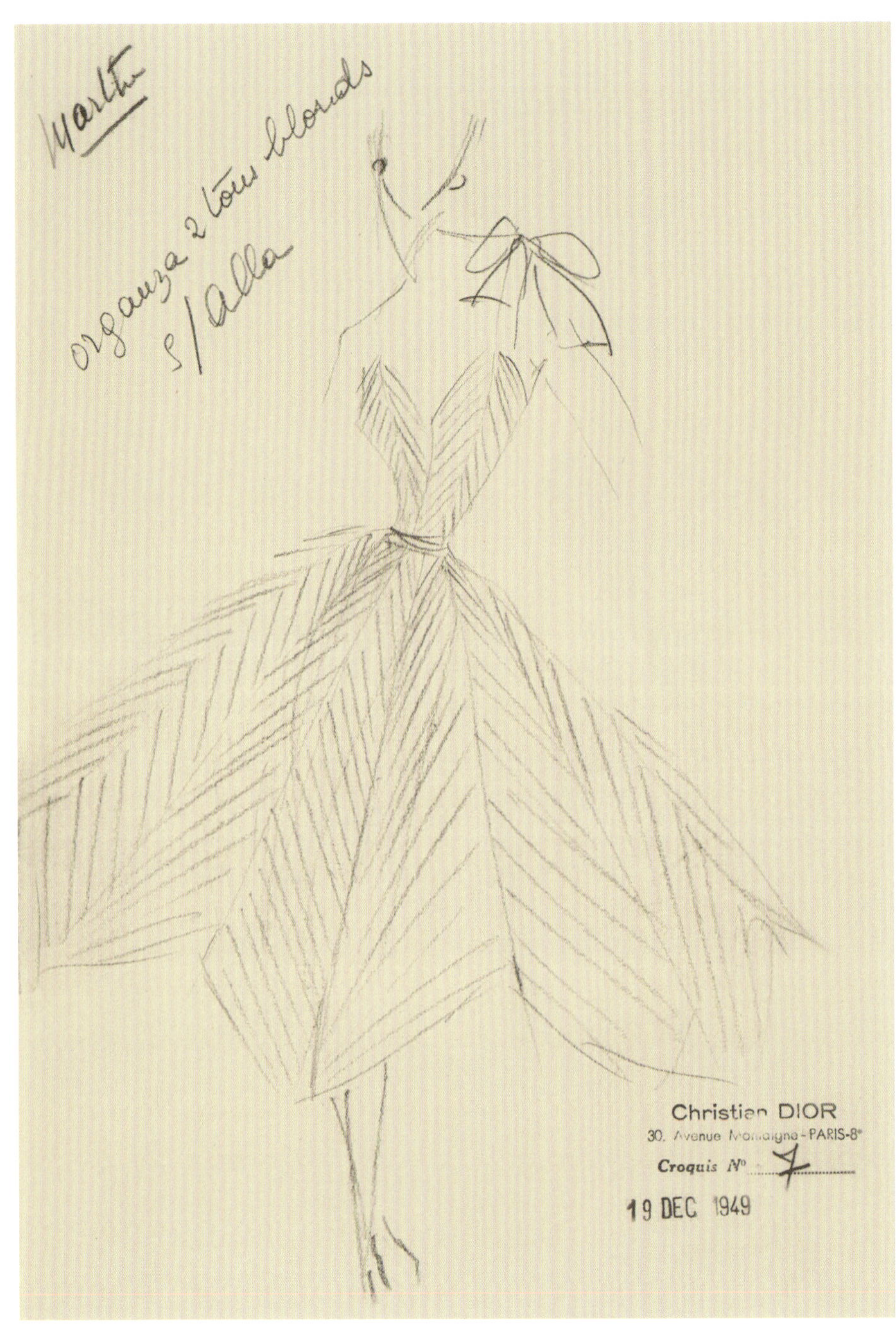

OPPOSITE
Christian Dior
Rose des vents

Evening dress in organza and
taffeta, Spring–Summer 1950
haute couture collection,
Verticale line. Paris,
Fondation Azzedine Alaïa.

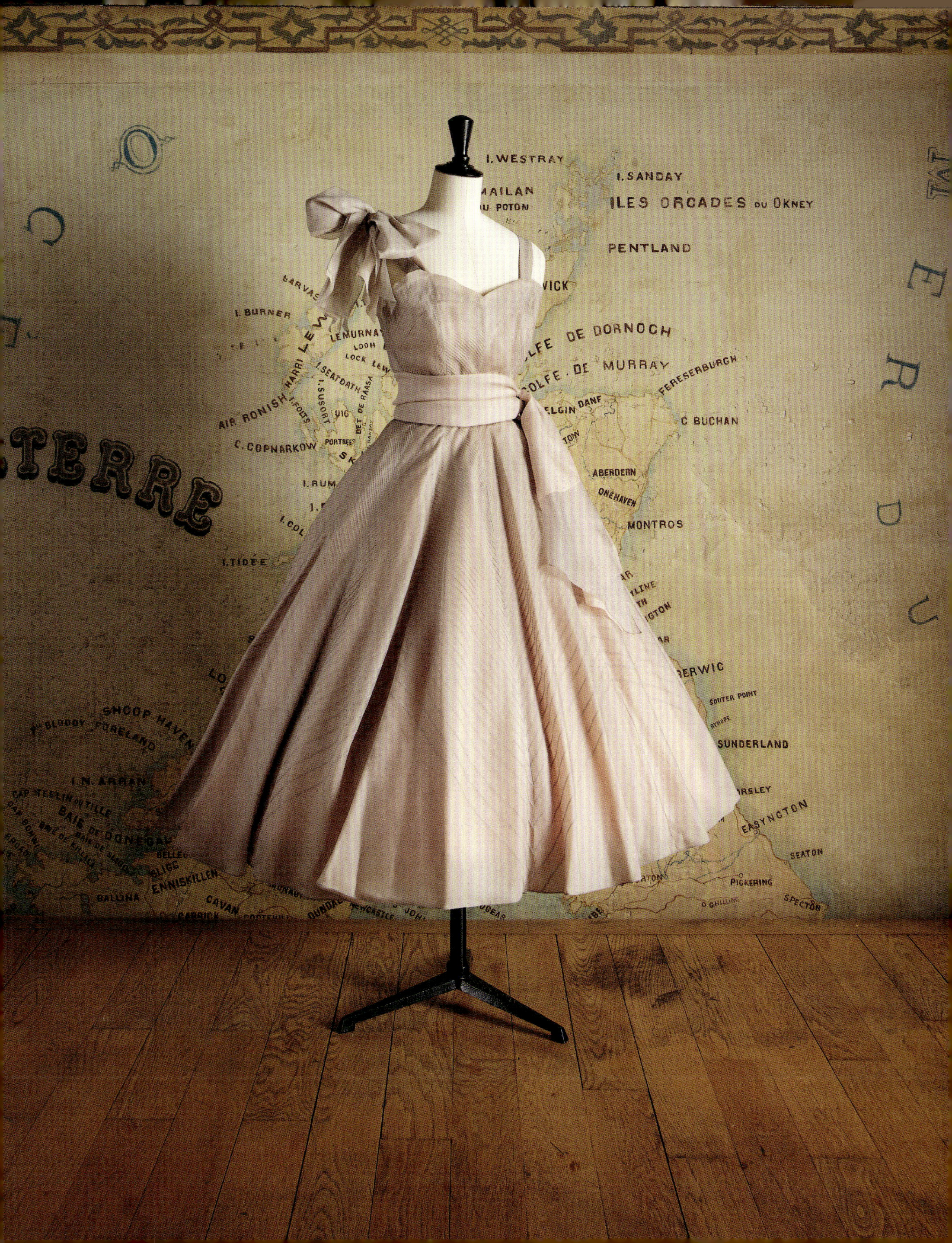

I. WESTRAY
I. SANDAY
MAILAN
DU POTON
ILES ORCADES DU OKNEY
PENTLAND

LARVAES
I. BURNER
LEMURNA
LOOH
LOCK LEW
I. SEATDATN
AIR. RONISH HARRI
I. SUSORT
DE DE RAASA
VIG
C. COPNARKOW
PORTREE
SK
I. RUM
I. COL
I. TIDÉE

GOLFE DE DORNOCH
GOLFE DE MURRAY
ELGIN DANF
FERESERBURGH
C BUCHAN
ABERDERN
ONEHAVEN
MONTROS

BERWIC
SOUTER POINT
RYHOPE
SUNDERLAND
ORSLEY
EASYNCTON
SEATON
PICKERING
GHILLING
SPECTON

SHOOP HAVEN
BLODDY FORELAND
I. N. ARRAN
CAP STEELIN DU TILLE
BAIE DE DONEGAL
BAIE DE SLIGO
BELLEG
SLIGG
ENNISKILLEN
CAVAN
BALLINA
CARRICK

STERRE

TERRE

DU

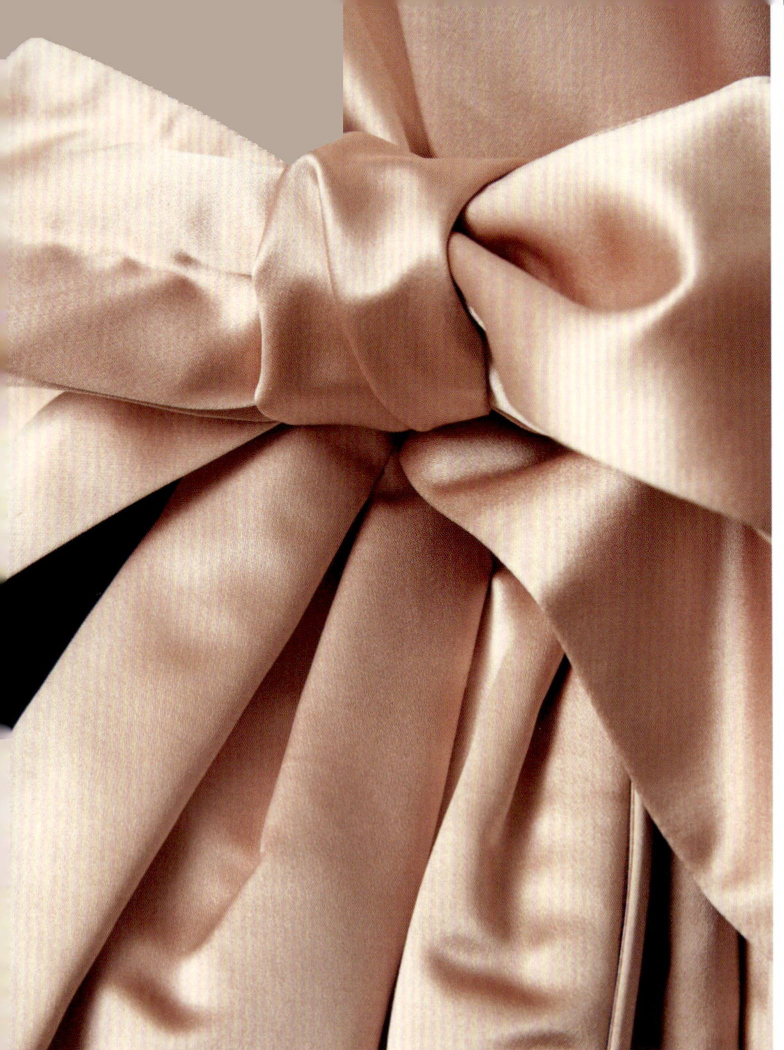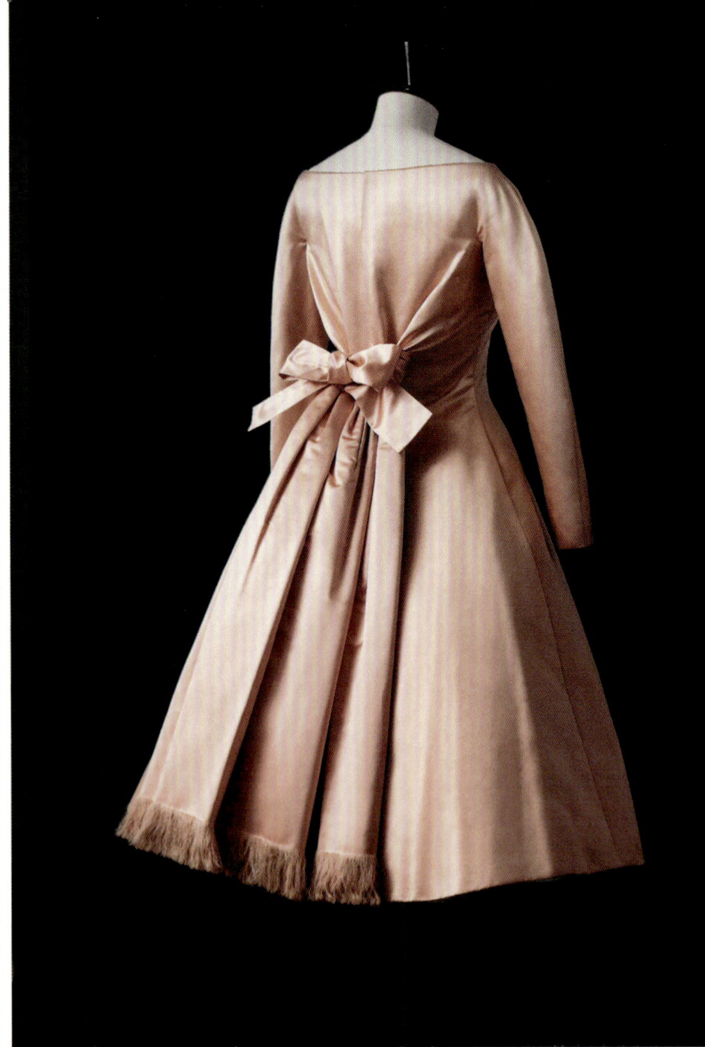

"PINK. THE SWEETEST OF ALL THE COLORS. EVERY WOMAN SHOULD HAVE SOMETHING PINK IN HER WARDROBE. IT IS THE COLOR OF HAPPINESS AND OF FEMININITY."

CHRISTIAN DIOR

Christian Dior
Caracas

Reception dress in silk satin
(with detail), Autumn–Winter 1956
haute couture collection,
Aimant line. Paris,
Fondation Azzedine Alaïa.

This dress, for a client, is a pink
version of the original model.

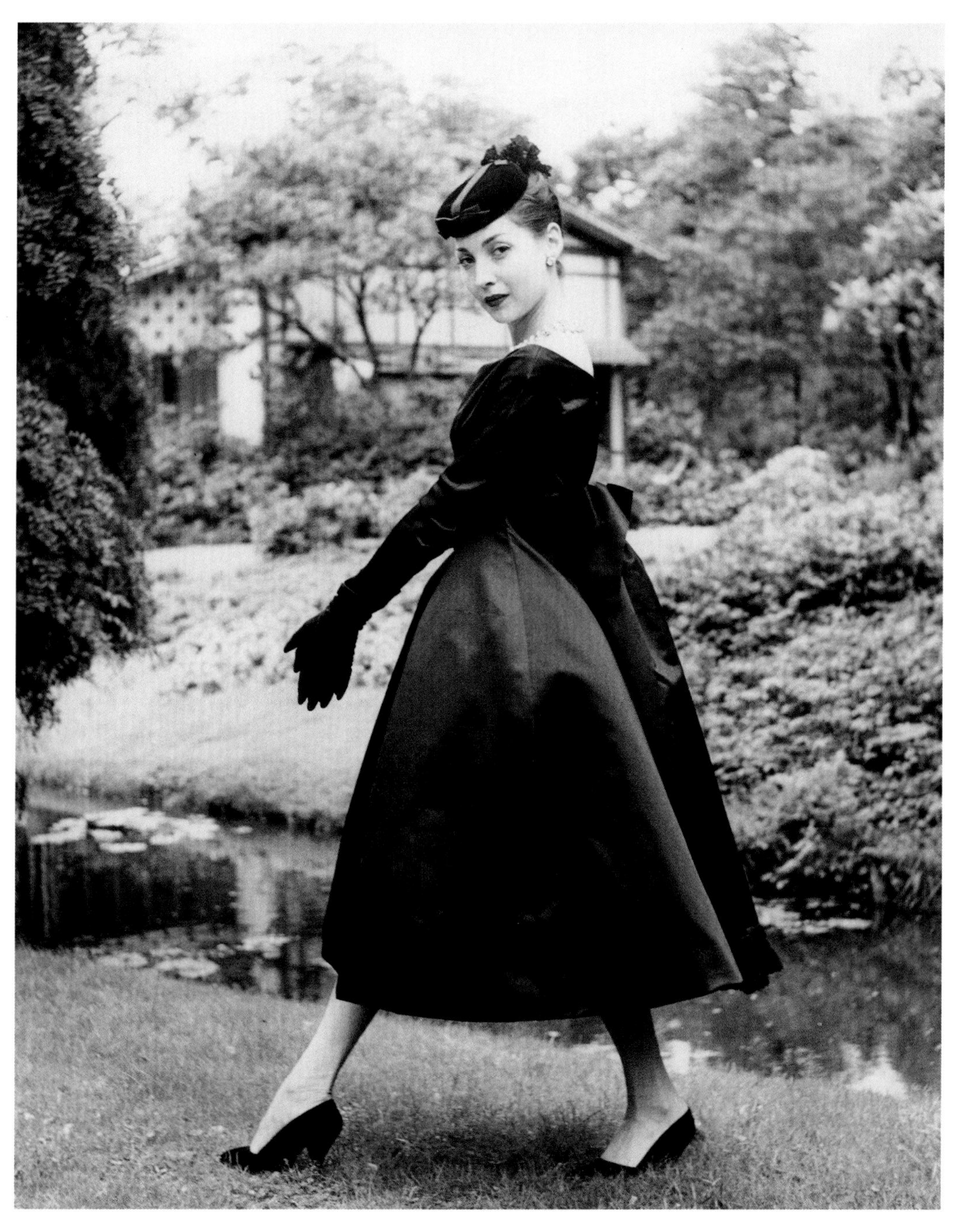

ABOVE
The model Renée wearing
the Christian Dior
Caracas reception dress.
Photograph by Willy Maywald.

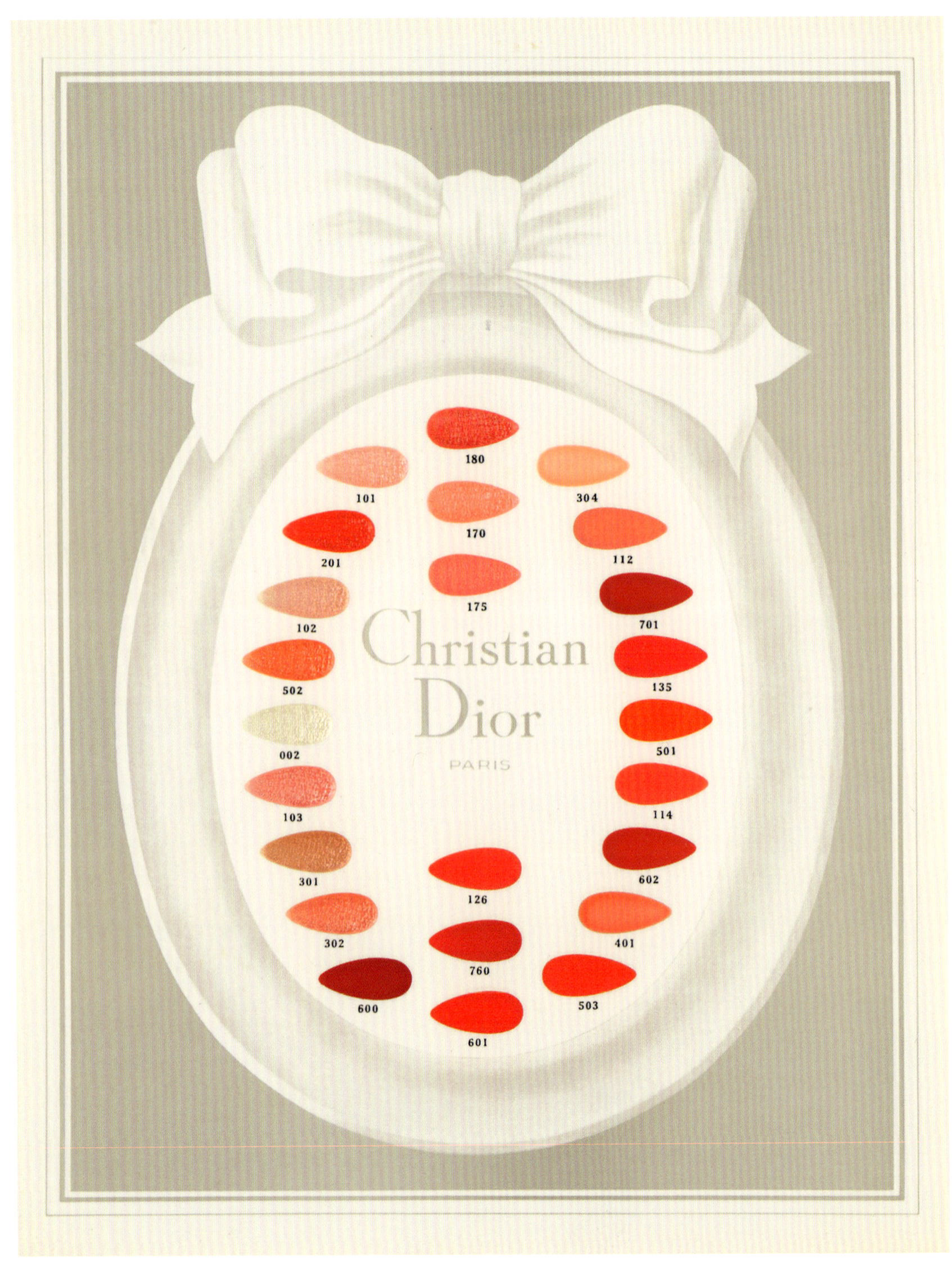

Color charts for *Dior* and *Ultra Dior*
nail polish and lipsticks, 1965.
Paris, Parfums Christian Dior.

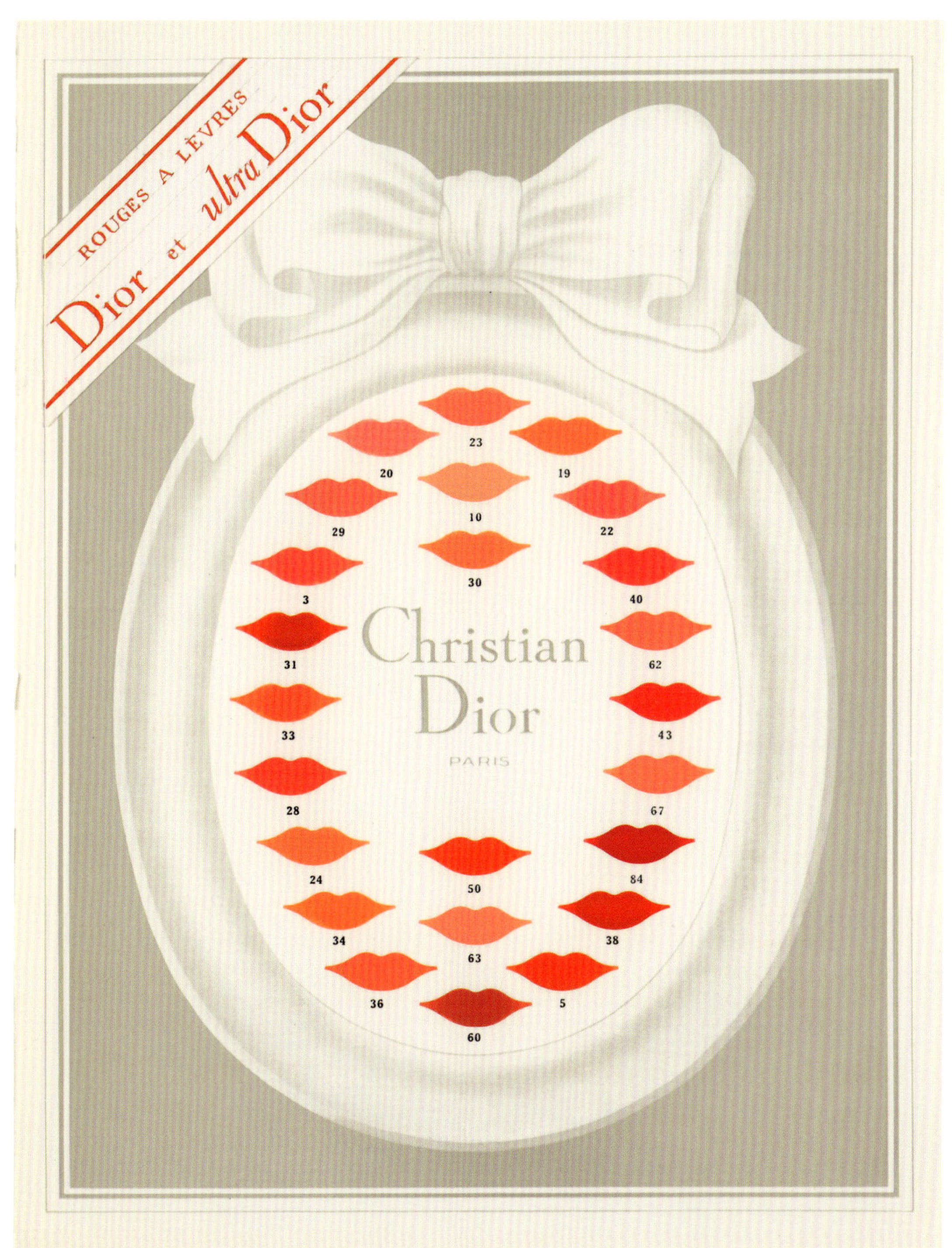

ROUGES A LÈVRES
Dior et ultra Dior
Christian
Dior
PARIS
23
20
19
29
10
22
3
30
40
31
62
33
43
28
67
24
50
84
34
38
36
63
5
60

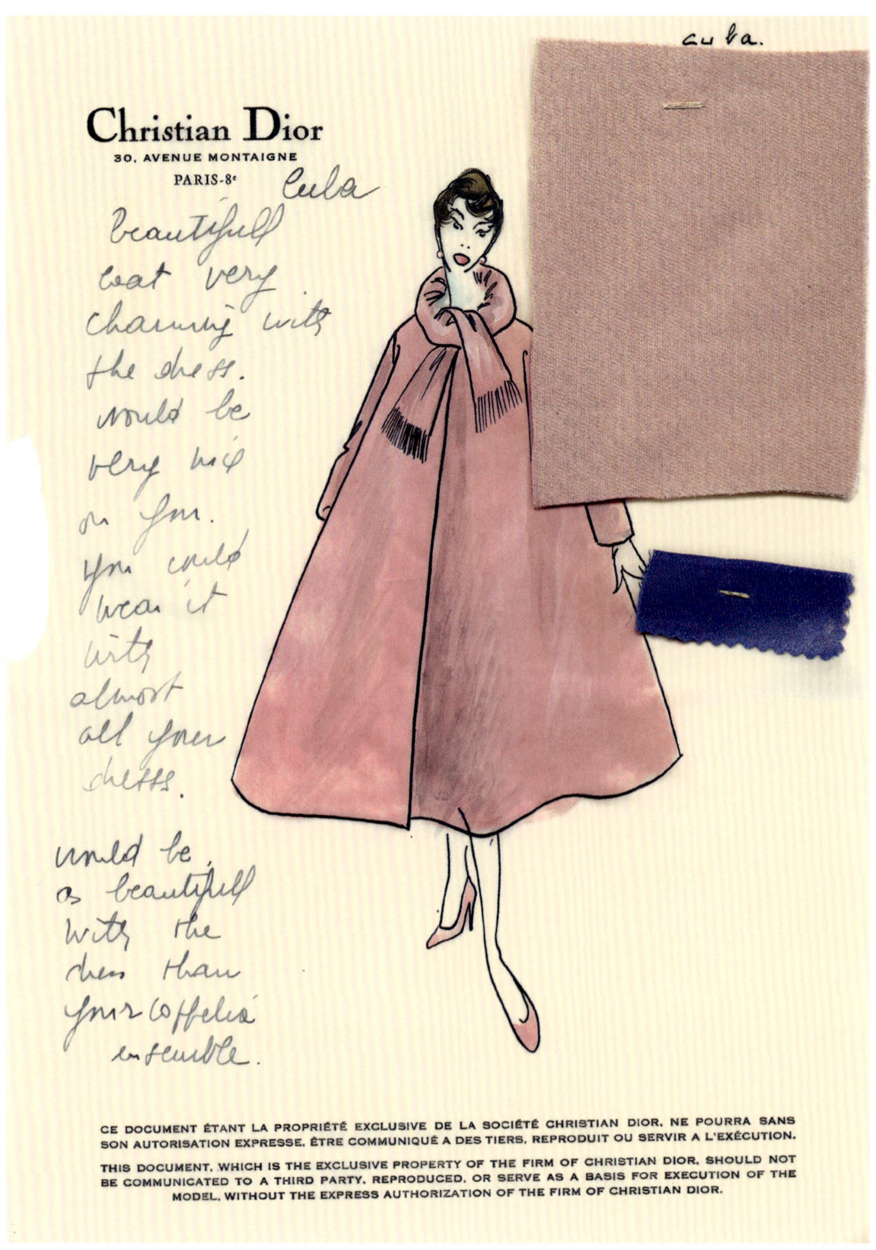

ABOVE
Sales sketch of the coat of the Christian Dior *Cuba* ensemble, Autumn–Winter 1954 haute couture collection, *H* line. Paris, Dior Héritage.

This annotated sketch with fabric samples attached is from a set of drawings of models recommended by a saleswoman for an American client who was unable to attend the presentation show.

OPPOSITE
René Gruau, advertising illustration used for the Dior perfumes, *Diorama* in 1955, then *Miss Dior* in 1960. Paris, Parfums Christian Dior.

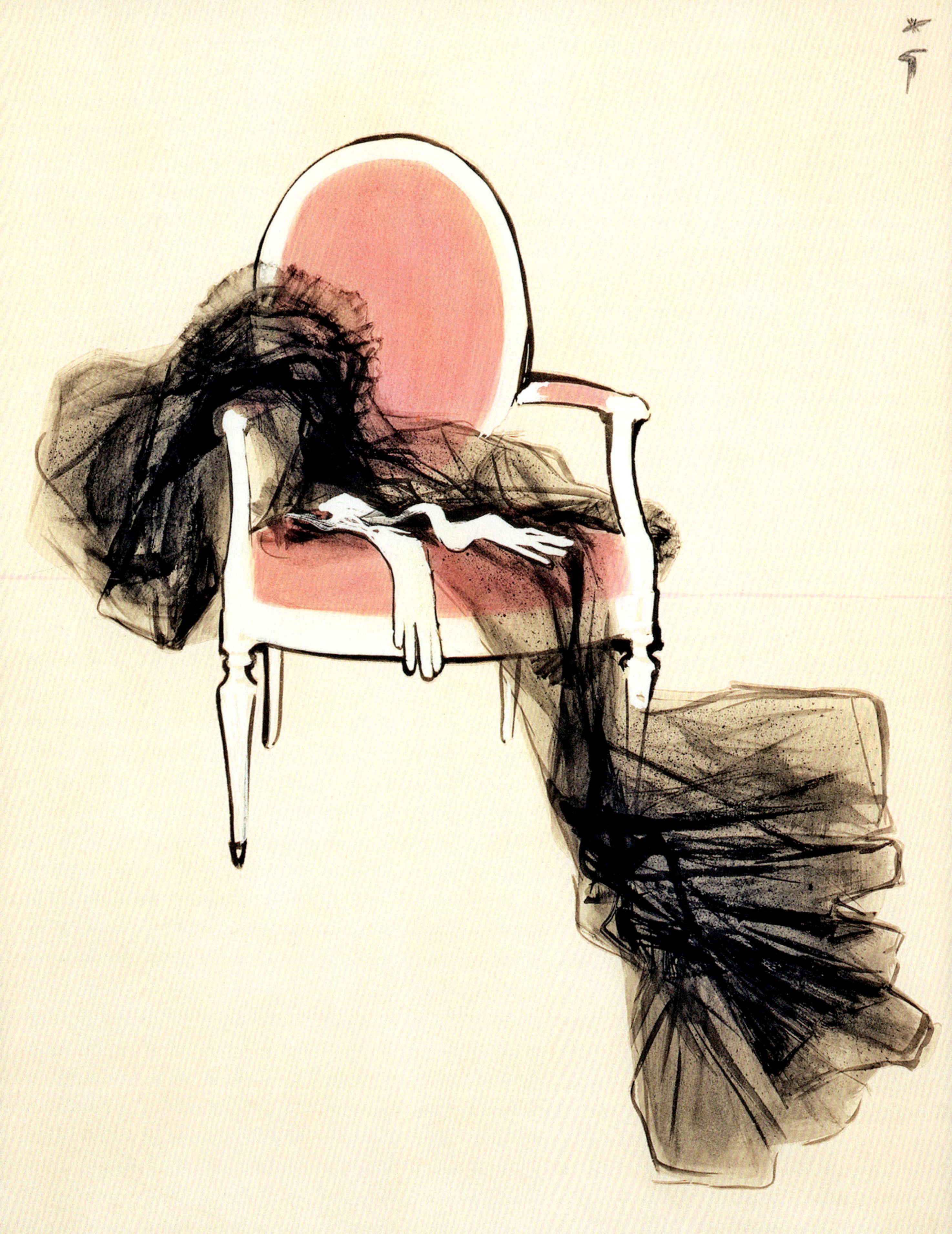

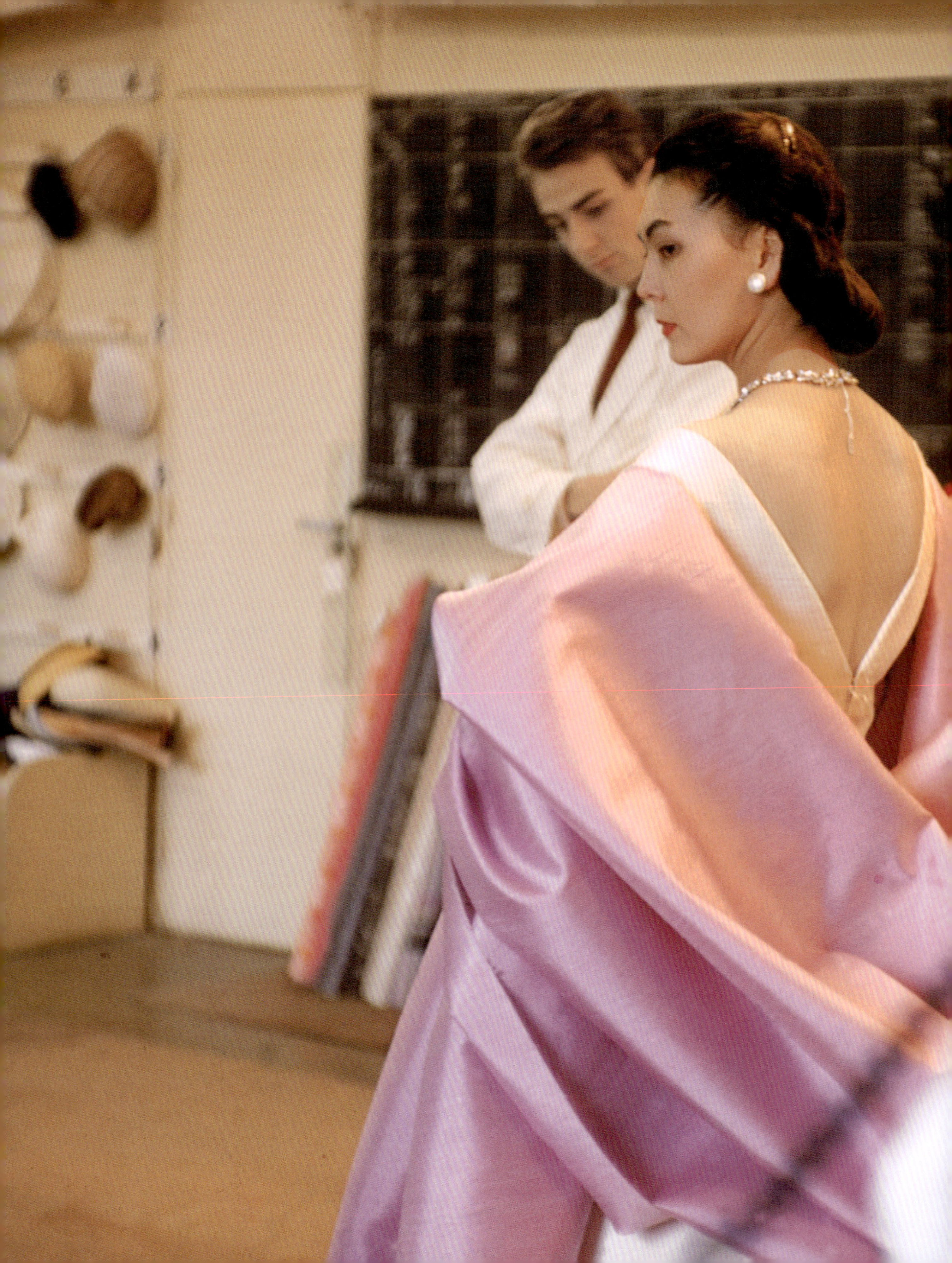

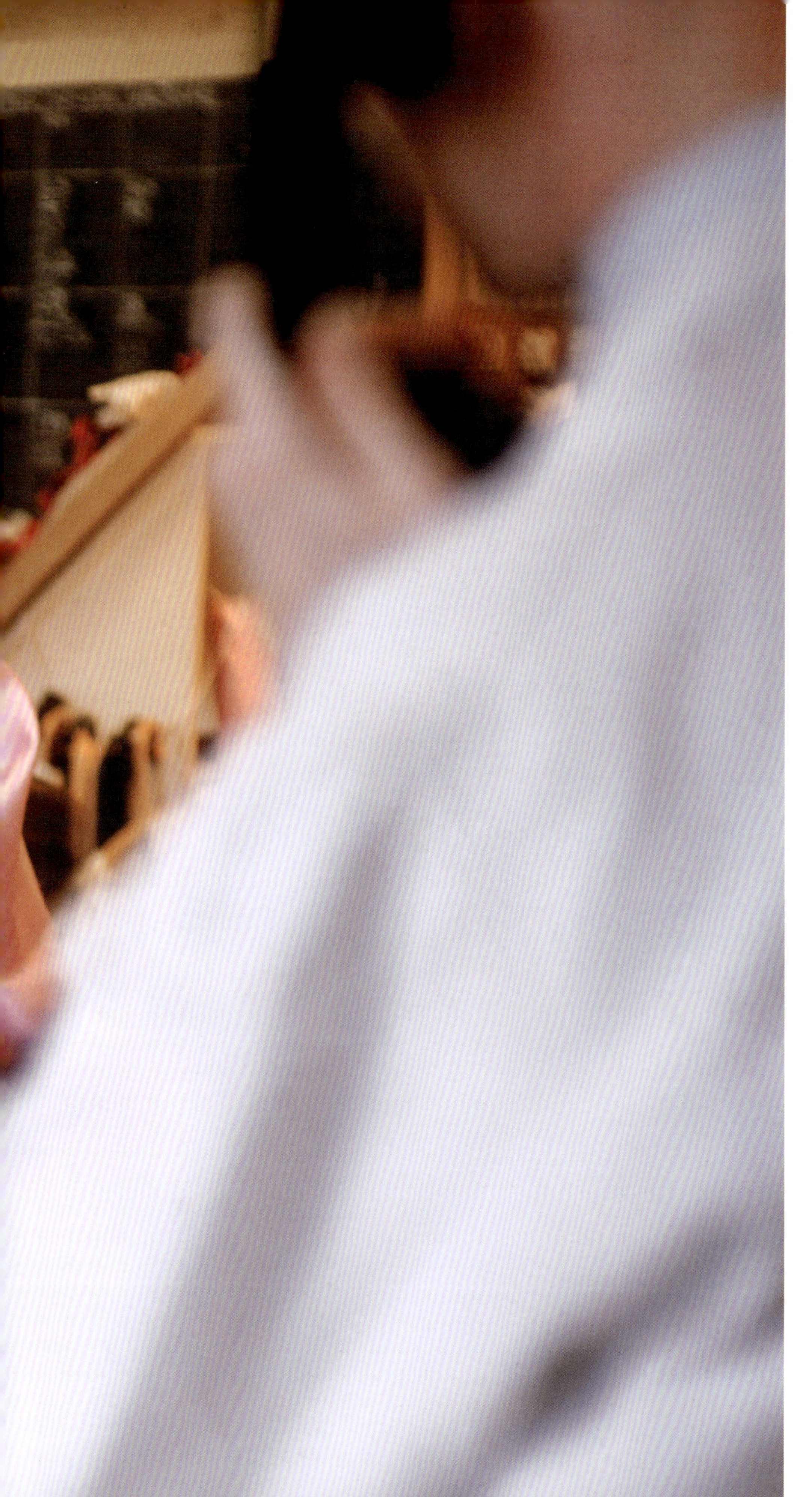

The model Alla during
a fitting session in the studio
at 30 Avenue Montaigne,
Paris, 1957. Photograph
by Loomis Dean.

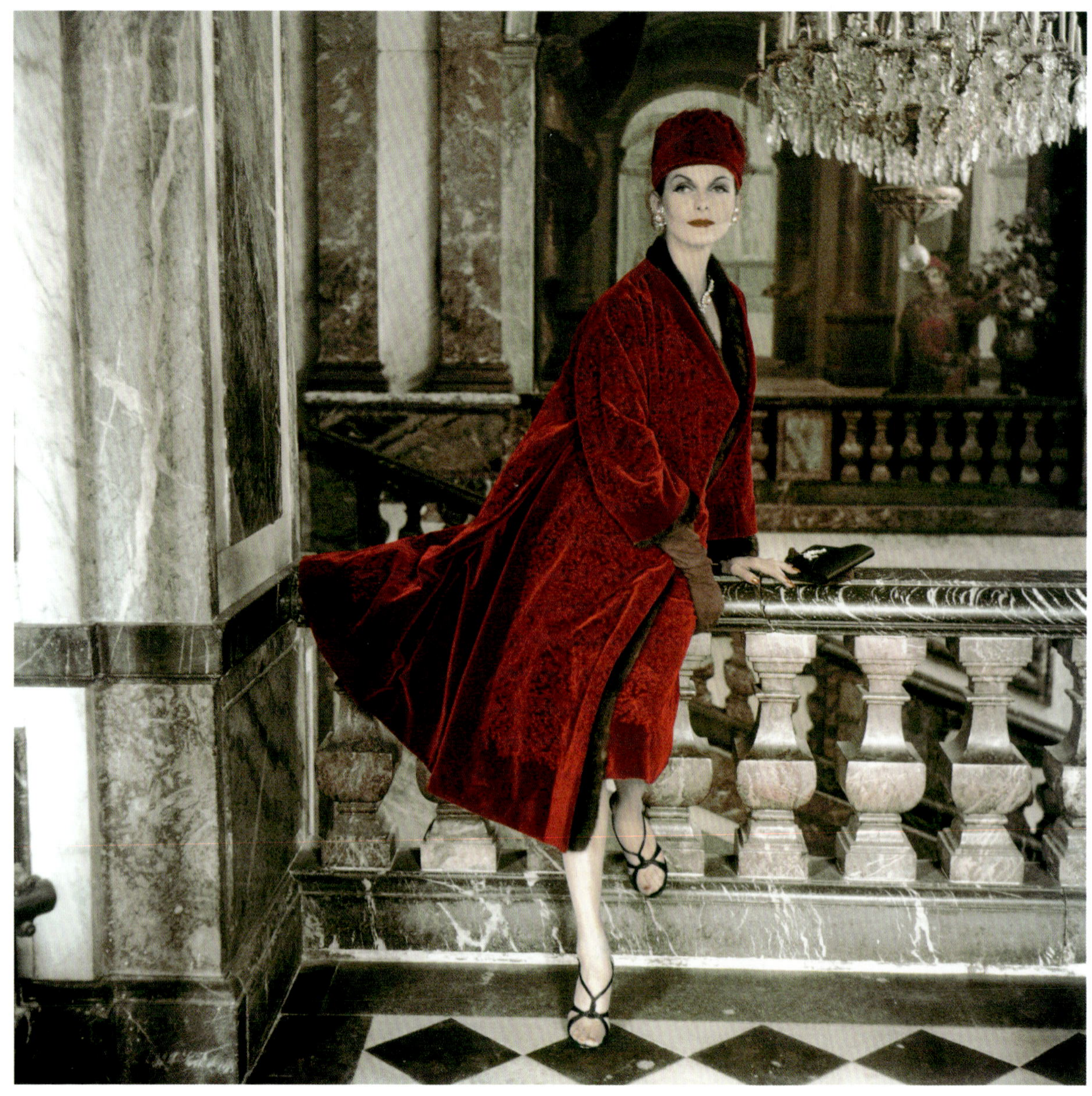

The model Anne Sainte-Marie wearing
the Christian Dior *Samarcande* evening coat,
Autumn–Winter 1955 haute couture collection,
Y line. Photograph by Henry Clarke, published
in *Vogue Paris*, November 1955.

The Fondation Azzedine Alaïa
has a longer version of this coat
without fur in its collections.

THE MANY LIVES
OF DRESSES

OLIVIER SAILLARD

Picture a dress, born of a couturier's drawing. Come what may, its chosen destiny will always be that of the women who, each in turn, sometimes unaware of its origins, adopt its silhouette as their own. It goes through several phases of life between the concept that makes it appear in a dream, and the *salons* where it commands the gaze of journalists and clients alike. But its vital record does not stop there. A loyal and constant friend through joys and troubles, it becomes intertwined with the adventures of its owner's daily life, but may then find itself alone after several years of cohabitation. Doomed by new fashions, forgotten in a closet, and confined to the shadows, it sets out on a long period of purgatory. Assigned to the cold metal of a coat hanger rather than warm human shoulders, it no longer gets to enjoy its owner's laughs and gestures. It may even be briskly whisked out of its sleepy closet to embark on a new life. Forgotten, passed on, or sold, the dress withdraws into folds and creases, and tries to forget what went before, in order to entice a new partner. It happens often. Working in concert with an enthusiastically steaming iron, the dress nurtures new hopes. It has won over other pairs of eyes and readies itself to make its way onto a different body.

As with an old master painting or a sculpture, there should be a list of all a dress's owners, who together constitute its prestigious pedigree. The names of the women who have shared its life should be embroidered in the lining of the dress itself. We could then follow its timeline, and imagine the catalog of emotions that it accompanied before the day it was put into total isolation.

There are dresses that everyone thought were dead and gone, lost forever, and then one of them appears again in an auction salesroom and is spotted by an expert. Collectors are overjoyed; historians and archivists buzz with excitement. As would be done with a rare flower that has fallen out of a fragile herbarium, they wear gloves to examine it. They unbutton and unhook the bodice like the binding of a book, keen to read its secrets. They unfold the tulle underskirts like the delicate pages of an ancient manuscript. The dress is reborn. Having not long ago been rejected and shut away amid the trunks and suitcases of a deserted attic, it makes a surprise reappearance, sometimes on the other side of the world. With the care of a doctor and the tenderness of a lover, impassioned collectors and historians fight to acquire it—the sole cure for their agitated state. The dress is an object of desire and has found a new platform to assert its dignity. All its inner seams, which had appeared broken and resigned to the prospect of never framing a movement again, straighten out one by one.

A benevolent army of individuals leaps into action, with the seriousness and focus of archeologists who are about to raise an ancient shipwreck from the depths of an unknown sea. Gathered in the archives of the very couture house that produced the dress,

"HIDDEN BEHIND THE GREY SATIN CURTAIN WHICH DIVIDES ME FROM THE *SALON*, I LISTEN EAGERLY TO THE GREETING ACCORDED TO THE FIRST SHOWING OF MY DRESSES: FOR THIS IS THE MOMENT OF THEIR TRUE DEBUT. THEY ONLY SPRING TO LIFE WHEN THEY ARE ADMIRED."[1]

CHRISTIAN DIOR

or employed in museums' conservation and documentation centers, they work in white coats and promise the salvaged dress new, sunnier horizons. A name running around the inside of the collar or waist fills them with joy: embroidered, printed, or woven, on a colored ribbon or just in black and white, these few letters certify its vital record and make the dress official. The sight of this signature, which is more precious than a label on a piece of marquetry, has the collector champing at the bit. It is the start of a research process that will reconstruct the dress's genealogy, step by step.

By consulting old magazines and scrutinizing articles from the periods concerned, the dress is brought back to life. Captured through a famous photographer's lens, it becomes a bas-relief in a frieze known as the history of fashion—a history in which it has played a part. In the course of a description—an abstract combination of a few words where fabrics and colors form the vocabulary—the

---

1   Christian Dior, *Dior by Dior: The Autobiography of Christian Dior* (London: V&A Publishing, 2025; orig. published in 1957), 80.

same dress offers itself up to be read. Its heart beats to the rhythm of these successive awakenings. With a level of commitment to rival that of a crew of paramedics, the specialists and conservators rally around press kits, old registers, and order statements, getting closer to discovering the name of the dress whose tracks they have been following. They identify the collection that it was part of when it was first paraded in a presentation show, they pinpoint the atelier that made it, and sometimes a hidden piece of wrapping attributes the dress to its mannequin and maker in the atelier. By taking the diametrically opposite path to the one that led it to oblivion, every landmark moment of its journey is methodically re-established. When a hand sifting through bundles of drawings has the good fortune to come across the sketch that set this particular dress's destiny in motion, the mystery of its origins is solved and the dress acquires its place in eternity. Shown to visitors, or carefully placed on the wooden mannequin in a museum display case, the dress is given its title and recognized as sacred. Thereafter, it might be returned to the atmosphere of the costume stores, where, in the darkness and luxury of a drawer softly lined in tissue paper and felt, it can be preserved forever, with all the necessary precautions.

This lengthy process of identification was scrupulously carried out for every one of the 596 signature Christian Dior pieces that Azzedine Alaïa examined from afar before eagerly acquiring them. He scoured salesrooms throughout his life, and consulted former clients, with the aim of assembling a fashion collection that now rivals those of the great museums. The catalog of couturiers' and couturières' names is too long to cite them all here. It covers all the shifts in fashion and dress, from the eighteenth century to the contemporary period, and allows all the fluctuations of French haute couture and designer ready-to-wear to be exhaustively represented. Scattered across several secret locations that were all near one another, day dresses, evening gowns, suits, and coats by the great Christian Dior lay in waiting. They had been accumulating ever since Alaïa had become caught up in the passion of collecting, although nobody could attest to it during his lifetime. They were all brought together when the foundation that he had envisaged was established on his death in 2017. The conservation teams noted nearly 600 pieces by the house of the couturier he had so admired, added to which were accessories, shoes, photographs, and rare drawings, such as the one that Dior himself signed when he was still an assistant with Lucien Lelong. Thanks to a collaboration that blossomed into an exhibition, the House of Dior enabled his collection to be better assessed. By resuming the research through images and documents preserved in the Dior collection, each dress's narrative, as described above, can be reconstructed in its most biographical form.

All of these exceptional pieces gradually revealed their full selves and were given a vital record—something that was only possible through a deep knowledge of Christian Dior's work.

That dusky pink organdy dress was called *Rose des vents* (Compass rose, Spring–Summer 1950 collection, pp. 98–99); that long, straw-colored silk sheath dress with asymmetric buttoning on the skirt is none other than the *Gruau* model (Autumn–Winter 1949 collection, pp. 118, 121), a worthy representative of the style of the famous illustrator it was named after. *Cygne noir* (Black swan, Autumn–Winter 1957 collection, pp. 74–75, 157), in ivory satin and ostrich feather, was the cocktail dress they came across a hundred times, hanging in a box. The evening dress with floral motifs on a yellow background was revealed to be the *Marcel Pagnol* model (Spring–Summer 1952 collection, pp. 46–47). The flurry of titles testifies to Christian Dior's uniquely poetic approach to naming his creations. Fine gowns and coats in Alaïa's collection were identified as having sometimes cheeky names redolent of their era. *Astarté* (Spring–Summer 1955 collection, pp. 40–41), *Ritz* (Autumn–Winter 1956 collection, pp. 42, 44–45), *Tolède* (Toledo, Autumn–Winter 1956 collection, pp. 78–79), *Sourire* (Smile, Autumn–Winter 1948 collection), *Zerline* (Zerlina, Autumn–Winter 1957 collection, p. 138), *Frondeuse* (Rebel, Autumn–Winter 1954 collection), *Chérie* (Darling, Spring–Summer 1948 collection, pp. 4, 70–71), *Bois de Boulogne* (Autumn–Winter 1949 collection, p. 53), *Grisette* (Autumn–Winter 1949 collection, pp. 148–149), *Zélie* (Autumn–Winter 1954 collection, pp. 144–145), *Élisabeth* (Autumn–Winter 1952 collection, p. 37), *Samarcande* (Samarkand, Autumn–Winter 1955 collection, pp. 108, 150–151), *Octave Feuillet* (Spring–Summer 1952 collection, p. 93) . . . Examples from the *Ailée*, *Milieu du siècle*, *Verticale*, *Sinueuse* or *Tulipe*, *H*, *A*, *Y*, *Flèche*, and *Aimant* lines, among others, indicate how exhaustively Alaïa pursued his goal as both collector and historian.

This orchestra of dresses that he brought together and saved for the fashion world and the French nation, now partially placed on display for the exhibition at La Galerie Dior, fosters an ever-broader awareness of Christian Dior's oeuvre. Between 1947 and 1957—a period of just ten years—he spawned the most beautiful creations in fashion history. His pursuit of sumptuousness, along with continuing to use traditional savoir-faire to articulate haute couture, influenced entire generations of designers aiming for excellence. Azzedine Alaïa was one of them, but his admiration extended to becoming a collector of the dresses that had sparked his youthful imagination. With the meticulousness of a conservator, he safeguarded the evidence of the greatest couturiers' output. Within the pantheon that he was constructing, Christian Dior was not only the most important of all in his eyes, but also represented the quintessence of French fashion, against which he measured his own work. By collecting the most iconic models, he identified an era's taste for particular colors—bright or muted but always timeless—detected the architectural prowess that went into a garment's cut, and gleaned tips on what it was that enabled these dresses to stand the test of time, outlasting fashion trends.

A true craftsman with virtuoso skills, Alaïa logged the names of the creations he admired, like those of the authors in an endlessly expanding library. He also liked to maintain the memory of the individuals in the ateliers who, beyond the isolated figure of the designer, had toiled to produce these dresses and coats that he had spotted and identified as unique. More than that, when he knew the identity of the women who had bought them in the past, he sought also to preserve the unique taste that the community of major clients taught through their individual decisions.

"THE PAST IS CLEAR, WE LIVE IN THE PRESENT, AND THE FUTURE IS OBSCURE. THIS PRESENT THAT WE'RE LIVING, WE MUST STRETCH IT OUT." AZZEDINE ALAÏA

Showcasing the collection of pieces by Christian Dior and by his successors at the helm of his couture house, now featured in the exhibition, has offered an opportunity to evaluate it. Rediscovering each dress's identity, exact date, and place within the unique creative output that is Dior's, has laid the foundations for them all to receive due recognition, their reputation restored after their years in anonymous boxes. Thanks to this collaborative effort, these creations, with their incalculable value to haute couture heritage, now enjoy both a sort of official blessing and a setting where they can be appreciated. This would have been a source of pride and satisfaction to Alaïa the couturier, and of relief to Alaïa the avid collector. "The past is clear, we live in the present, and the future is obscure," he said. "This present that we're living, we must stretch it out."[2] Building and nurturing his field's legacy, and setting out the memory of his peers and predecessors, including Christian Dior, was also one of his greatest contributions. Long may the history of fashion—of all fashions—be grateful to him for it.

---

2   Azzedine Alaïa in conversation with Donatien Grau, in *Taking Time* (New York: Rizoli, 2020), 16.

The model Victoire wearing the Christian Dior
Curaçao short evening dress, Autumn–Winter 1954
haute couture collection, *H* line.
Photograph by Henry Clarke, published
in *Vogue Paris*, September 1954.

The Fondation Azzedine Alaïa
has a version of this dress, for a client,
in its collections.

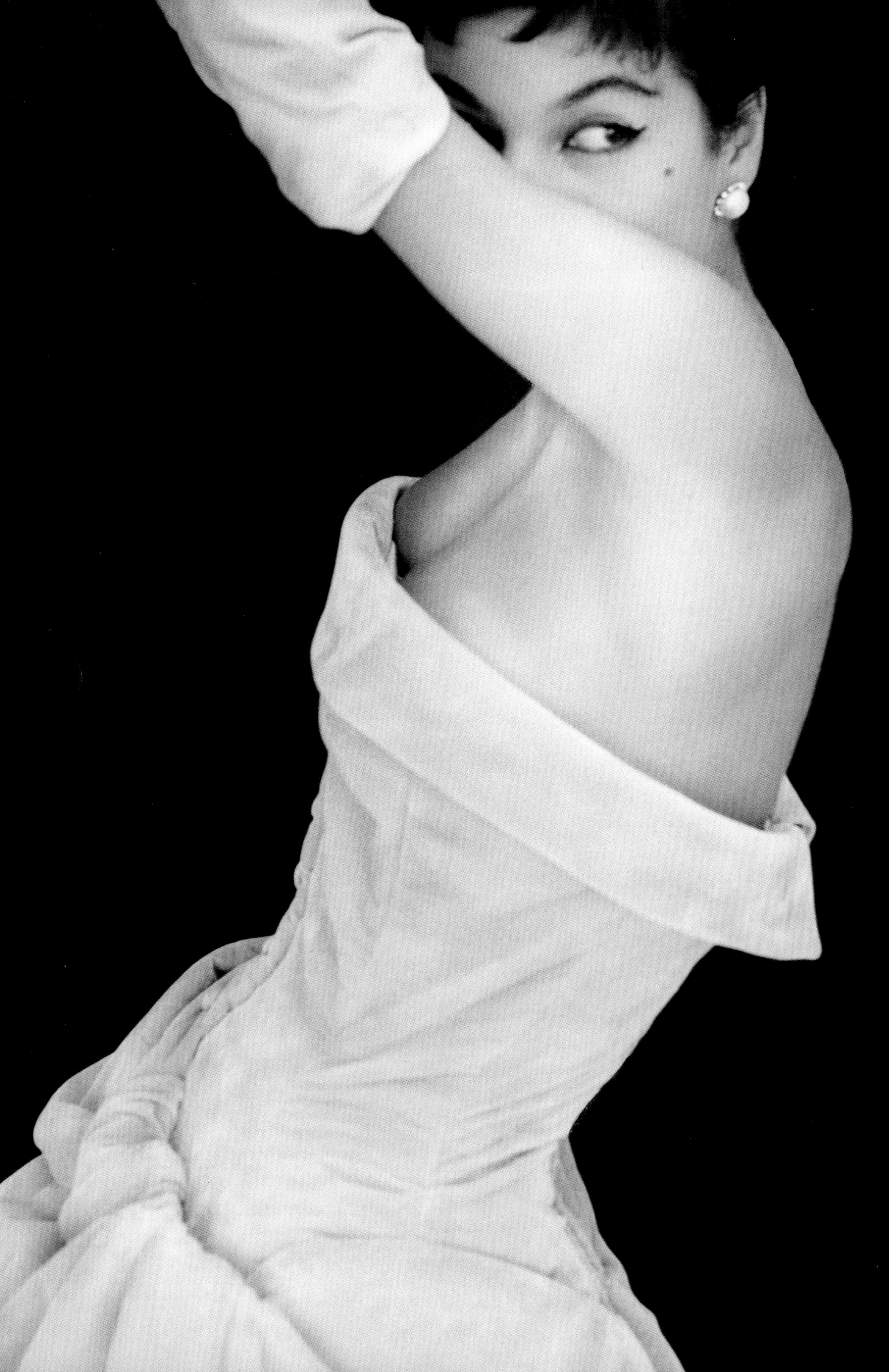

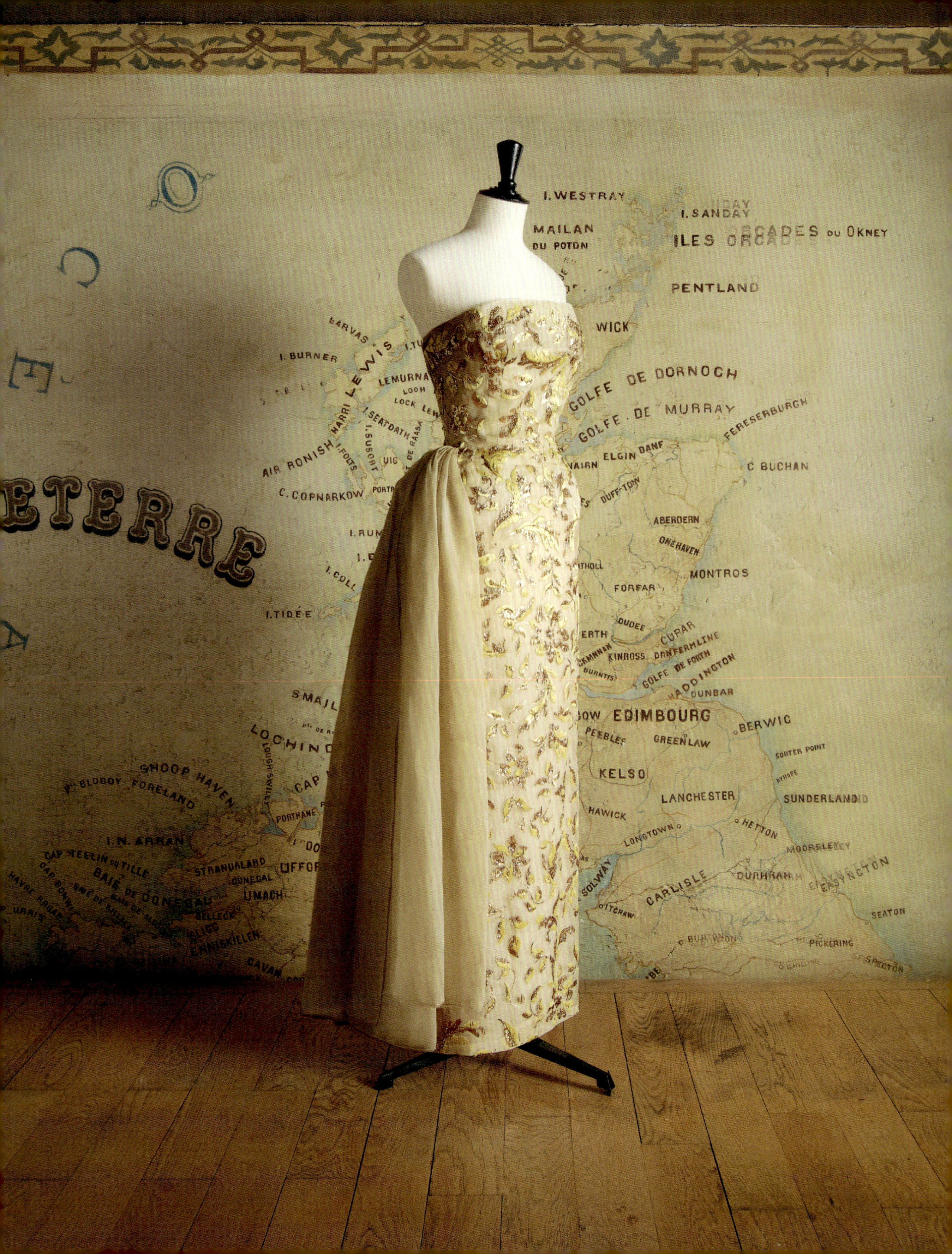

O
C
E
ETERRE
A
I. WESTRAY
I. SANDAY
MAILAN
DU POTON
ILES ORCADES DU OKNEY
PENTLAND
WICK
LARVAS
I. BURNER
I. TU
LEWIS
LEMURNA
LOOH
LOCK LEW
GOLFE DE DORNOCH
GOLFE DE MURRAY
FERESERBURGH
AIR RONISH HARRI
I. SEATDATH
I. SUSONT
VIG DE RAASA
FORS
NAIRN
ELGIN DANF
C. BUCHAN
C. COPNARKOW
PORTR
DUFF-TON
ABERDERN
I. RUM
ONEHAVEN
I. B
I. COLL
PITHOLL
FORFAR
MONTROS
I. TIDÉE
DUDEE
PERTH
CUPAR
CKMANNAN
KINROSS
DINFERMLINE
BURNTIS
GOLFE DE FORTH
HADDINGTON
SMAIL
DUNBAR
LOCHINO
PIE DE R
OW
EDIMBOURG
BERWIC
LOUGH SWILLY
SHOOP HAVEN
PEEBLES
GREENLAW
SOUTER POINT
PIE BLODOY FORELAND
CAP
KELSO
NYPOPE
PORTKANE
HAWICK
LANCHESTER
SUNDERLANDID
I. N. ARRAN
DO
LONGTOWN
HETTON
CAP TEELIN
TILLE
STRANUALARD
MOORSLEIEY
BAIE DE DONEGAU
DONEGAL
UFFORD
DURHRANAM
EASYNGTON
HAVRE BREAD
BAIE DE SLIGO
UMACH
SOLWAY
CARLISLE
URRIS
BELLECK
OITCHAW
SEATON
SLIGO
ENNISKILLEN
BURWTON
PICKERING
CAVAN
BE
GHILIN
S.PRILTON

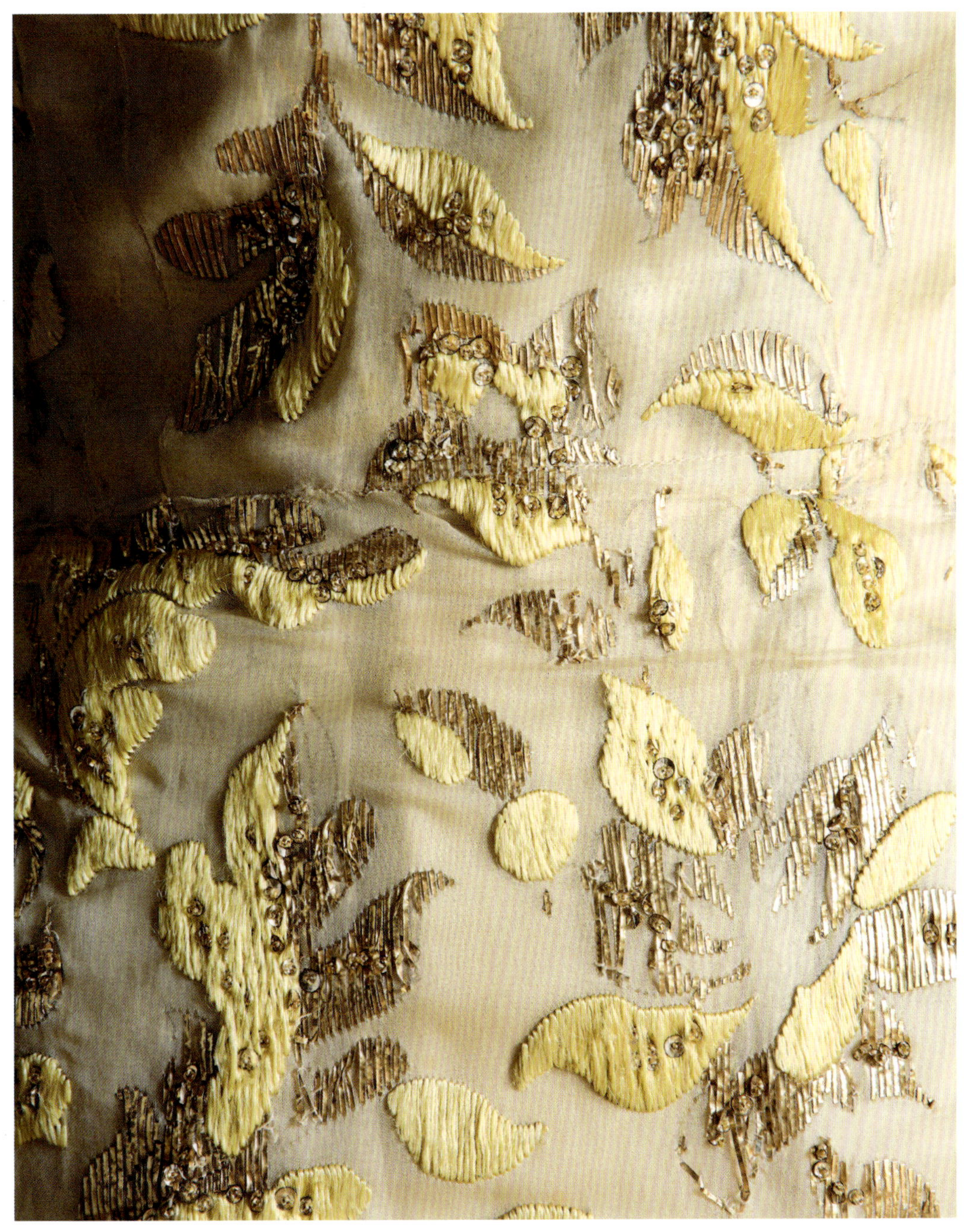

OPPOSITE AND ABOVE
Christian Dior
Muriel

Sheath dress in embroidered
organza (with detail),
Spring–Summer 1953 haute
couture collection, *Tulipe* line.
Paris, Fondation Azzedine Alaïa.

FOLLOWING PAGES
Spread from *Harper's Bazaar* showing
the *Gruau* formal evening gown (left) and
the *Pavane* dress (right) by Christian Dior,
Autumn–Winter 1949 haute couture
collection, *Milieu du siècle* line.
Photographs by Richard Avedon,
published in the October 1949 issue.

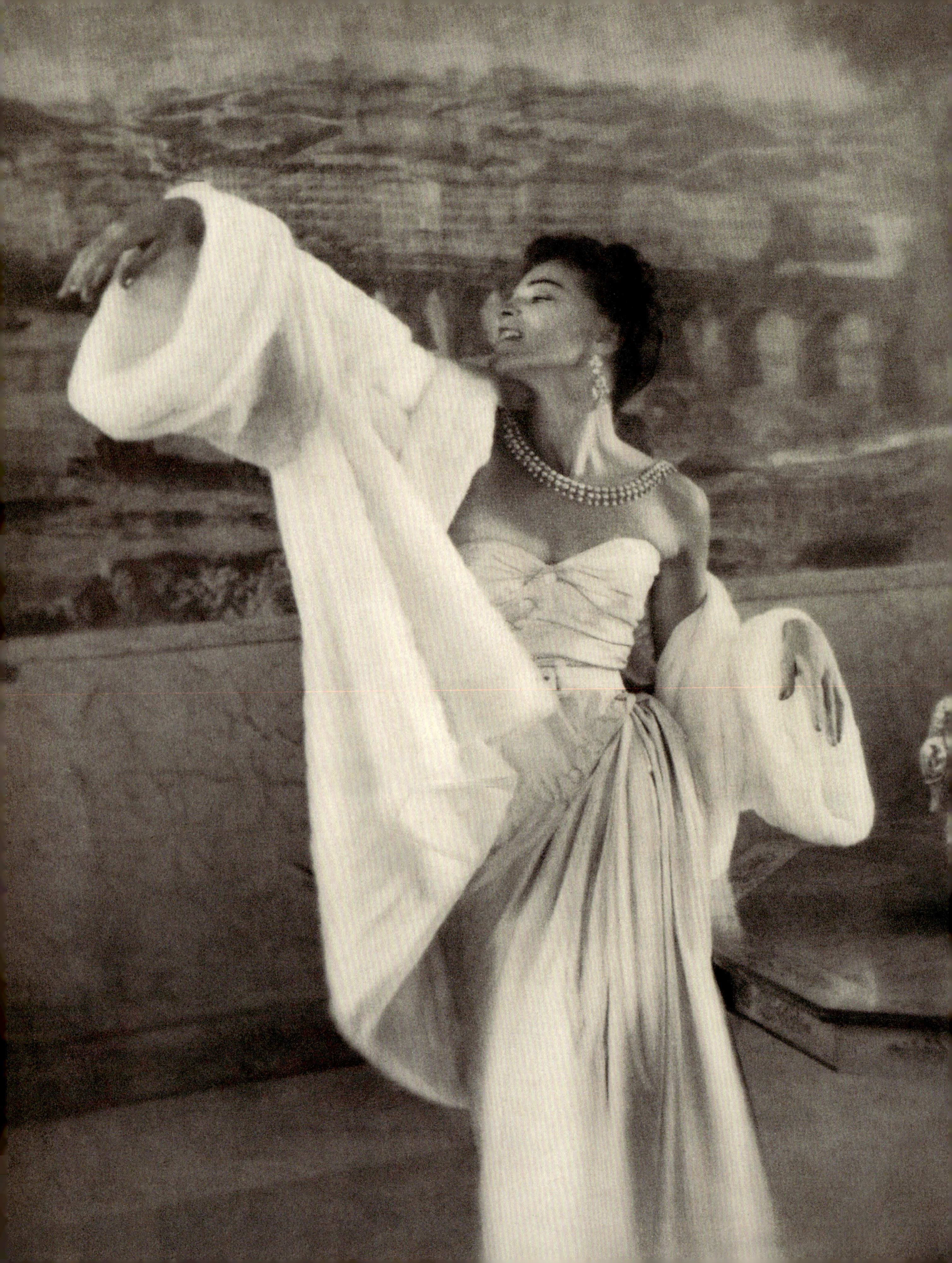

DIOR

SLIM LINE · CHEMISE DRESS

(*Continued from page 129*) coats, the loose coats and especially the *immensely loose coats* belong in the headlines. So does the *forward-moving hat,* worn tipped or straight, shading the eyes, as if Dior had just plucked it out of the attic and made it a fashion. *Day-skirt lengths are unchanged—for evening, day length or full length, but never ankle length.*

THE SLIM SILHOUETTE—What do I mean by a slim silhouette? I don't mean the hobble skirt, though some of Fath's models did totter into the showroom. The dress may have plenty of ease, even tremendous fullness. It may be pleated. It may have a tight skirt with a slit in back. Or Balenciaga's dress that wraps tightly around the figure and flies out to one side, without a bit of draping. Or Fath's sheath with a fan of pleats at the side. In any case, it looks straight. This means an end to the tiny-waist, padded-hip silhouette of the last two years. The waistline is normal, sometimes a little lower in back, and it is still small, but you no longer yank in your belt to the last hole or lace your waist with a tiny waistband. The new girdles must control the hips and behind, and the new brassieres must give a rounded, alluring line, but without point and without undue accent.

MEMORIES OF THE TWENTIES—Now of course some of this recalls the twenties. But we are not going back to John Held, Jr., dresses or the Gentlemen Prefer Blondes figure, as some would have you believe. We *are* going to be reminded again and again of our flaming youth. I felt a pleasant shock of (*Continued on page 132*)

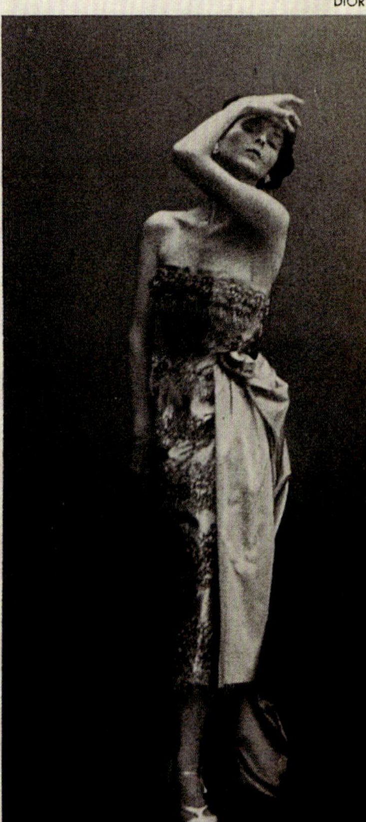

DIOR

"WE ARE GOING TO BE REMINDED AGAIN AND AGAIN OF OUR FLAMING YOUTH."
RIGHT, DIOR'S CHEMISE DRESS OF SILVER ⟶
GRAY SATIN EMBROIDERED WITH
GRAY PEARLS AND STEEL BEADS,
WITH BEAD FRINGE AT THE BOTTOM AND A SATIN
SASH IN SHADES OF GRAY. I. MAGNIN.

⟵ "FOR BALL DRESSES, SHINY, SUPPLE, FINE-SPUN SATIN."
OPPOSITE, DIOR'S WHITE SATIN COLUMN,
THE SKIRT PULLED SHARPLY TO ONE SIDE,
WORN WITH A VOLUPTUOUS ERMINE JACKET.
NOTE THE DIOR NECKLACE, A LEI OF BRILLIANTS.
DRESS: BONWIT TELLER CUSTOM-MADE SALON;
I. MAGNIN; WOODWARD AND LOTHROP.

PHOTOGRAPHS BY RICHARD AVEDON

Christian Dior

COLLECTION MILIEU DU SIÈCLE

MODE " MILIEU DU SIÈCLE "

Cette ligne d'Automne-Hiver 1949-1950, qui sera pour nous celle du milieu de ce XXe siècle, est essentiellement un système de coupe basé sur la géométrie interne des tissus. Droit-fil et biais s'entrecroisent en « **ciseaux** » ou rayonnent en « **moulins à vent** » dans un style **purement de notre époque**.

La taille, bien à sa place, reste toujours mince.

La longueur et l'ampleur des jupes sont essentiellement variables selon les modèles et les mannequins. Nous n'avons de préférence, ni pour une ligne étroite, ni pour une ligne large, mais pour une ligne avant tout seyante et **souple**.

D'ailleurs, si la coupe des jupes garde une grande importance, **les effets de volume sont**, en général, **réservés au buste** dont la carrure est encore accentuée par l'importance des manches.

Robes simples et deux-pièces empruntent au style chemisier sa **souplesse** et sa **désinvolture**. Nombreuses jupes plissées.

Les épaules, tout en restant fuyantes, retrouvent une nouvelle carrure qui leur est restituée par la façon dont les manches sont montées. Il n'y a presque pas de manches à même.

Les poches, peu apparentes sur les jupes, gardent leur importance sur le corsage où elles sont placées assez bas pour accentuer la **souplesse** du buste et affectent, volontiers, la forme d'un croissant.

Pour les robes plus habillées de fin d'après-midi ou de demi-soir, le traitement des tissus est en général, **oblique**. Sur les bustes et les jupes, s'entrecroisent les « **ciseaux** » ou rayonnent les « **moulins à vent** » que viennent souligner des oppositions de tissus tels que gros grain et velours, velours et lainage, satin et velours. C'est là un des thèmes principaux de la collection.

De grands cols montés en triangle encadrent le visage et retombent en arrière en découvrant la nuque, ce sont les cols « **coupe vent** ».

Les décolletés, en général moins généreux, ont tendance à basculer dans le dos.

Si les robes de grand soir sont toujours longues, les modèles de dîner et de **demi-soir** sont toujours courts. Nous avons attaché beaucoup d'importance au **demi-soir** qui, sauf exceptions, correspond mieux au besoin de la vie moderne.

Cette collection est, avant tout, celle du MILIEU DU SIÈCLE dont elle doit représenter le style et le mode de vie.

Les tailleurs empruntent aux deux-pièces leur souplesse. Même les plus classiques ne moulent plus le buste. Leurs manches sont toujours montées, souvent assez bas sur l'épaule.

De nombreux paletots vagues s'apparentent aux houppelandes de « **berger** ». Ce style volontairement rude et primitif est également celui des manteaux presque tous vagues. Quelques manches courtes, d'autres très longues, toujours très amples.

COULEURS

Avant tout :
— le noir, souvent approfondi par des contrastes de tissus.

Pas de tons sombres, sauf un gris assez foncé, le gris « Uranium ».
— un rouge auquel nous sommes fidèles : le rouge Dior.
— l'or qui fait sa réapparition dans de nombreux modèles de demi-soir.
— un rose tendre : le rose « Bonheur ».
— un bleu vert : le bleu « Email ».
— du marron, du marine, touches d'orange et de vert.

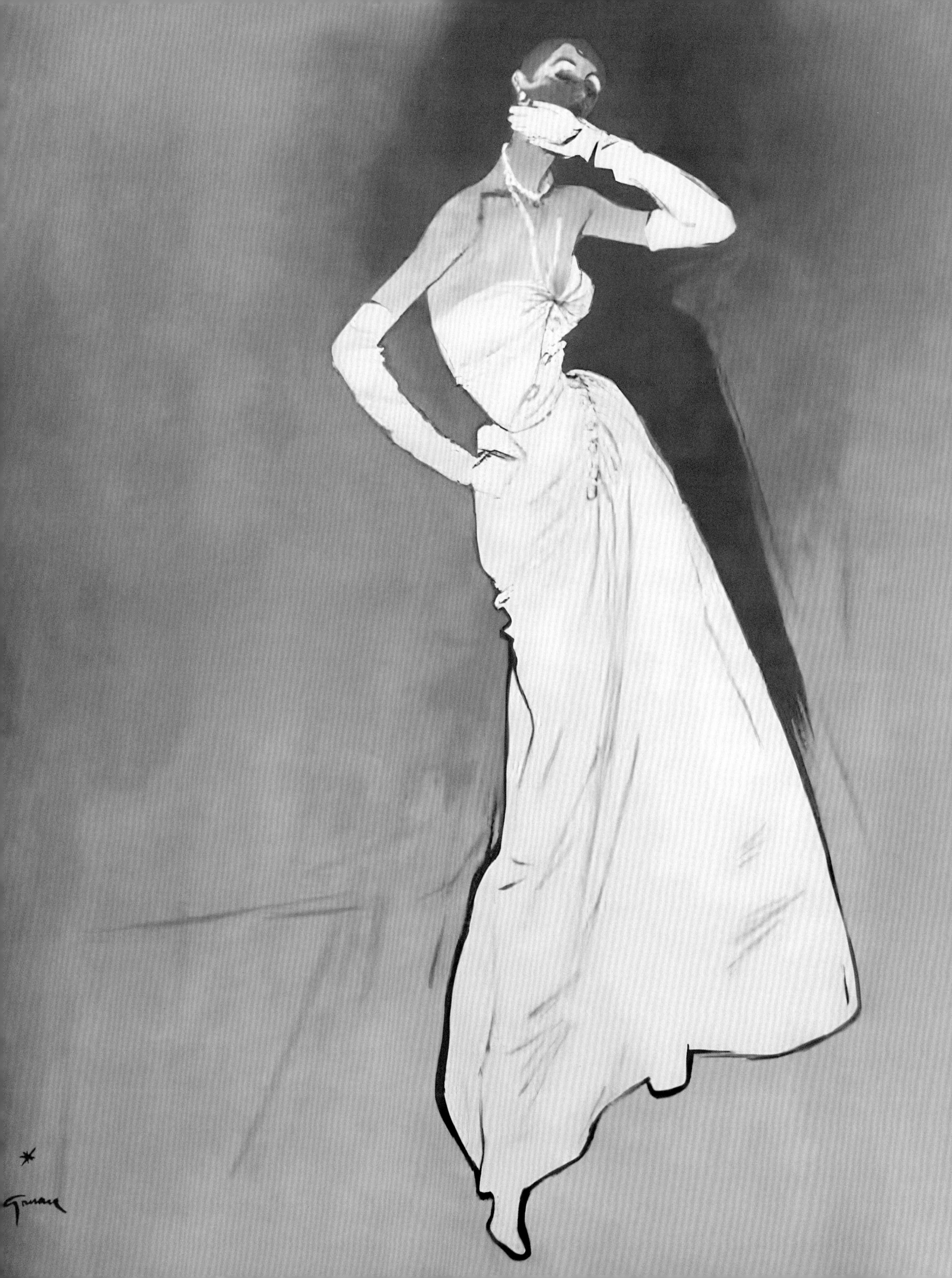

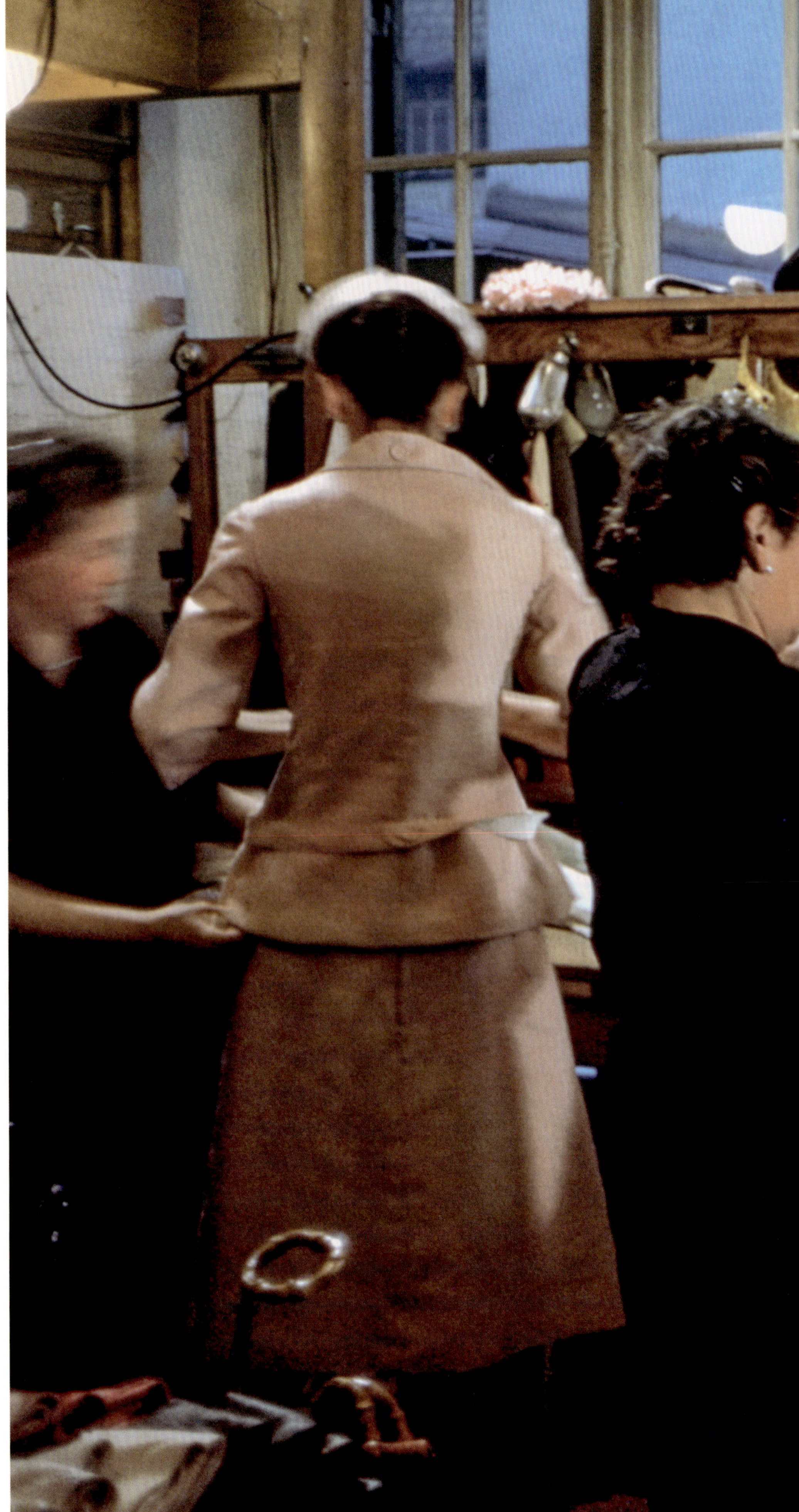

The models' fitting room at the Christian Dior couture house, 30 Avenue Montaigne, Paris, circa 1950. Photograph by Eugene Kammerman.

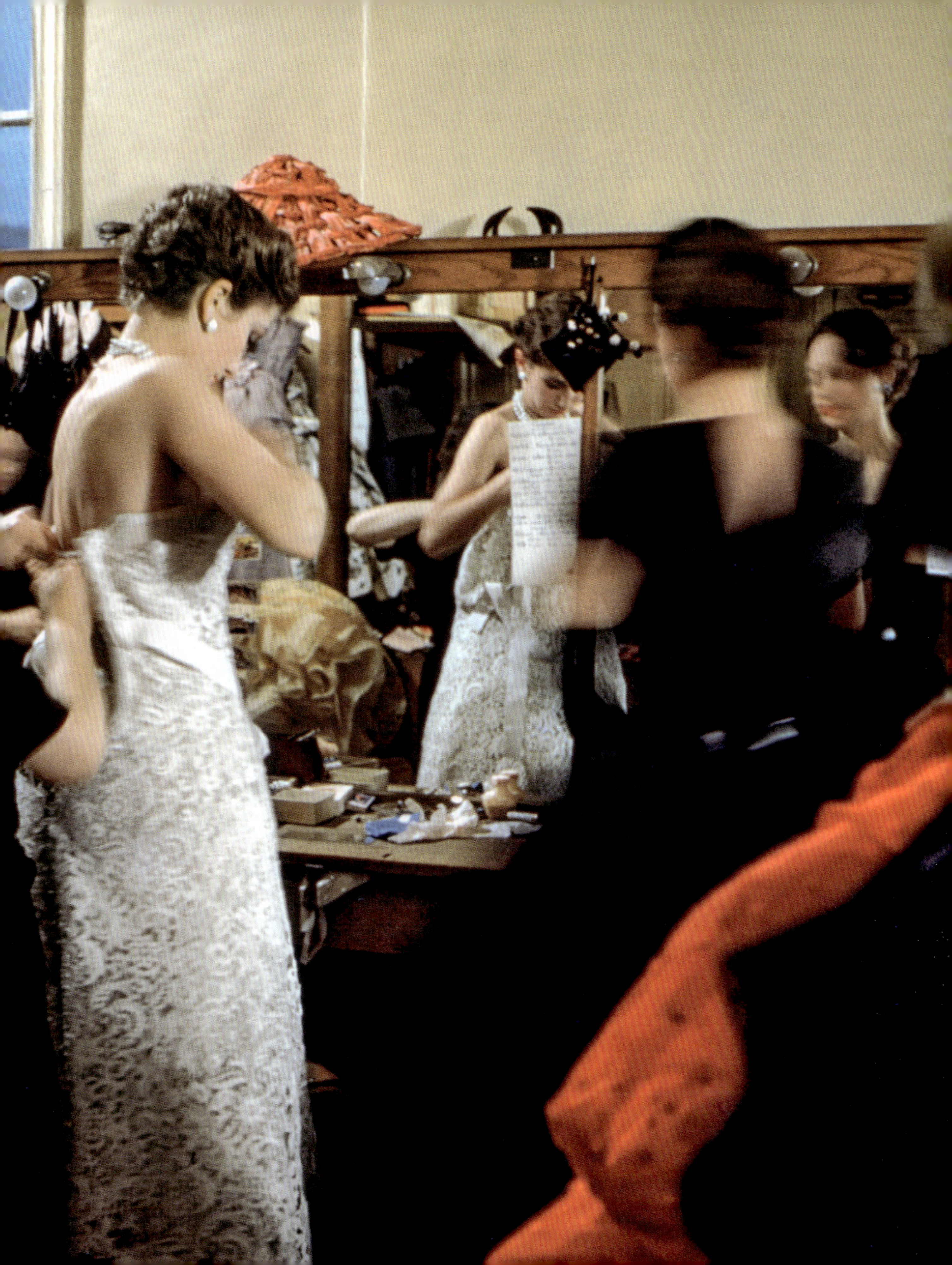

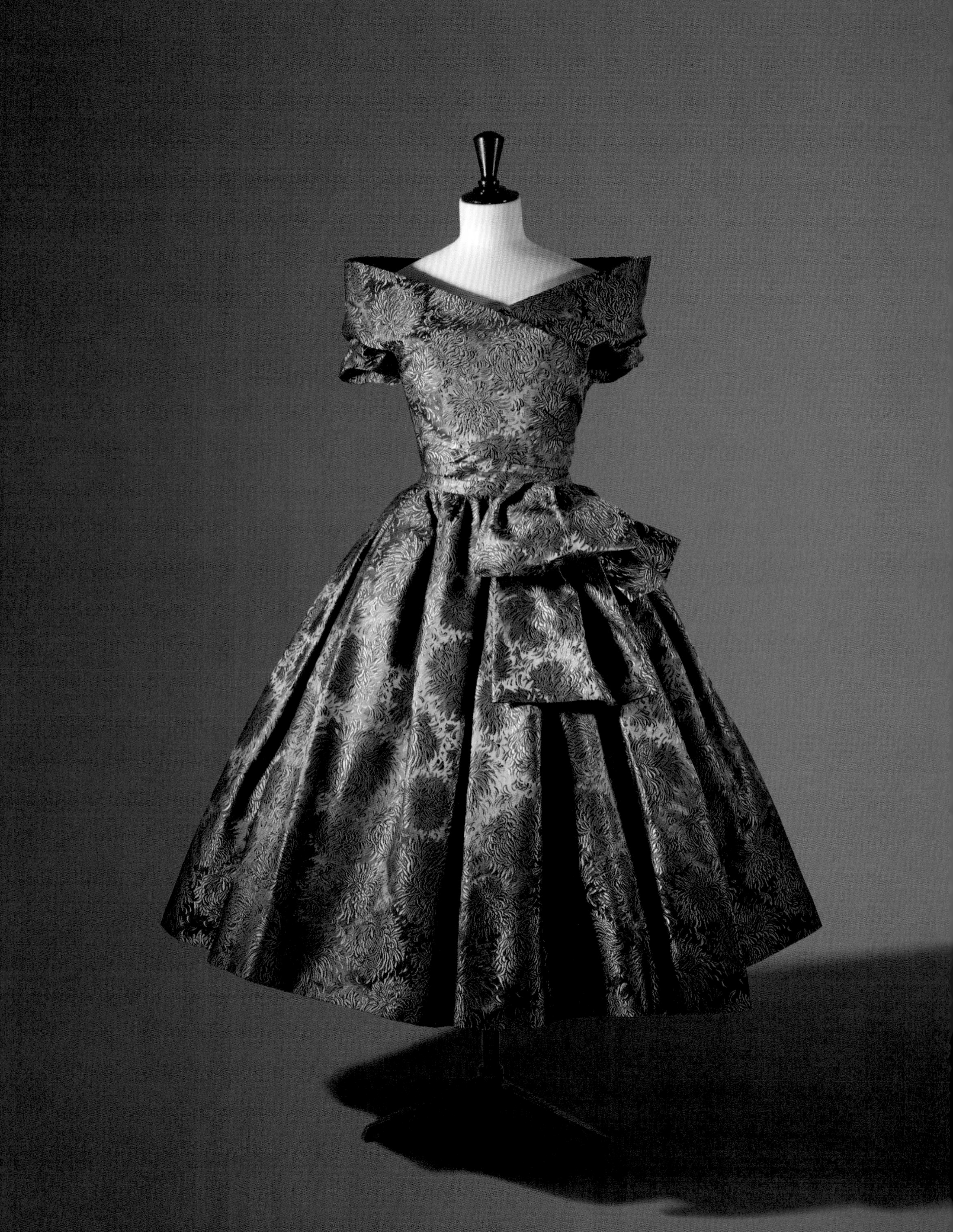

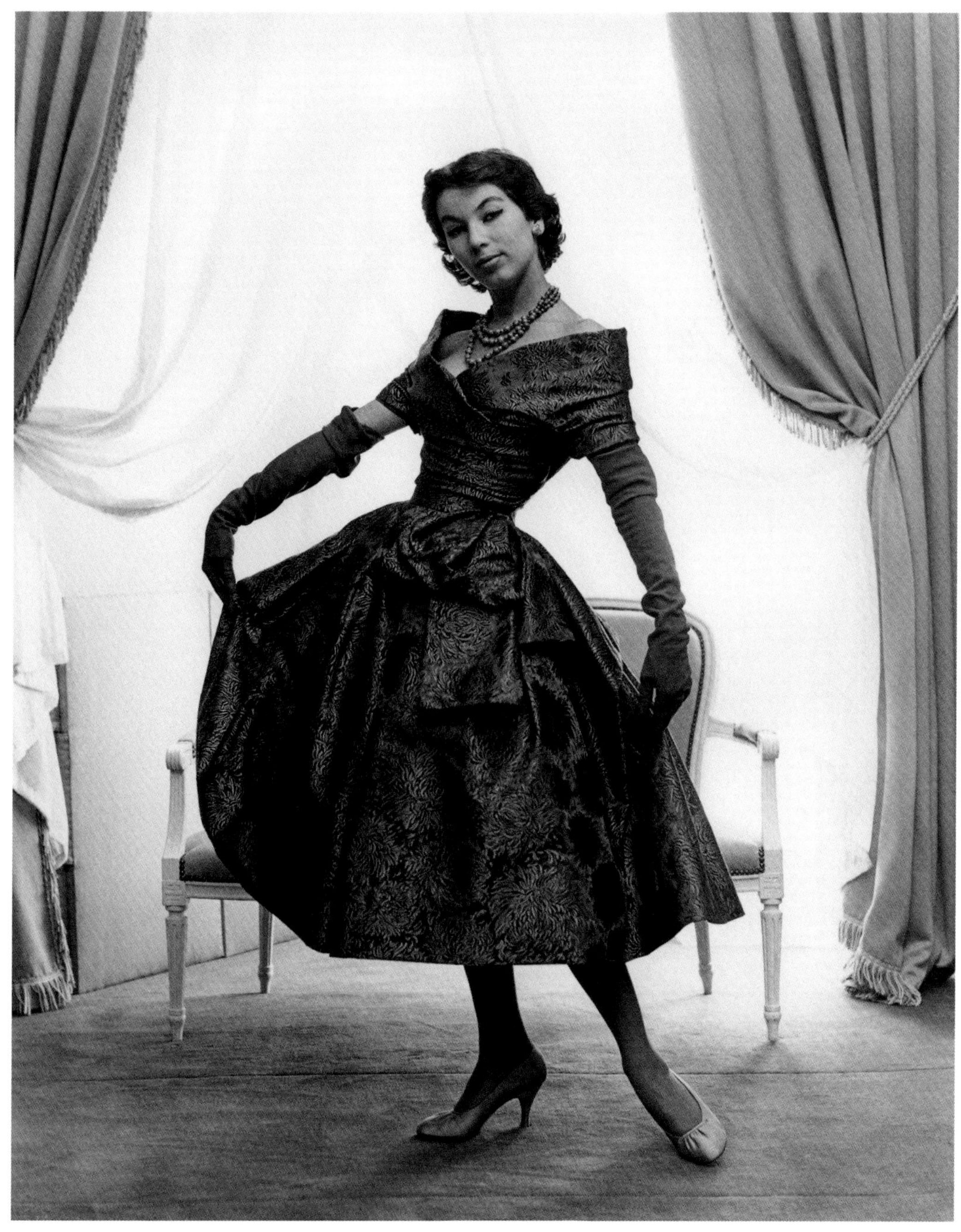

OPPOSITE
Christian Dior
Tokio

Dress in silk brocade, Autumn–Winter 1955
haute couture collection, *Y* line.
Paris, Fondation Azzedine Alaïa.

ABOVE
The model Victoire wearing
the Christian Dior *Tokio* dress in
the presentation salons
at 30 Avenue Montaigne, Paris.

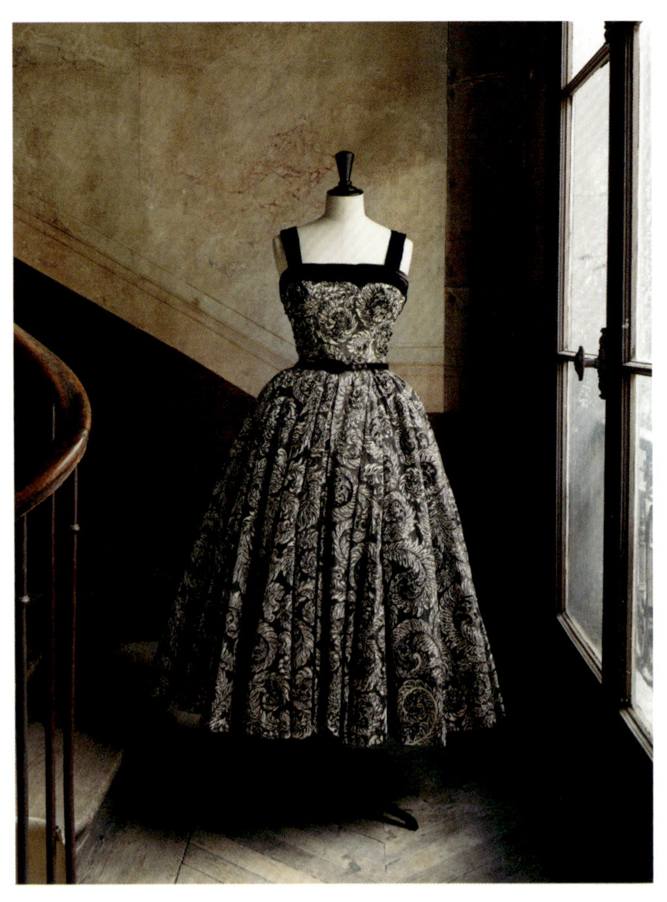

"IT IS NOT SUFFICIENTLY UNDERSTOOD THAT EMBROIDERY IS STILL DONE BY HAND, AS IN THE EIGHTEENTH CENTURY. A BALL DRESS MAY BE ENTIRELY COVERED WITH MILLIONS OF *PAILLETTES*, OR PEARLS, EACH ONE HAS TO BE PUT ON SEPARATELY AS IF THEY HAD BEEN SEWN BY FAIRIES."

ABOVE AND OPPOSITE
Christian Dior
Favorite

Semiformal evening dress in embroidered lace
(with detail), Autumn–Winter 1949 haute couture collection,
Milieu du siècle line. Paris, Fondation Azzedine Alaïa.

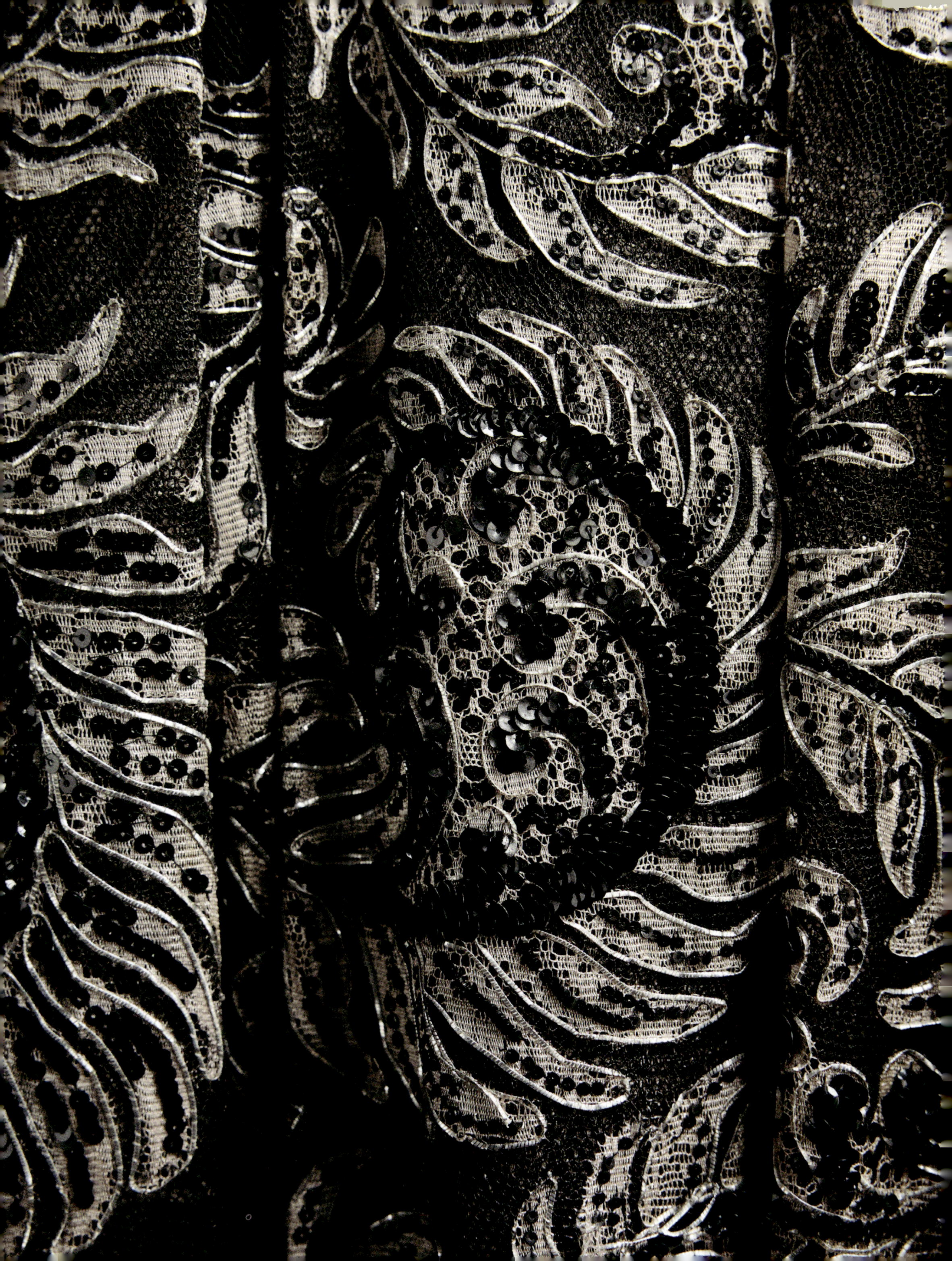

Christian Dior

AUTOMNE-HIVER 1955-1956

LIGNE Y

C'est encore à une lettre de l'alphabet, l'**Y,** qu'il revient d'exprimer l'essentiel de la nouvelle Collection.

Réaction contre les basques longues, les tailles basses, les tailles trop lâches, les chapeaux qui n'en sont pas.

Evolution que pouvaient laisser prévoir les jeux de taille de la dernière Collection vers une taille plus mince, plus haute et une poitrine plus marquée que soulignent presque tous les effets de coupe.

La poitrine **haut placée** s'épanouit entre les branches de l'**Y** qui aboutissent à la base des épaules naturelles et menues. Une nouvelle emmanchure a pour mission de préciser cette ligne.

La taille amincie, plus que serrée, reste en fait à sa place naturelle, mais avec une tendance à s'indiquer plus haute, ce qui donne aux jupes, donc aux jambes bases de l'**Y** un maximum d'allongement.

Les **basques** des **tailleurs** sont courtes et parfois presque absentes.

Très peu de **poches.**

Souvent les vestes sont remplacées par des **camisoles** boutonnées dans le dos, en général bien appuyées au-dessus de la ceinture, et décollant en remontant légèrement dans le dos.

Encolures très simples, revers tailleurs, au ras du cou, souvent complétées d'une **guimpe** donnant un effet souple de col chandail roulé.

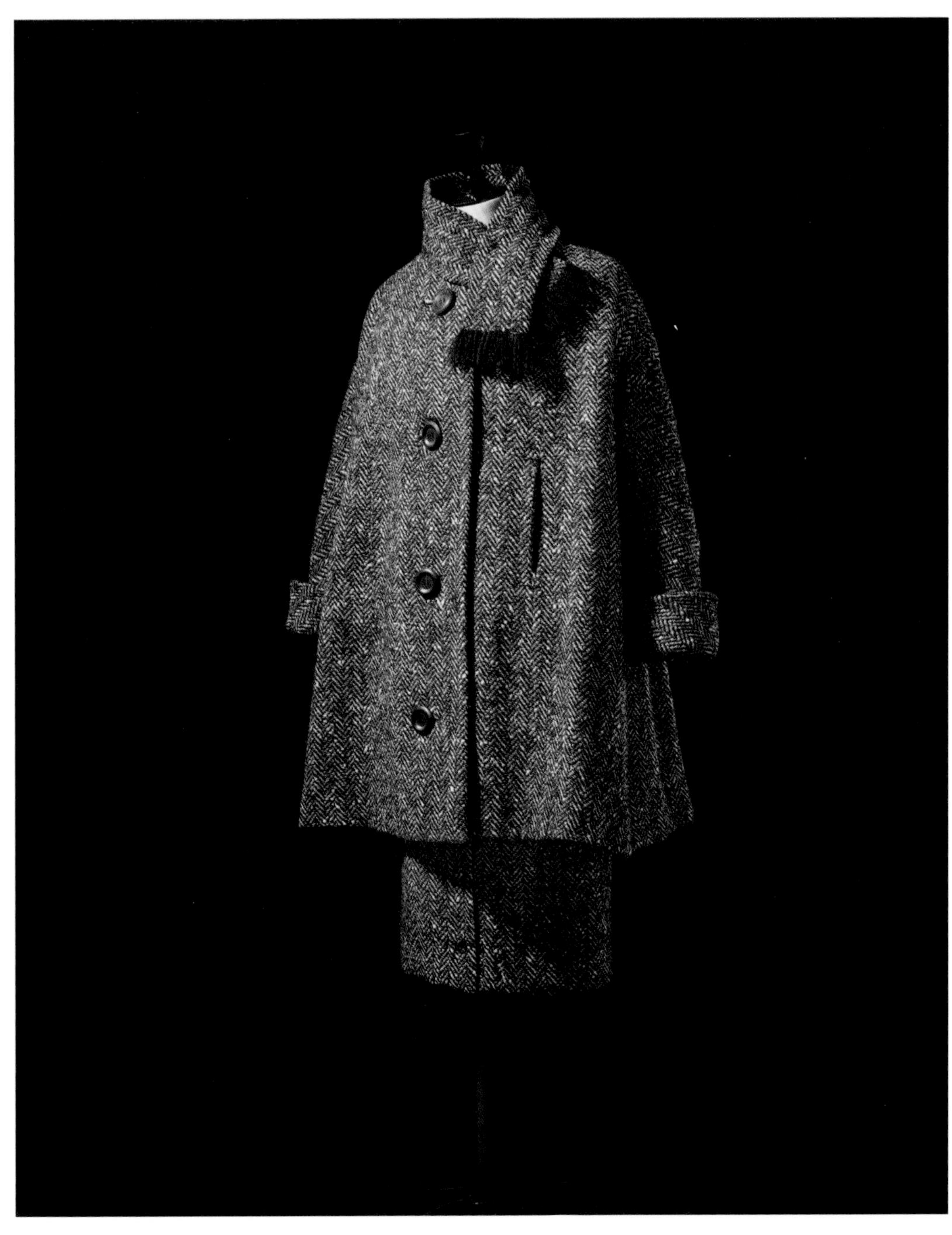

ABOVE
Christian Dior
Alibi

Ensemble in tweed,
Autumn–Winter 1955 haute couture
collection, *Y* line. Paris,
Fondation Azzedine Alaïa.

OPPOSITE
First page of the press release
for the Christian Dior Autumn–Winter 1955
haute couture collection, *Y* line.
Paris, Dior Héritage.

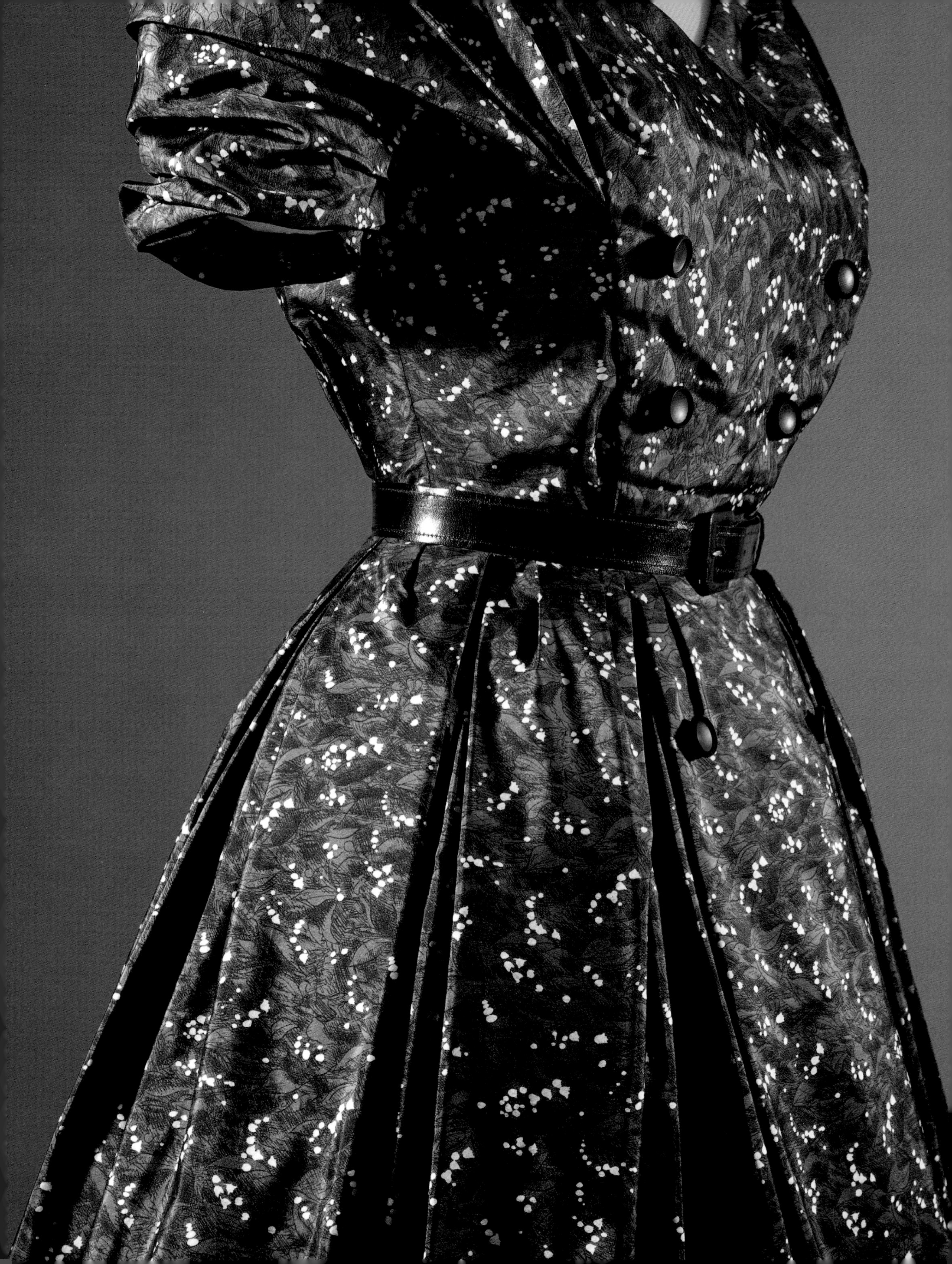

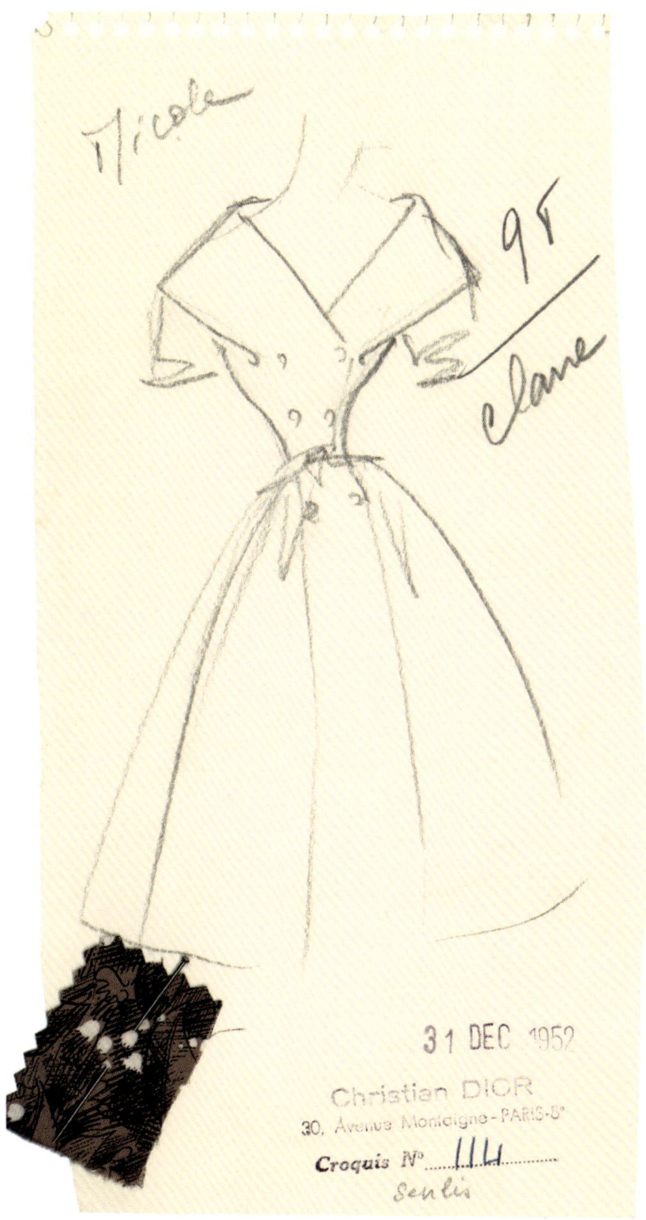

Christian Dior
Senlis

Town dress in printed taffeta,
Spring–Summer 1953 haute
couture collection, *Tulipe* line.
Paris, Fondation Azzedine Alaïa.

Christian Dior, original sketch,
with fabric sample,
for the *Senlis* town dress.
Paris, Dior Héritage.

131

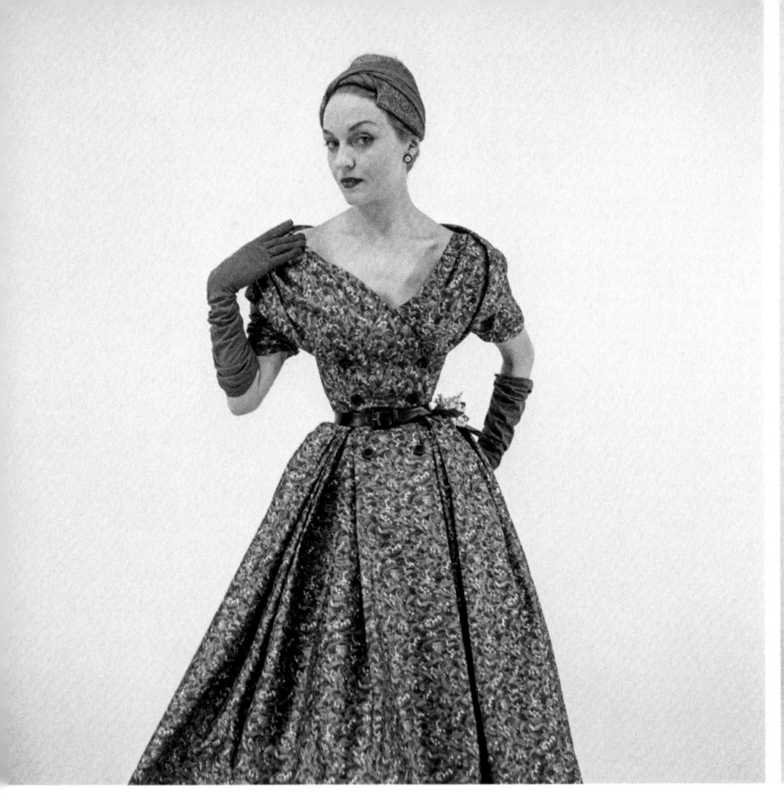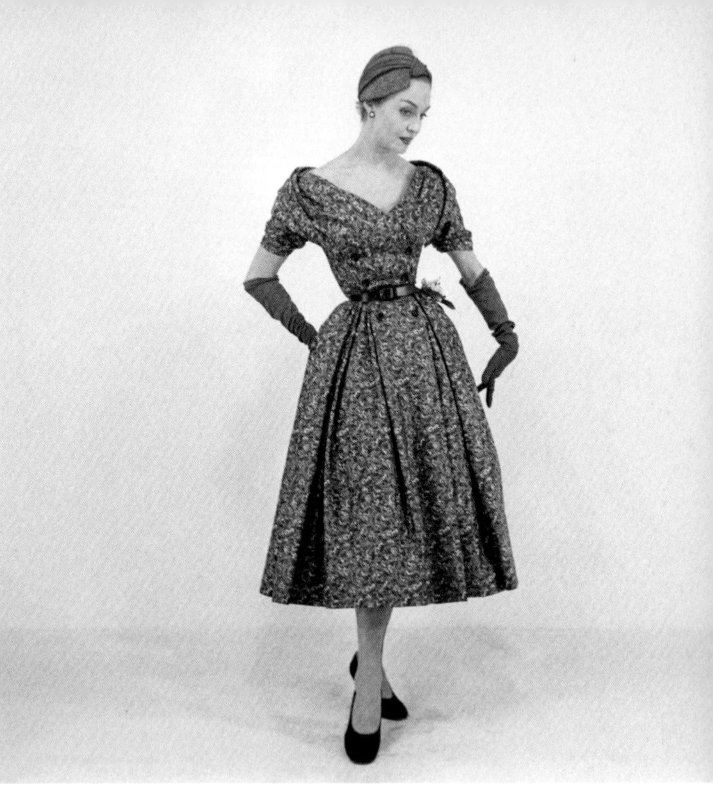

Model wearing the Christian Dior
Senlis town dress, Spring–Summer 1953
haute couture collection, *Tulipe* line.
Photographs by André Ostier.

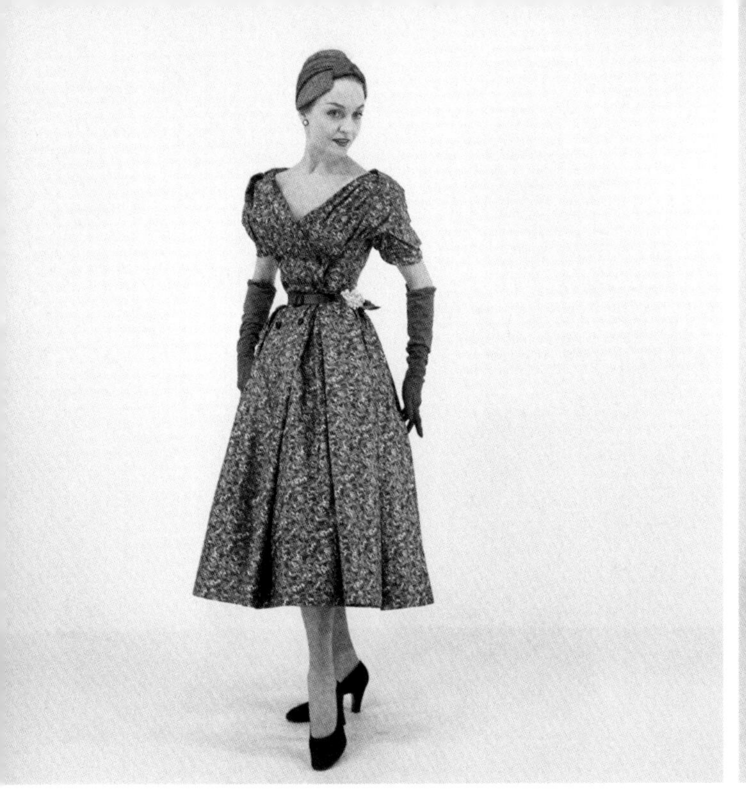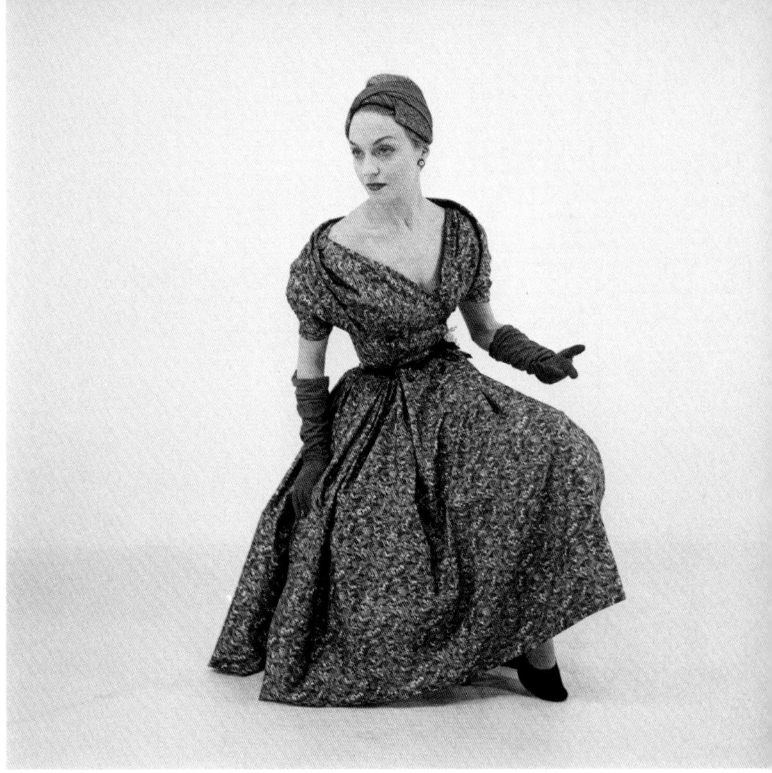

"THE FOLLOWING SPRING, APPEARED THE *TULIPE* LINE, MARKED BY THE DEVELOPMENT OF THE BUST AND THE NARROWING OF THE HIPS. LITTLE BY LITTLE THE WAIST WAS BEING FREED. COLORS WERE INSPIRED BY THE PICTURES OF THE IMPRESSIONISTS, AND EVOKED THE FIELDS OF FLOWERS DEAR TO RENOIR AND VAN GOGH." **CHRISTIAN DIOR**

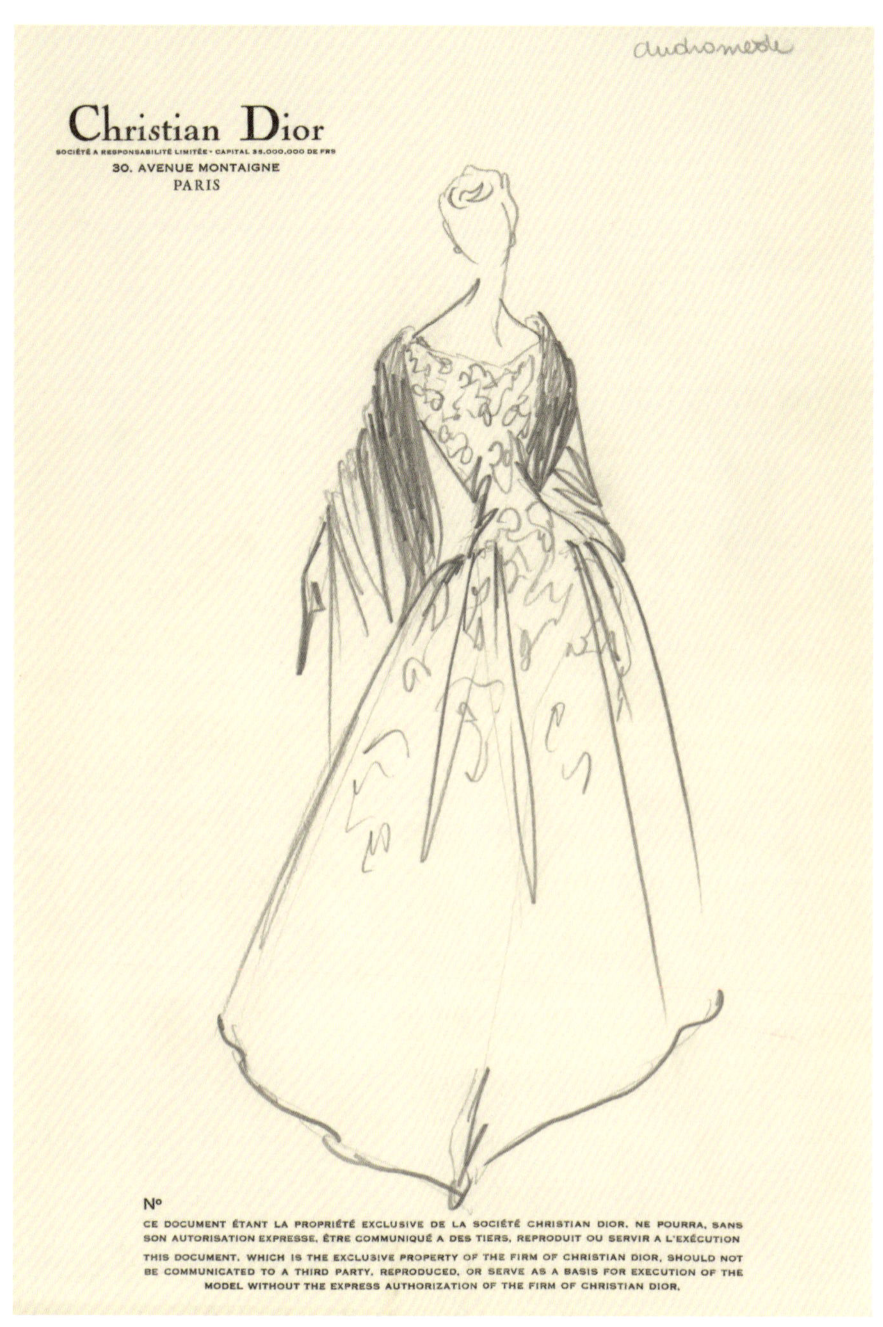

Andromède

Christian Dior
SOCIÉTÉ A RESPONSABILITÉ LIMITÉE · CAPITAL 35.000.000 DE FRS
30, AVENUE MONTAIGNE
PARIS

Nº
CE DOCUMENT ÉTANT LA PROPRIÉTÉ EXCLUSIVE DE LA SOCIÉTÉ CHRISTIAN DIOR, NE POURRA, SANS
SON AUTORISATION EXPRESSE, ÊTRE COMMUNIQUÉ A DES TIERS, REPRODUIT OU SERVIR A L'EXÉCUTION
THIS DOCUMENT, WHICH IS THE EXCLUSIVE PROPERTY OF THE FIRM OF CHRISTIAN DIOR, SHOULD NOT
BE COMMUNICATED TO A THIRD PARTY, REPRODUCED, OR SERVE AS A BASIS FOR EXECUTION OF THE
MODEL WITHOUT THE EXPRESS AUTHORIZATION OF THE FIRM OF CHRISTIAN DIOR.

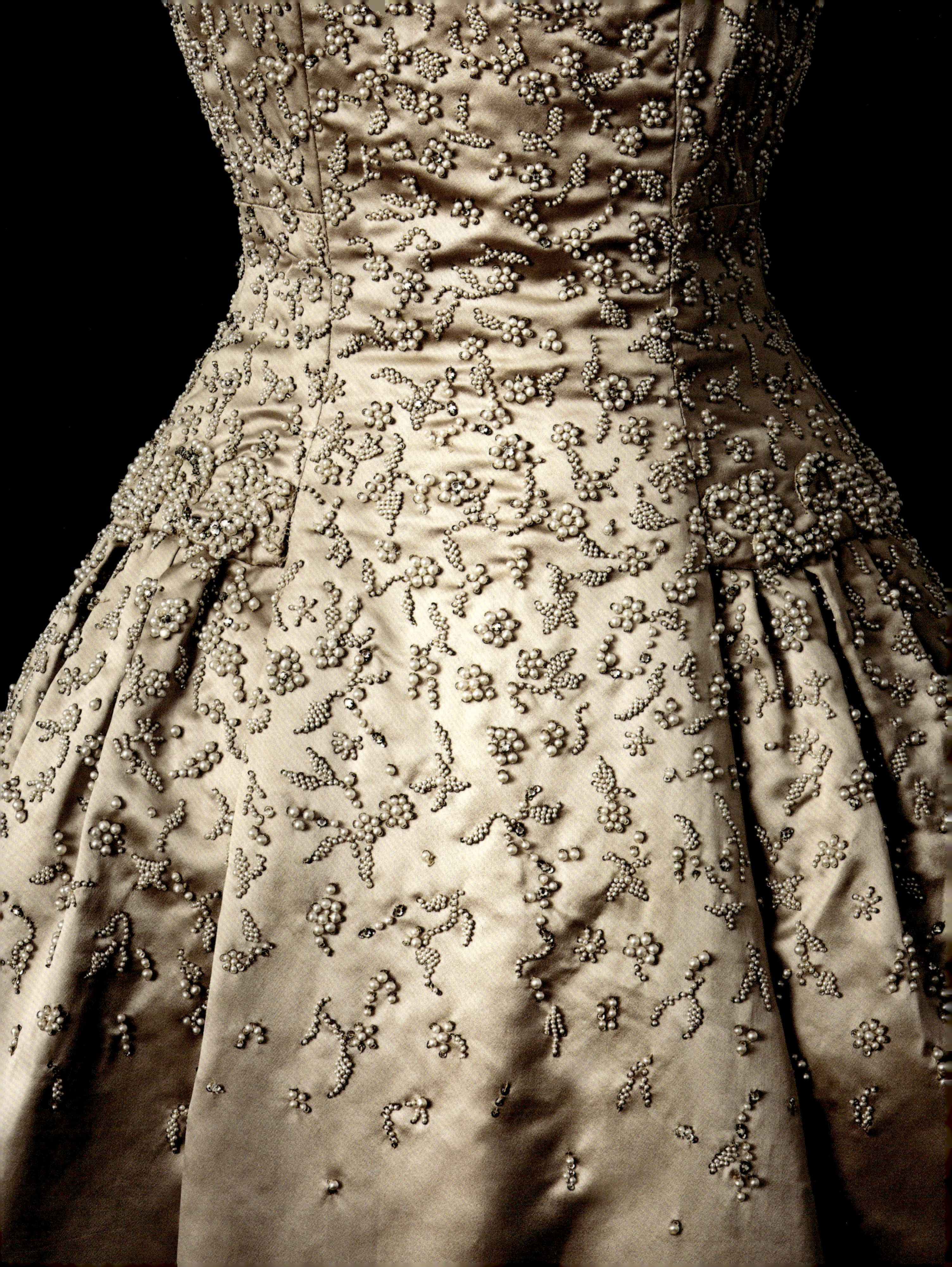

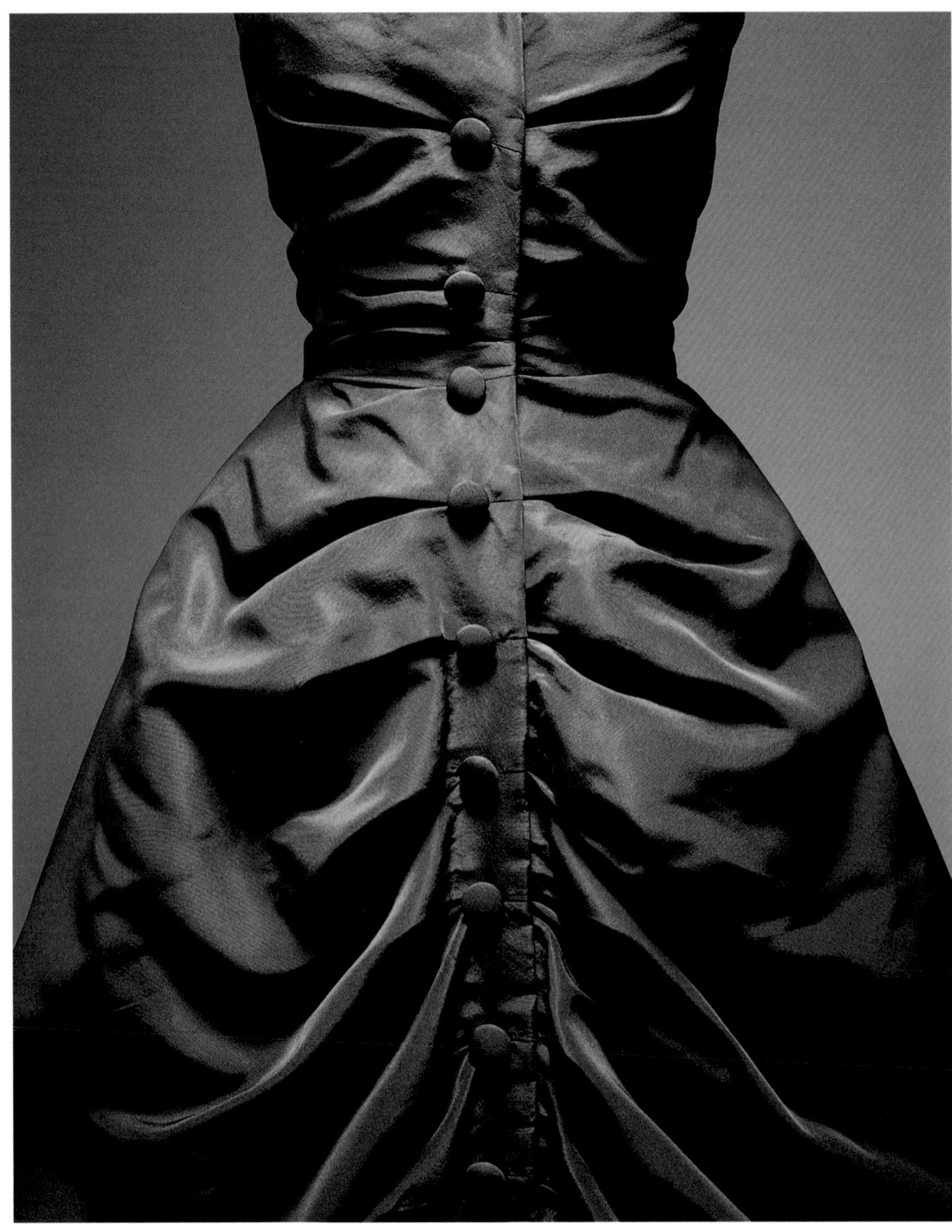

ABOVE
Christian Dior
Manon

Short evening dress
in *poult-de-soie* (detail),
Christian Dior–New York
Autumn–Winter 1957 collection.
Paris, Fondation Azzedine Alaïa.

OPPOSITE
The model Victoire wearing the Christian Dior
Venezuela reception dress, Autumn–Winter 1957
haute couture collection, *Fuseau* line.
Photograph by Guy Bourdin, published
in *Vogue Paris*, October 1957.

The Fondation Azzedine Alaïa has
an example of this dress in its collections.

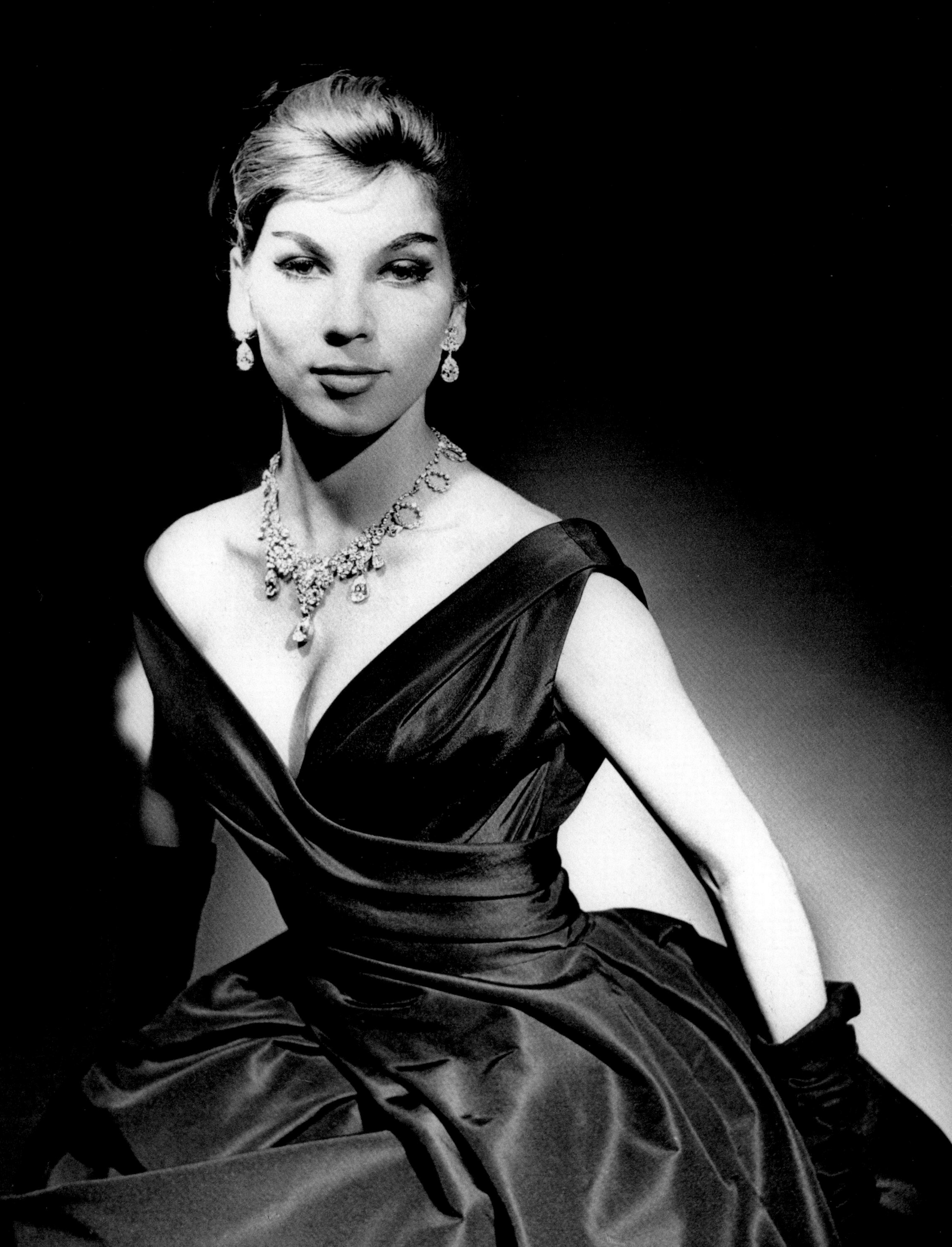

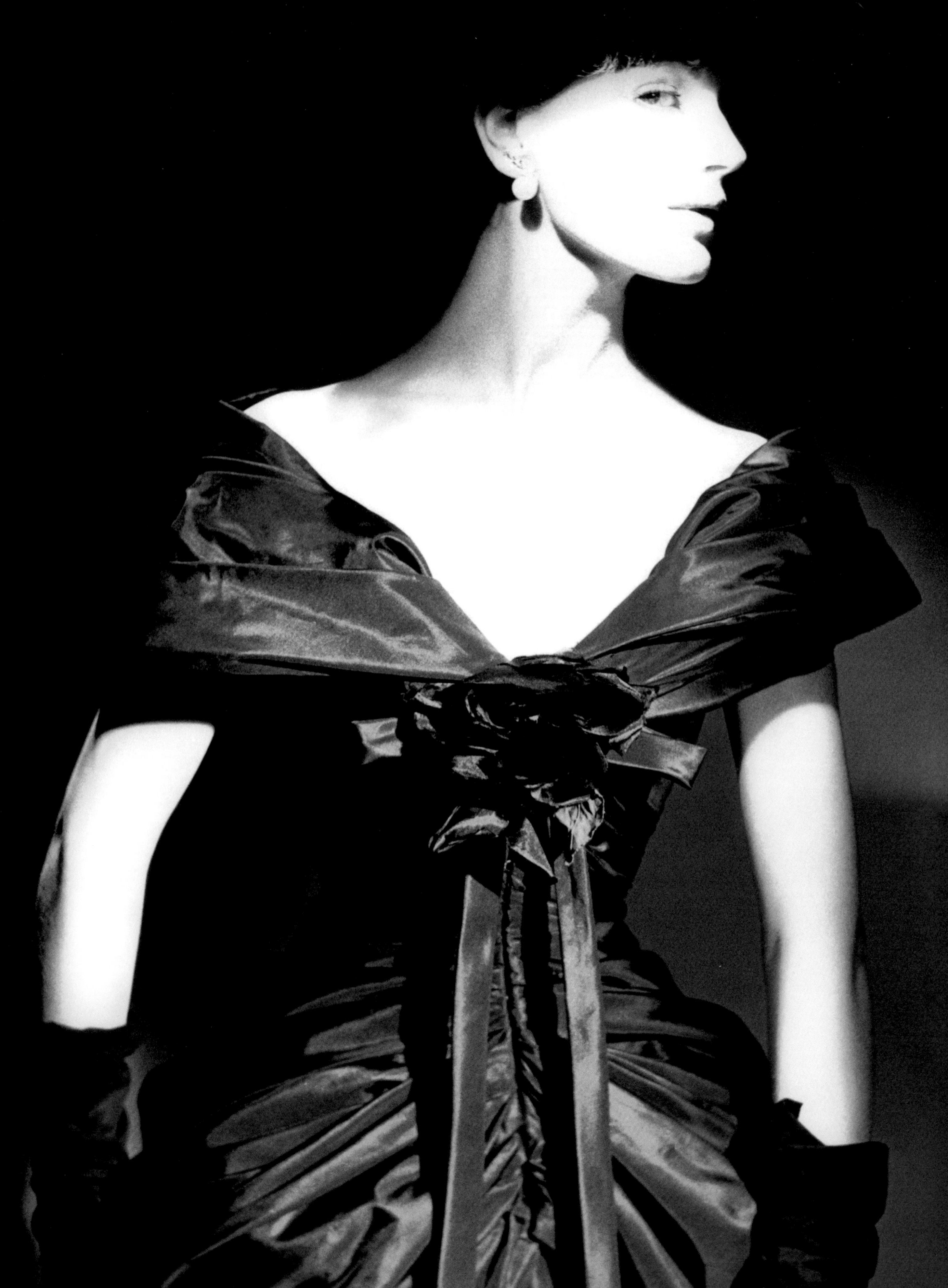

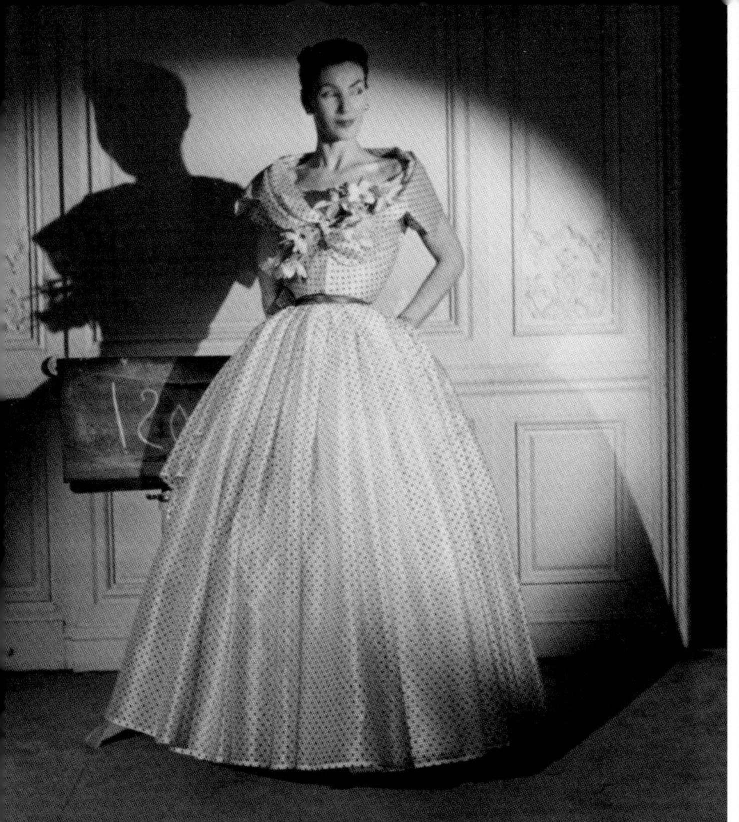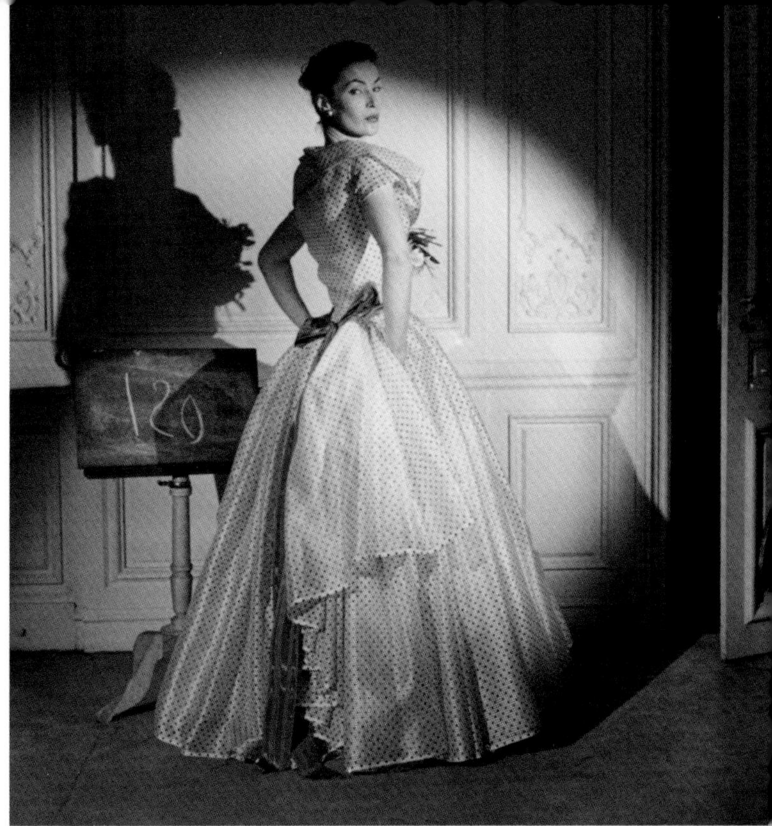

"AS THE HOURS GO BY, THE DRESSES BEGIN TO BECOME MORE ELABORATE AND FULL, THEIR SKIRTS LENGTHEN, AND WE IMPERCEPTIBLY SHIFT FROM THE DINNER DRESS TO THE FORMAL EVENING GOWN, WHICH ENJOYS TOTAL FREEDOM IN TERMS OF SILHOUETTE AND VOLUME." **CHRISTIAN DIOR**

OPPOSITE
Model wearing the Christian Dior *Zerline* reception dress, Autumn–Winter 1957 haute couture collection, *Fuseau* line. Photograph by Guy Bourdin, published in *Vogue Paris*, October 1957.

ABOVE
The model Lucky wearing the Christian Dior *Victorien Sardou* evening dress, Spring–Summer 1952 haute couture collection, *Sinueuse* line, in the presentation salons at 30 Avenue Montaigne, Paris.

The Fondation Azzedine Alaïa has an example of these two dresses in its collections.

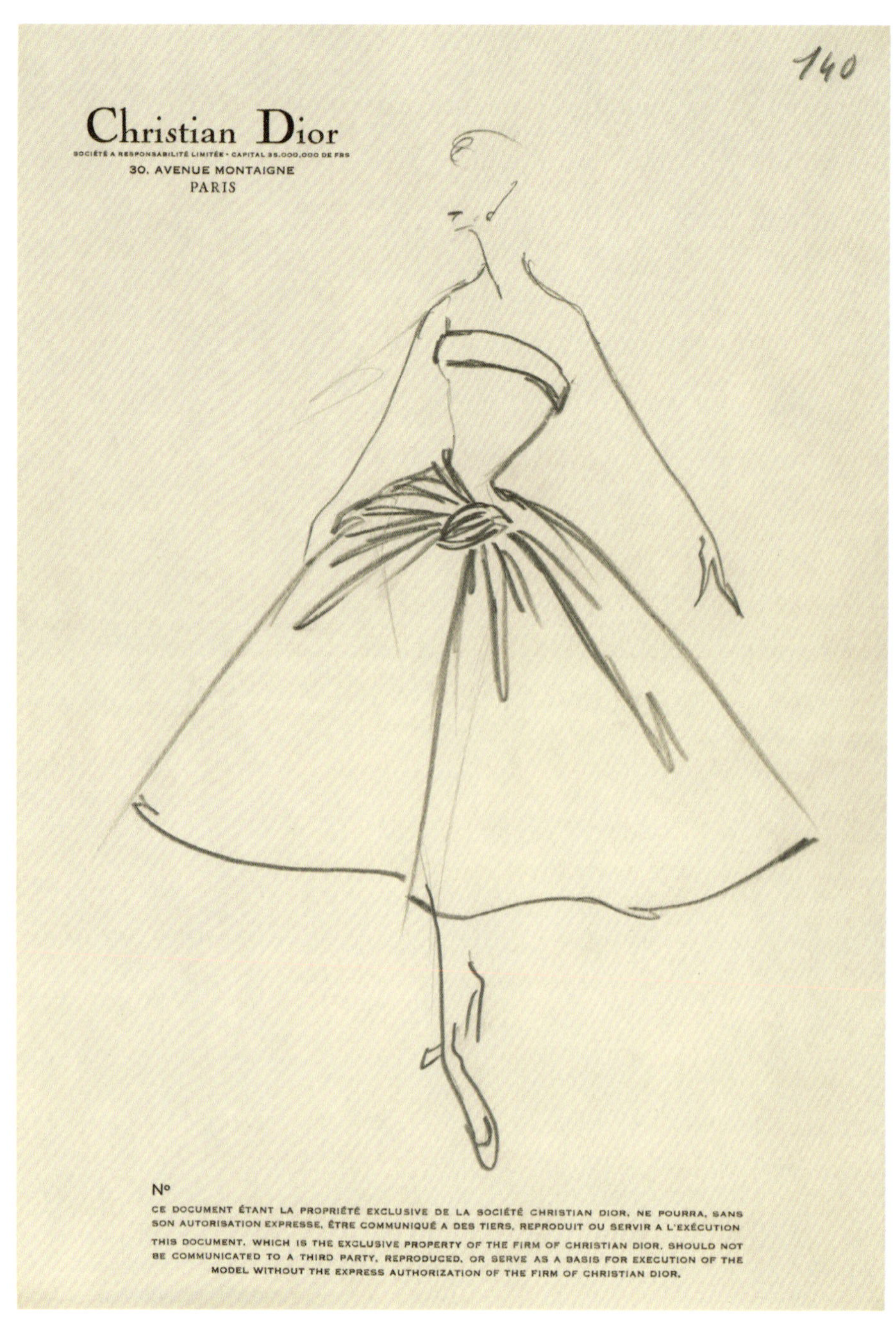

The model Victoire presenting the Christian Dior
Curaçao short evening dress with its mink stole,
Autumn–Winter 1954 haute couture collection, *H* line,
in the salons at 30 Avenue Montaigne, Paris.
Photograph by Mark Shaw.

The Fondation Azzedine Alaïa has a version
of this dress, for a client, in its collections.

Press sketch for the Christian Dior *Curaçao*
short evening dress. Paris, Dior Héritage.

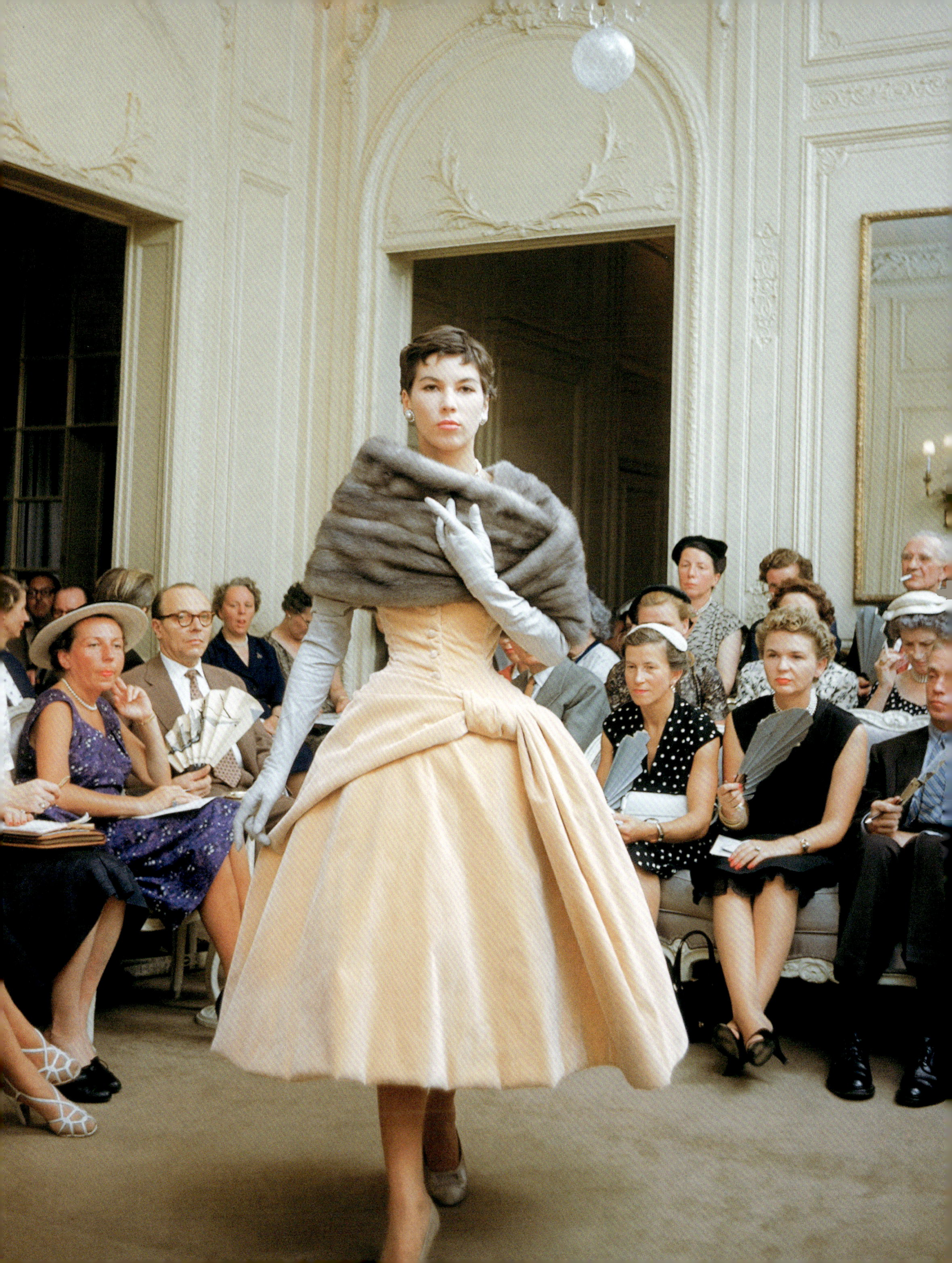

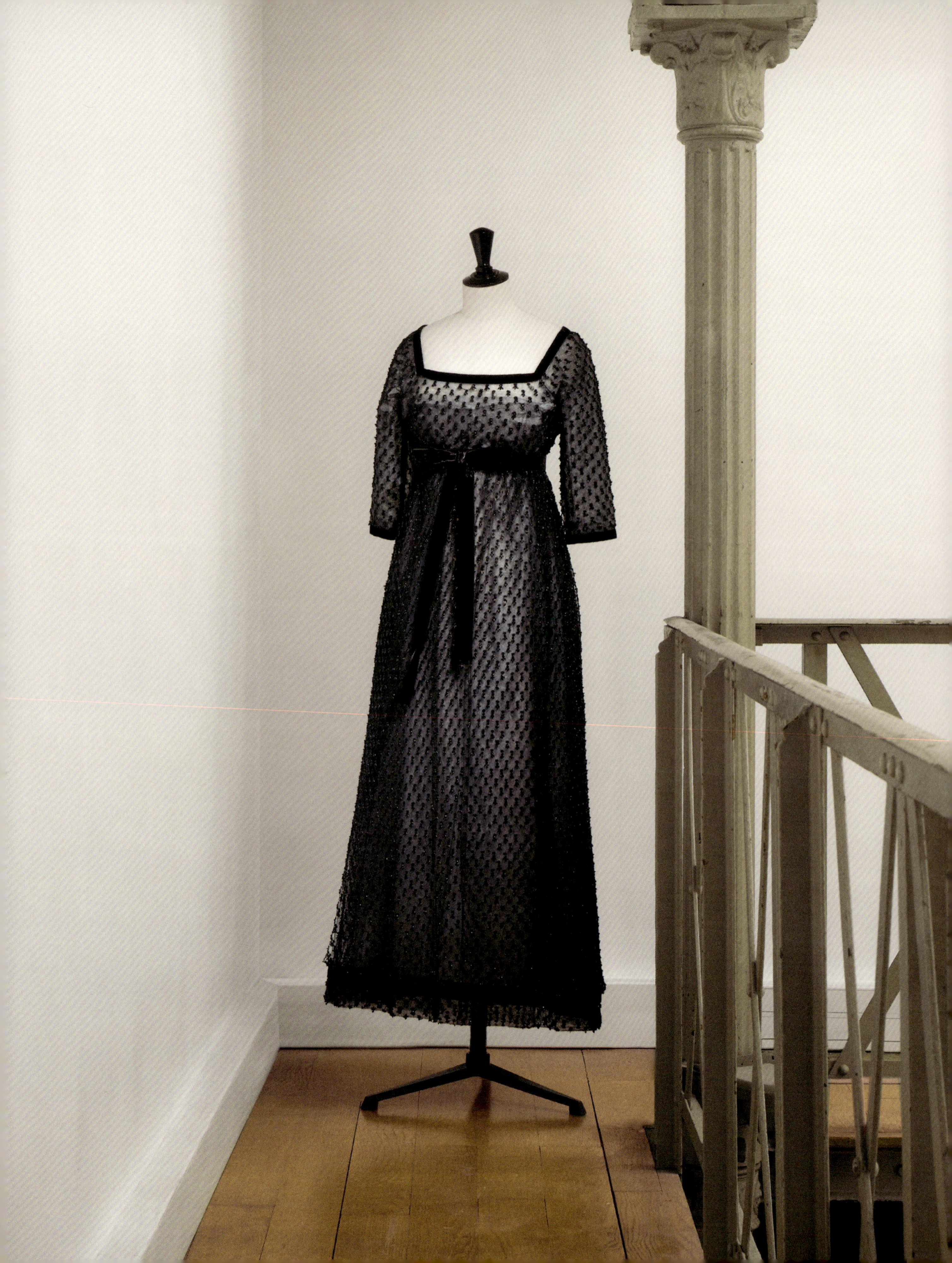

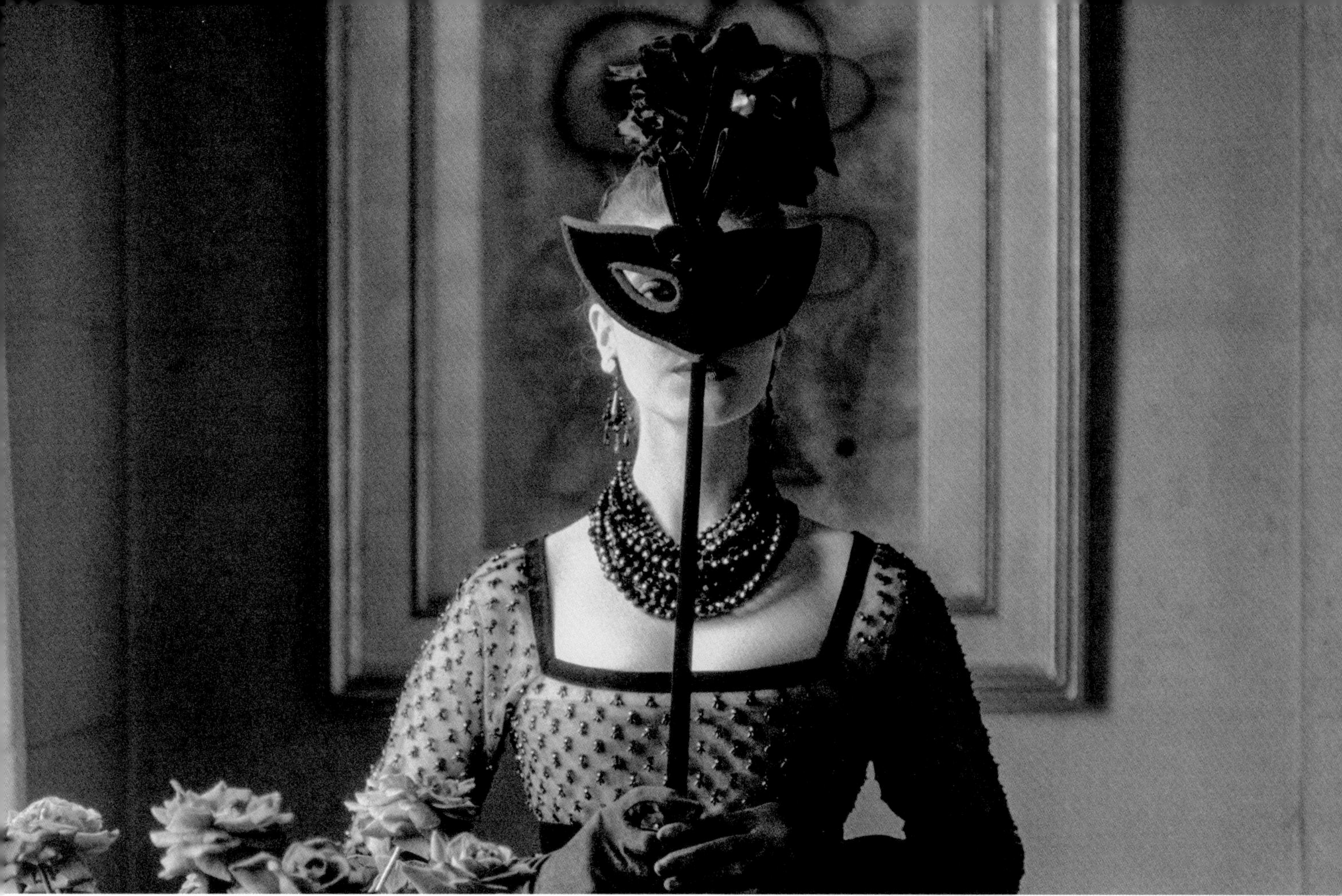

Yves Saint Laurent for Christian Dior
Lola

Long evening dress in embroidered
point d'esprit tulle, Autumn–Winter 1958
haute couture collection, *Courbe* line.
Paris, Fondation Azzedine Alaïa.

Model wearing the
Yves Saint Laurent for
Christian Dior *Lola*
long evening dress.
Photograph by Mark Shaw.

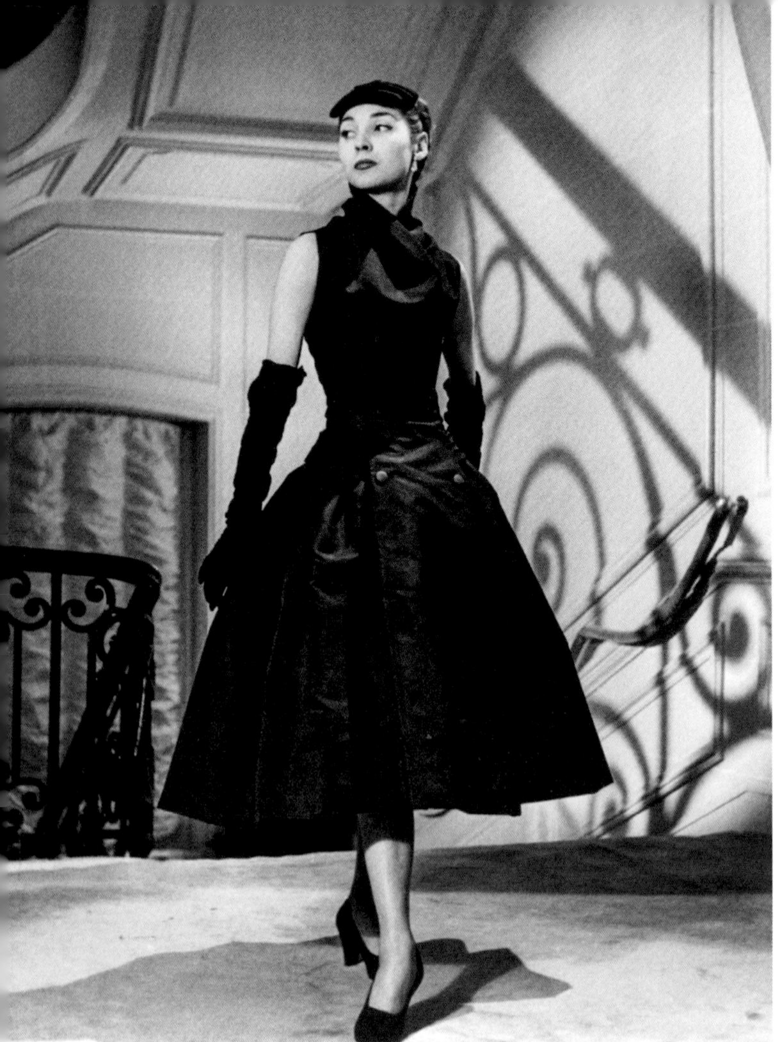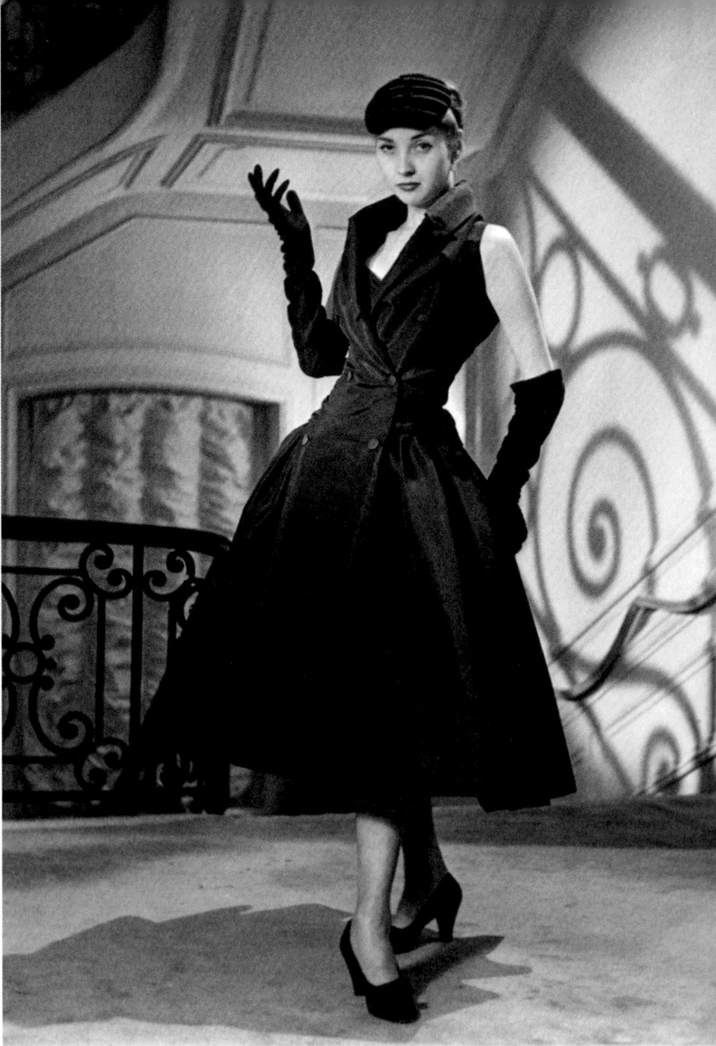

ABOVE
The model Renée wearing
the Christian Dior *Zélie* late-afternoon
dress in the grand staircase
at 30 Avenue Montaigne, Paris.
Photographs by Willy Maywald.

OPPOSITE
Christian Dior
Zélie

Late-afternoon dress in silk faille,
Autumn–Winter 1954 haute couture
collection, *H* line. Paris, Dior Héritage.

The Fondation Azzedine Alaïa has
an example of this dress in its collections.

144

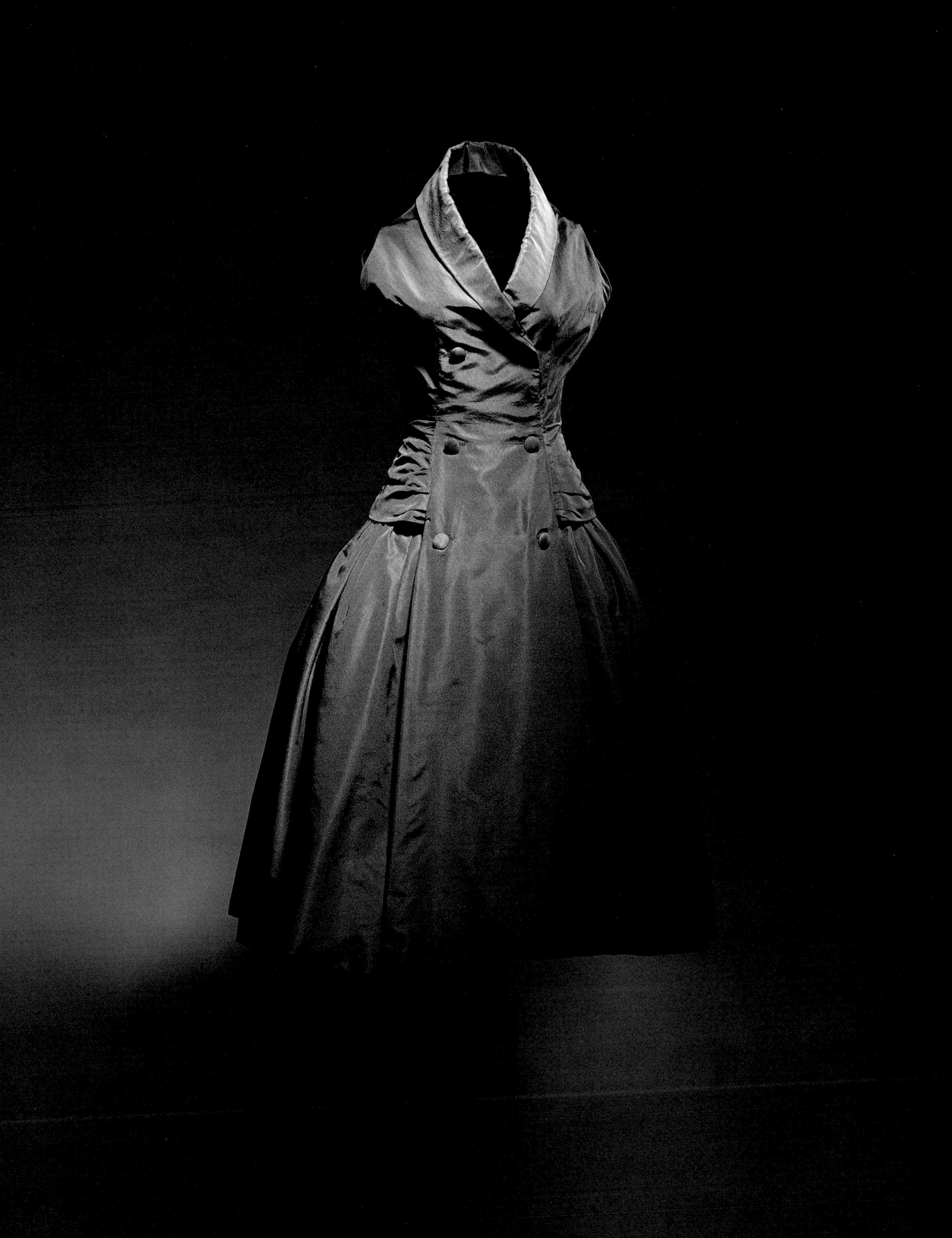

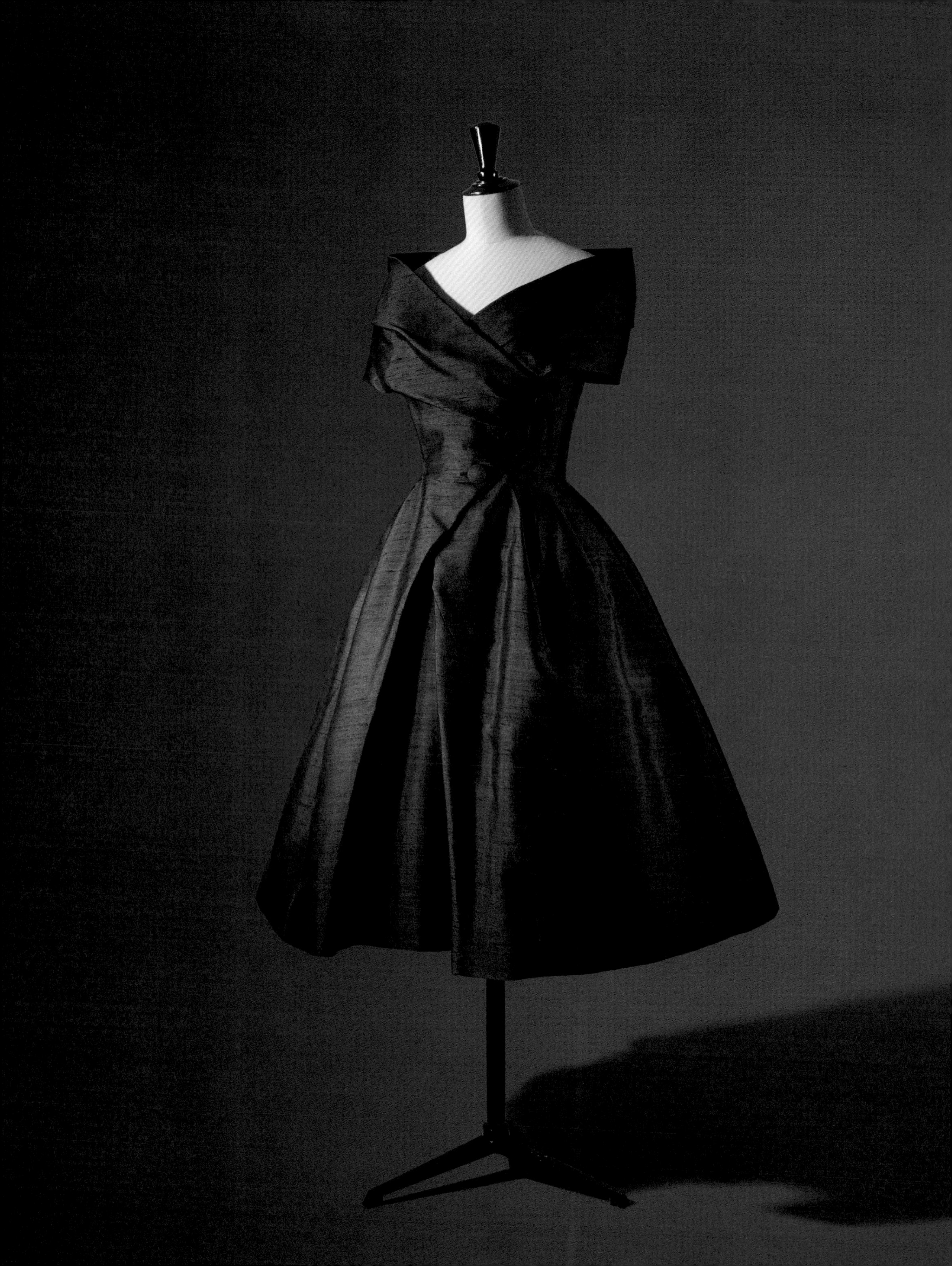

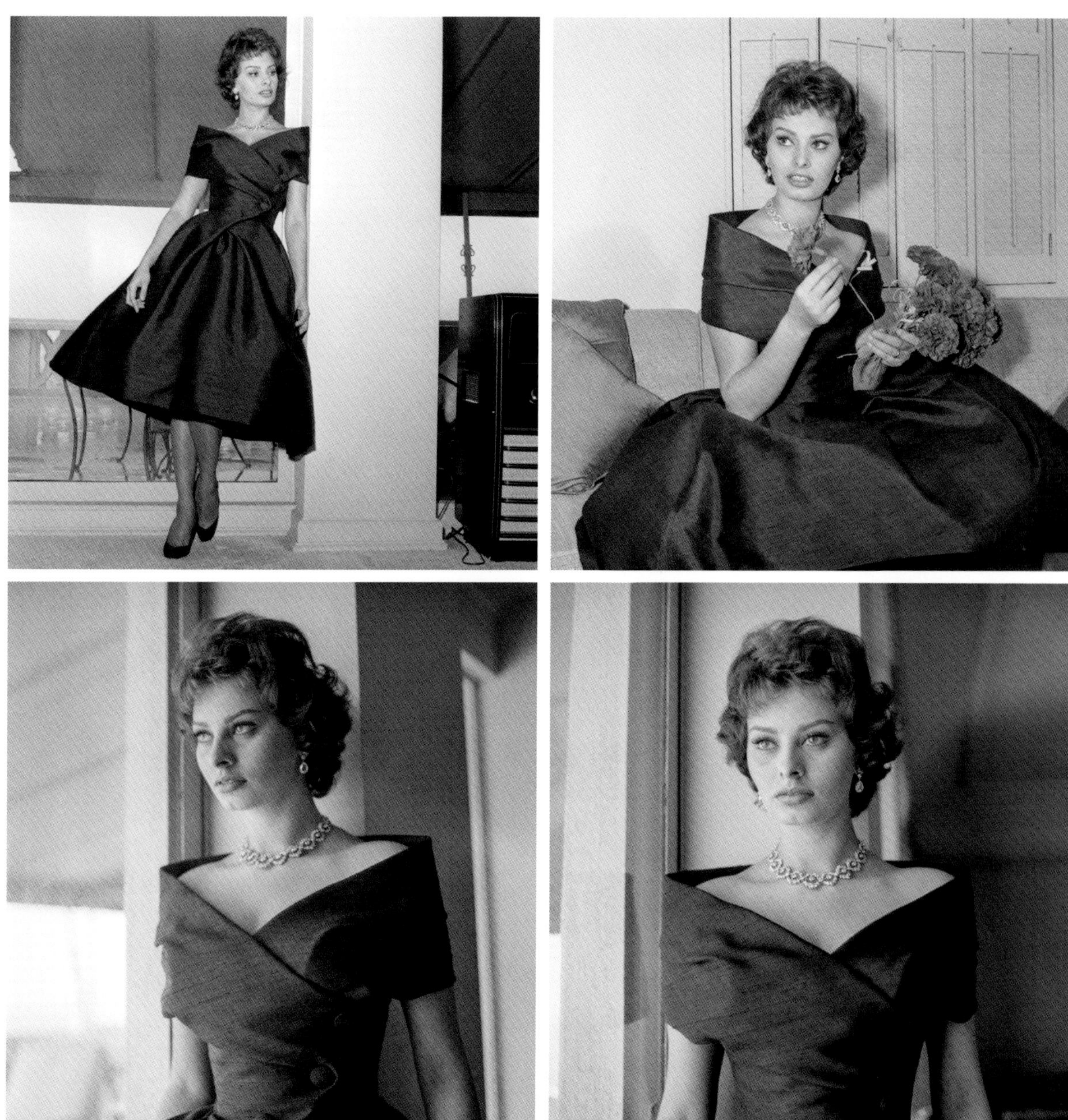

OPPOSITE
Christian Dior
Caracas

Afternoon dress in Aleoutienne,
Spring–Summer 1957 haute couture
collection, *Libre* line. Paris,
Fondation Azzedine Alaïa.

ABOVE
The actress Sophia Loren
wearing the Christian Dior
Caracas afternoon dress.

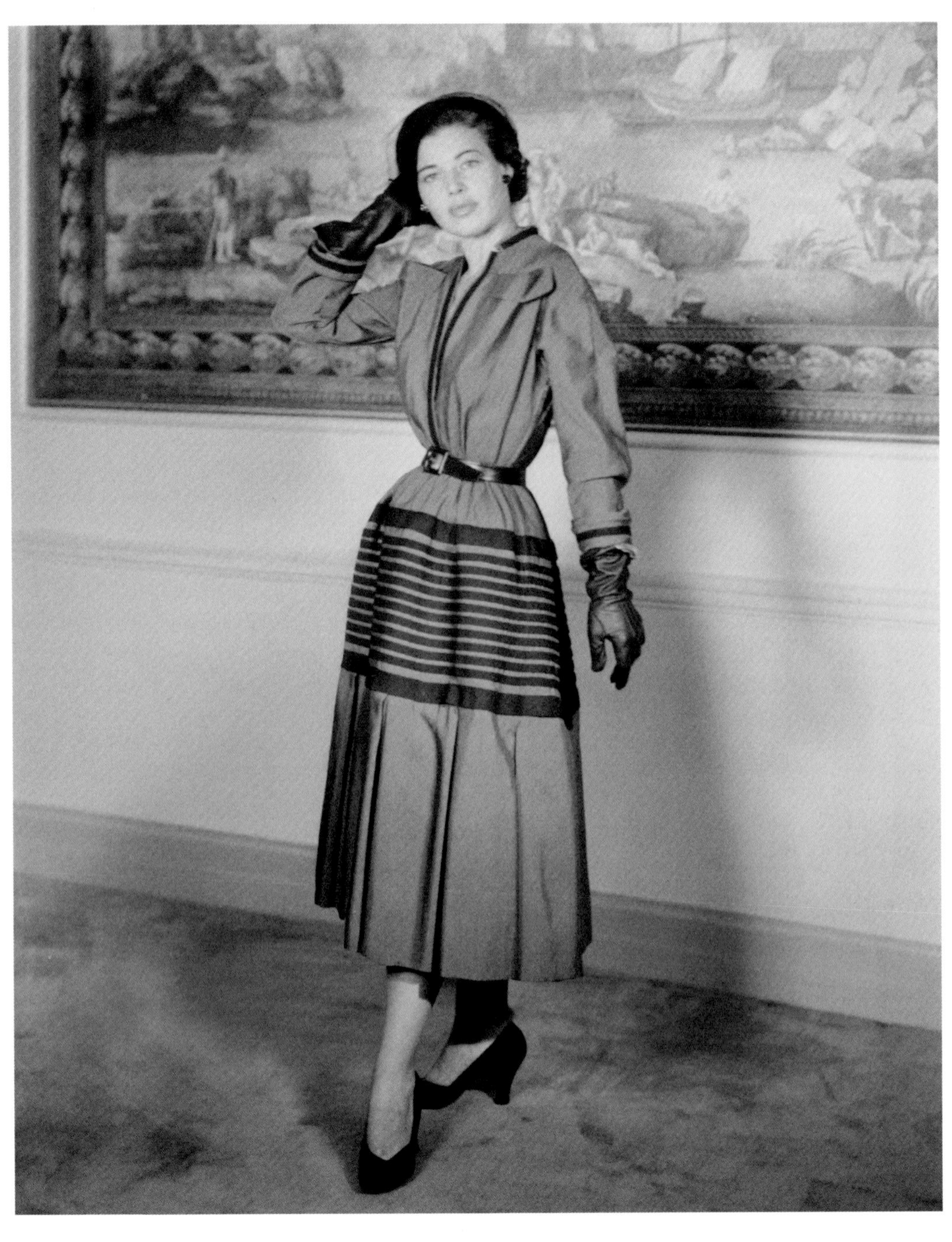

Christian Dior
Grisette

Dress in wool,
Christian Dior–New York
Autumn–Winter 1949 collection.
Paris, Fondation Azzedine Alaïa.

ABOVE
Model wearing the *Grisette* dress,
by Christian Dior.

148

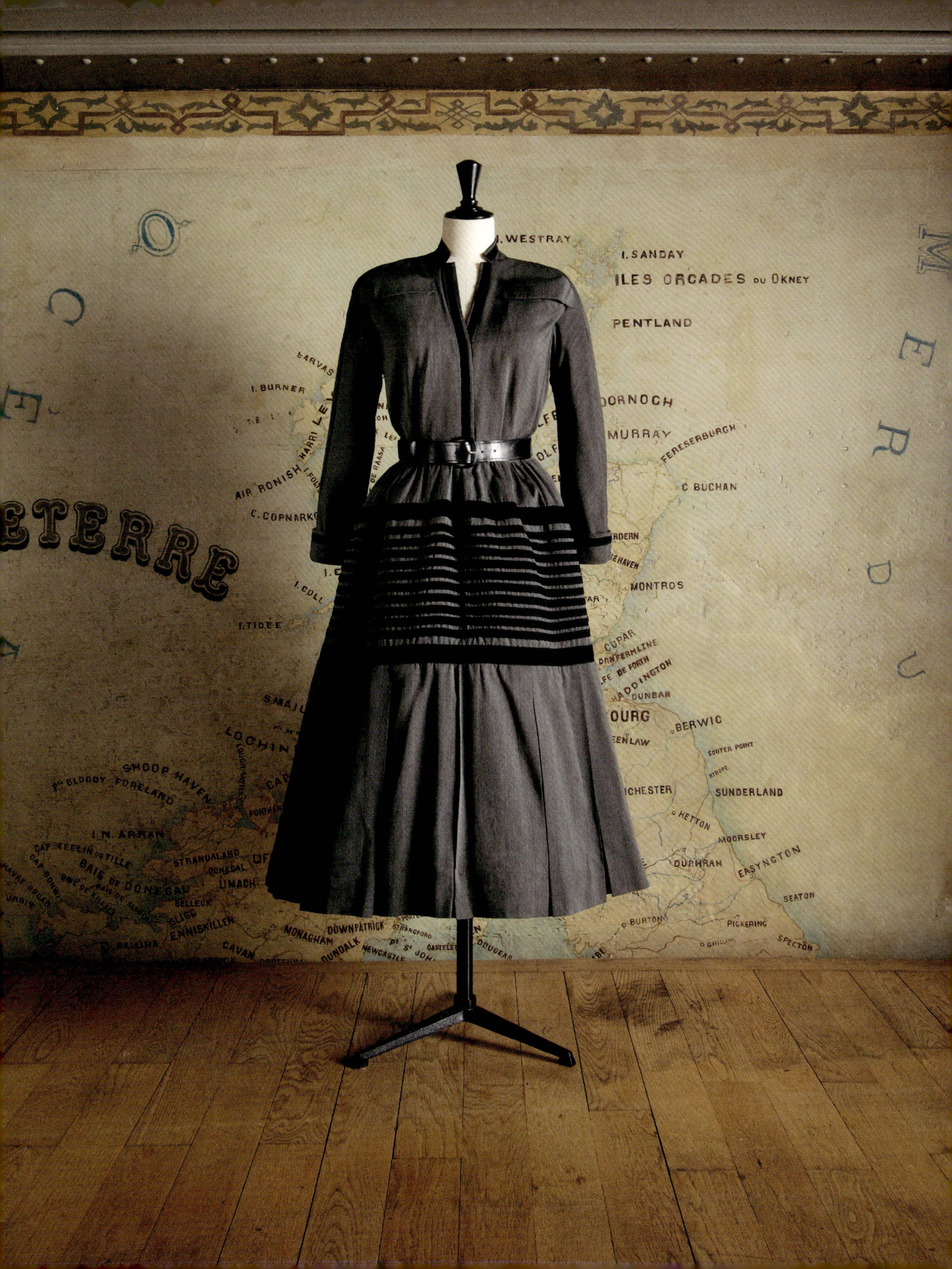

OCÉAN
MER DU
ANGLETERRE
I. WESTRAY
I. SANDAY
ILES ORCADES du OKNEY
PENTLAND
LARVAS
I. BURNER
DORNOCH
MURRAY
FERESERBURGH
C. BUCHAN
AIR. RONISH HARRI LE
C. COPNARKO
MONTROS
I. COLL
CUPAR
DANFERMLINE
I. TIDEE
LFE DE FORTH
ADDINGTON
DUNBAR
S. MAJU
OURG
BERWIG
EENLAW
LOCHIN
SOUTER POINT
SHOOP HAVEN
ATROPE
FORELAND
ICHESTER
SUNDERLAND
I.N. ARMAN
HETTON
MOORSLEY
CAP TEELIN TILLE
EASYNGTON
BAIE DE DONEGAL
DURHRAM
UMACH
SEATON
STRANDALARD
DONEGAL
BELLECK
SLIGO
D. BURTON
ENNISKILLEN
PICKERING
SPECTON
BALLINA
CAVAN
MONAGHAM
DOWNPATRICK
STRANGFORD
DUNDALK
NEWCASTLE
DOUGEAS

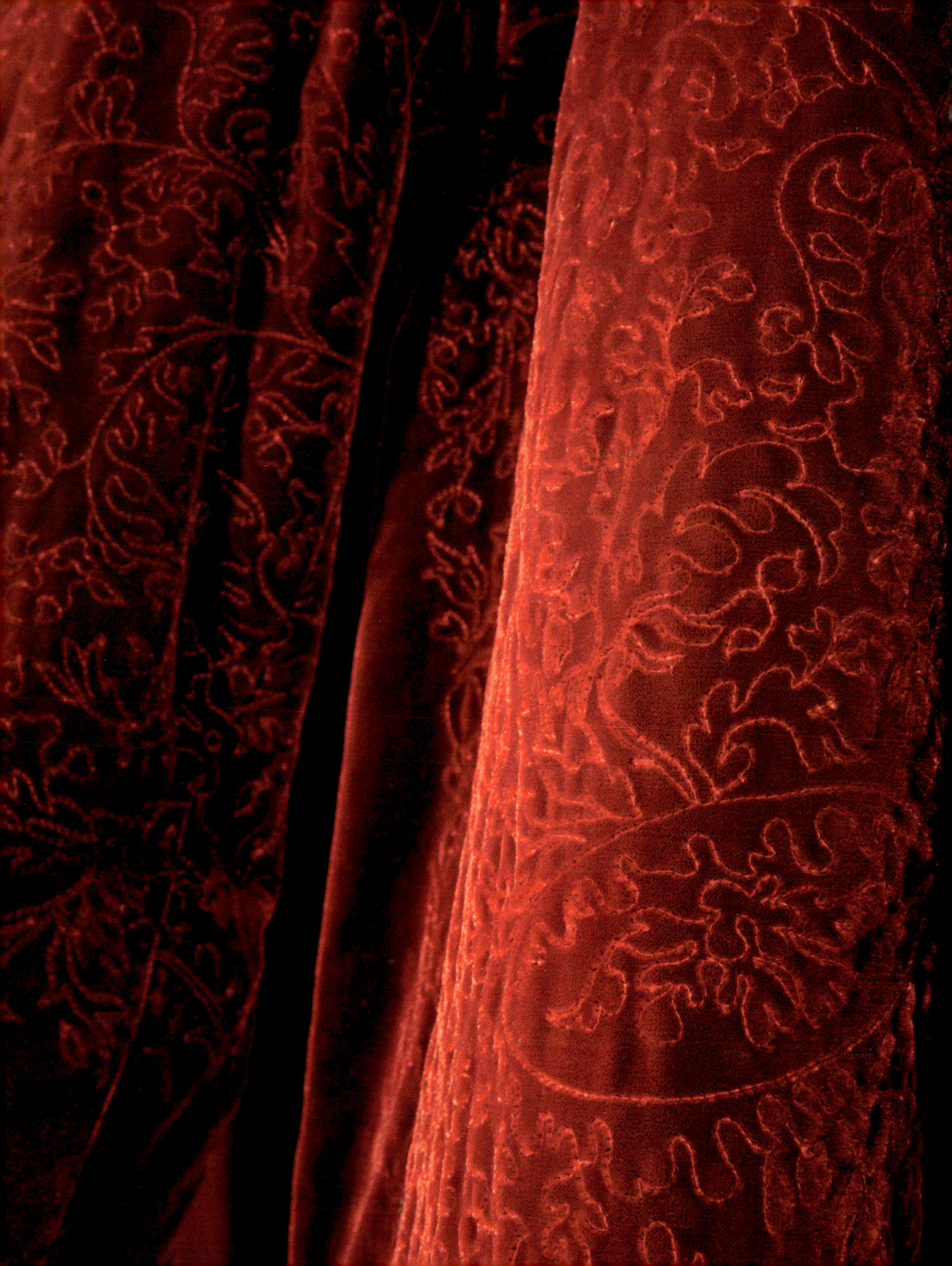

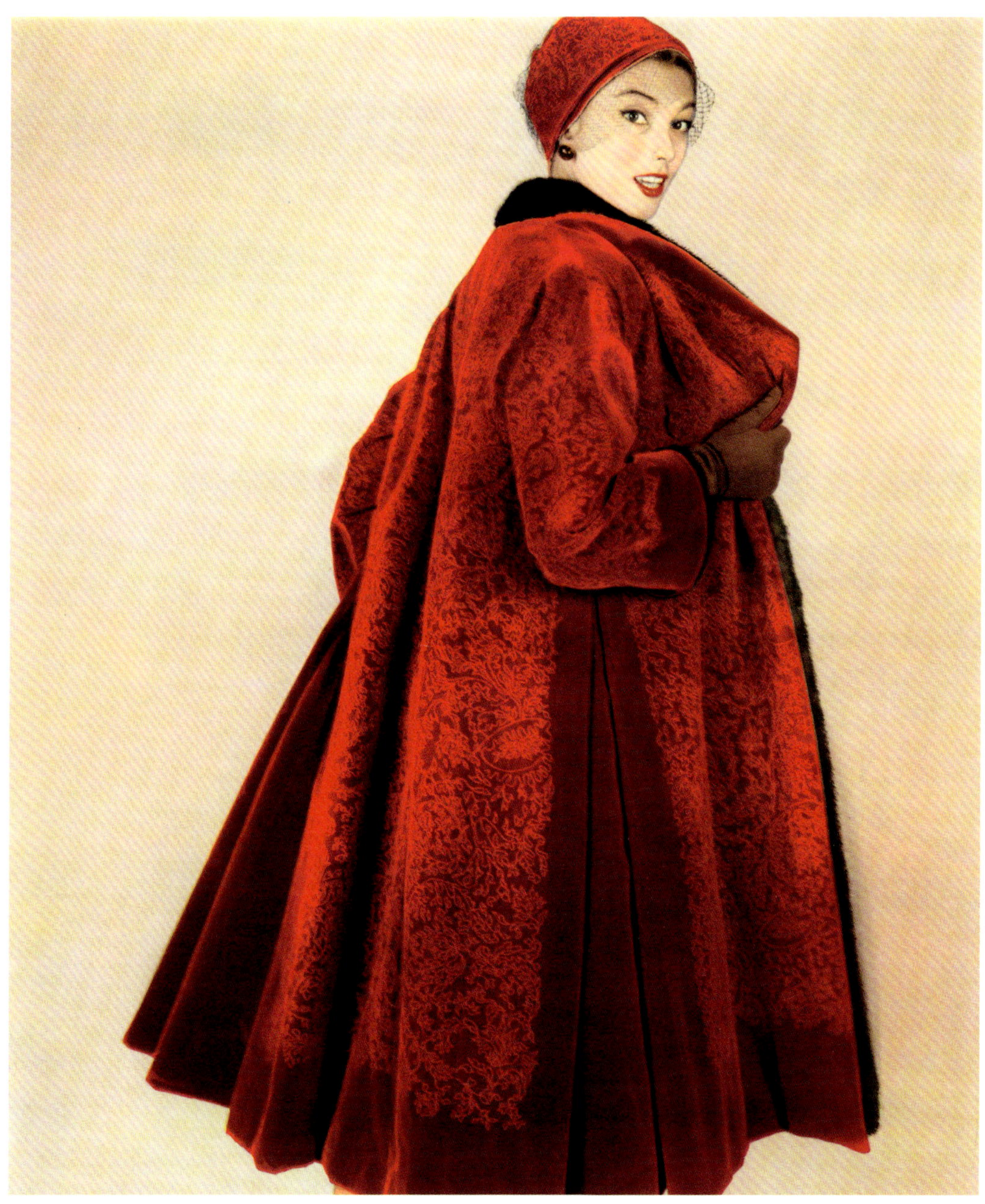

OPPOSITE
Christian Dior
Samarcande

Evening coat in embroidered silk
velvet (detail), Autumn–Winter 1955
haute couture collection, *Y* line.
Paris, Dior Héritage.

The Fondation Azzedine Alaïa
has a longer version of this coat
without fur in its collections.

ABOVE
Model wearing the Christian Dior
Samarcande evening coat.
Photograph by Philippe Pottier,
published in *L'Officiel*, September 1955.

151

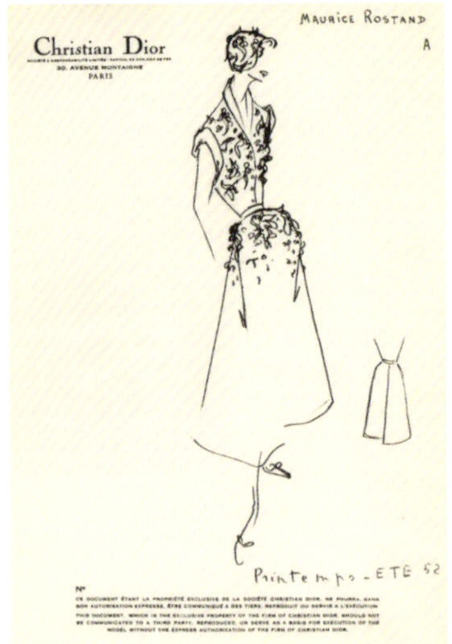

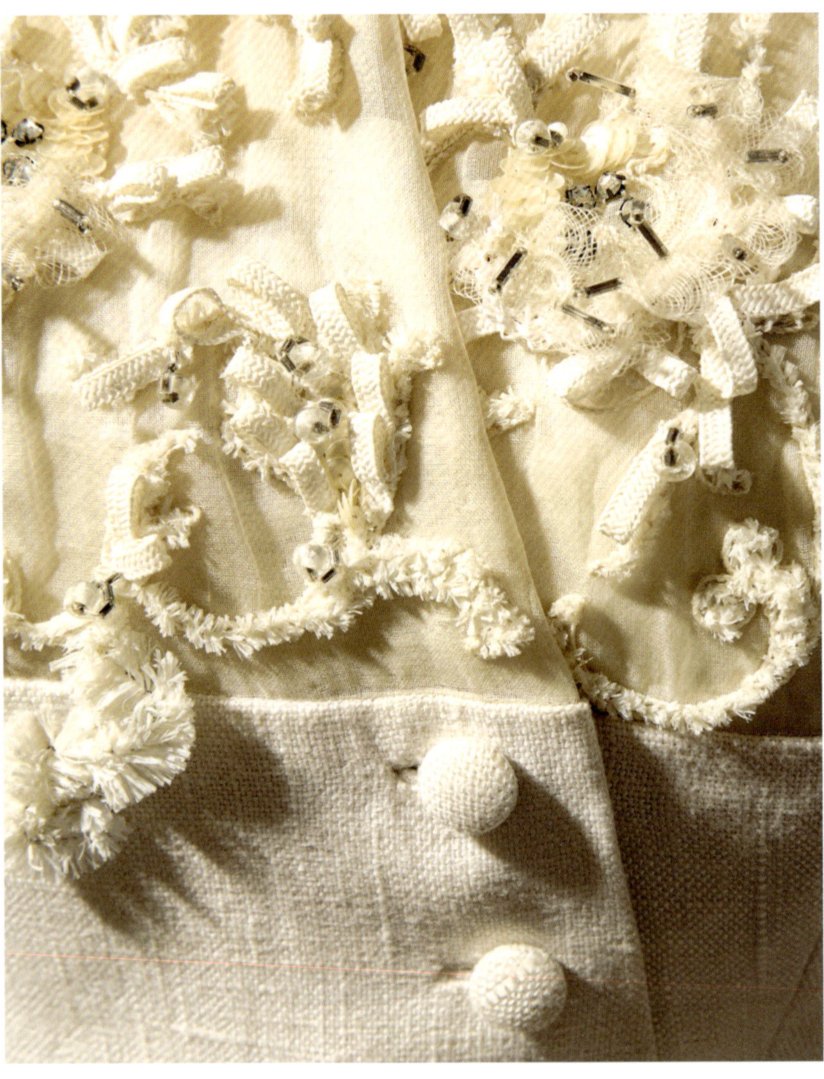

Christian Dior
MAURICE ROSTAND
A
Printemps–ETÉ 52

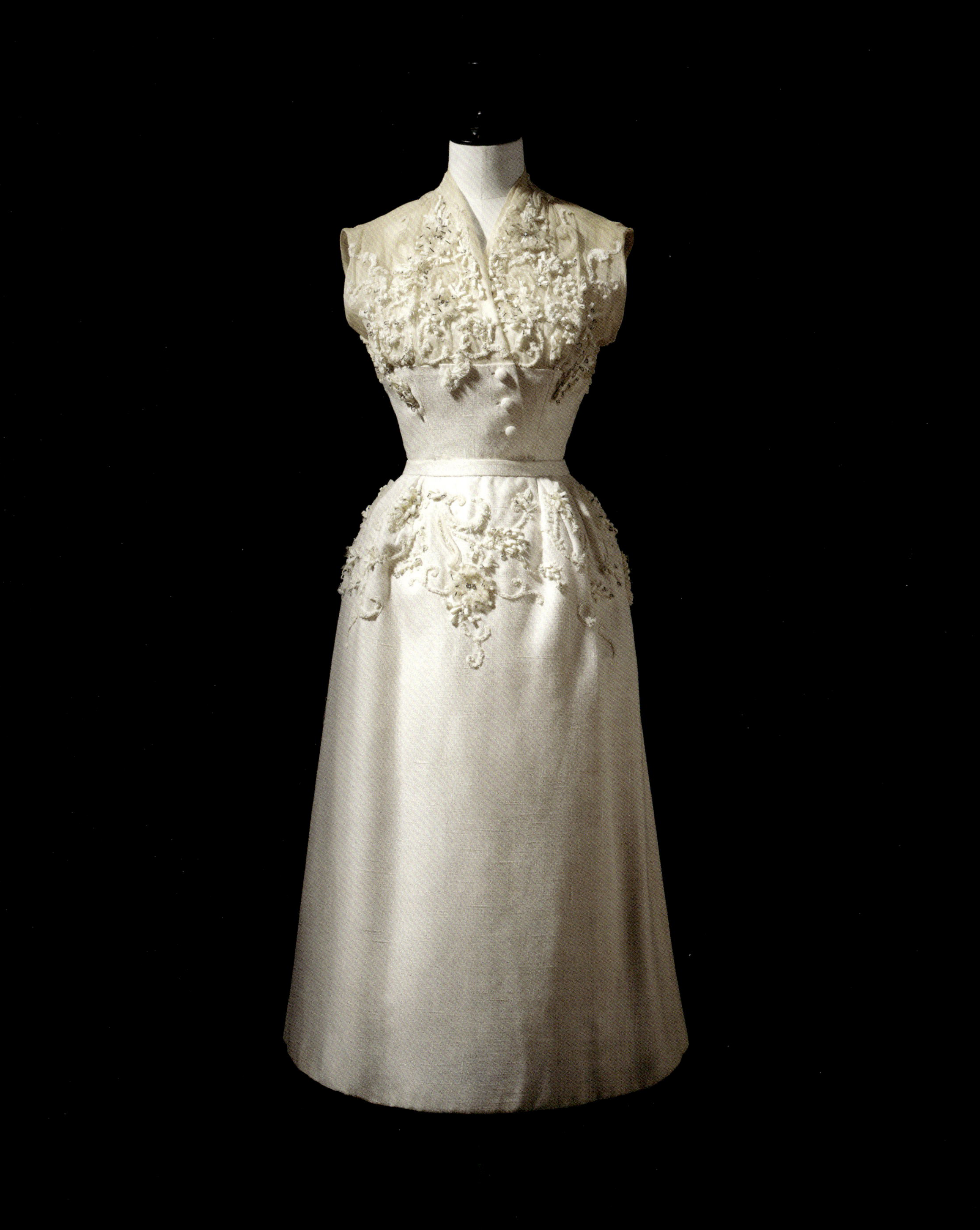

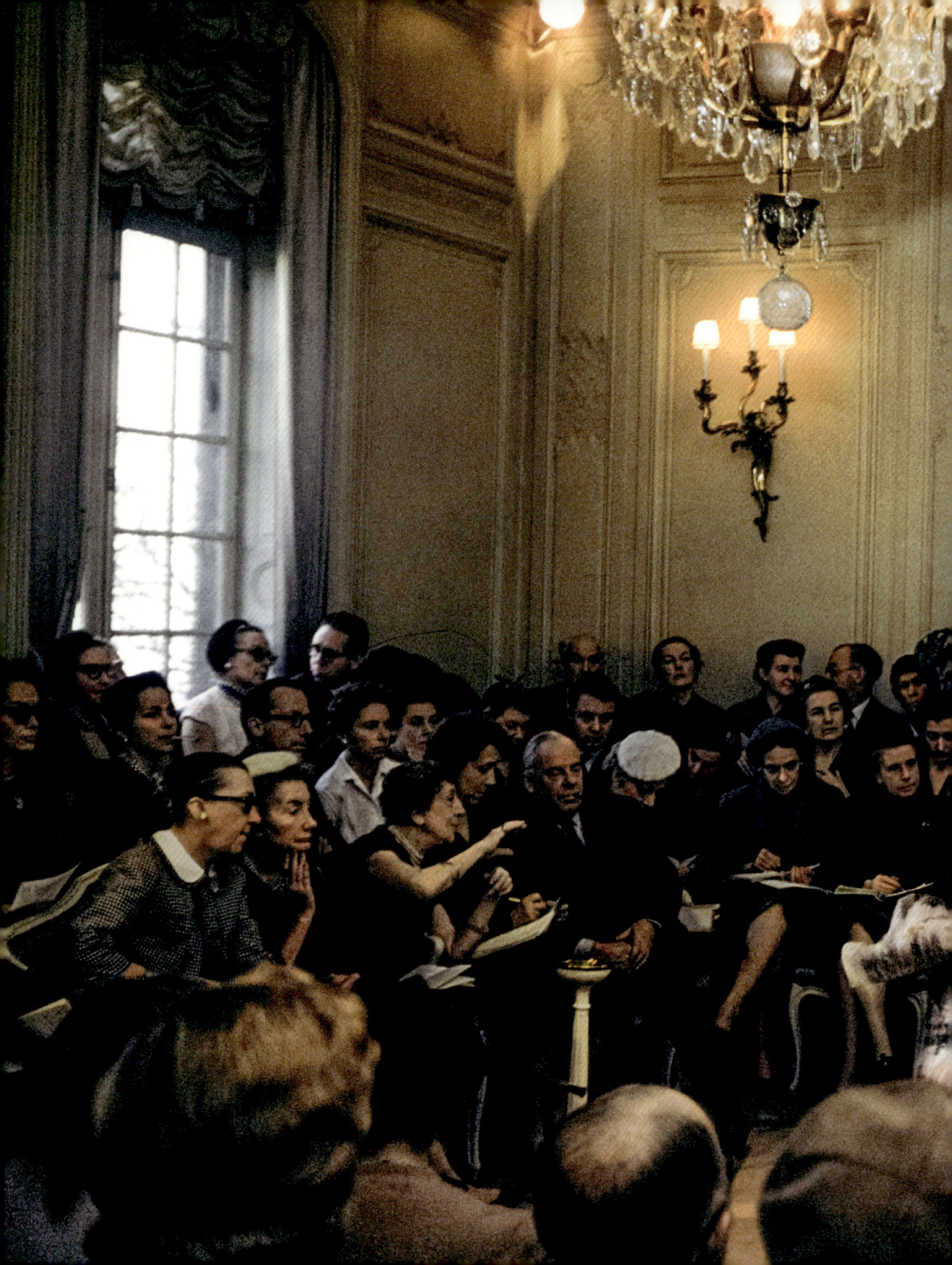

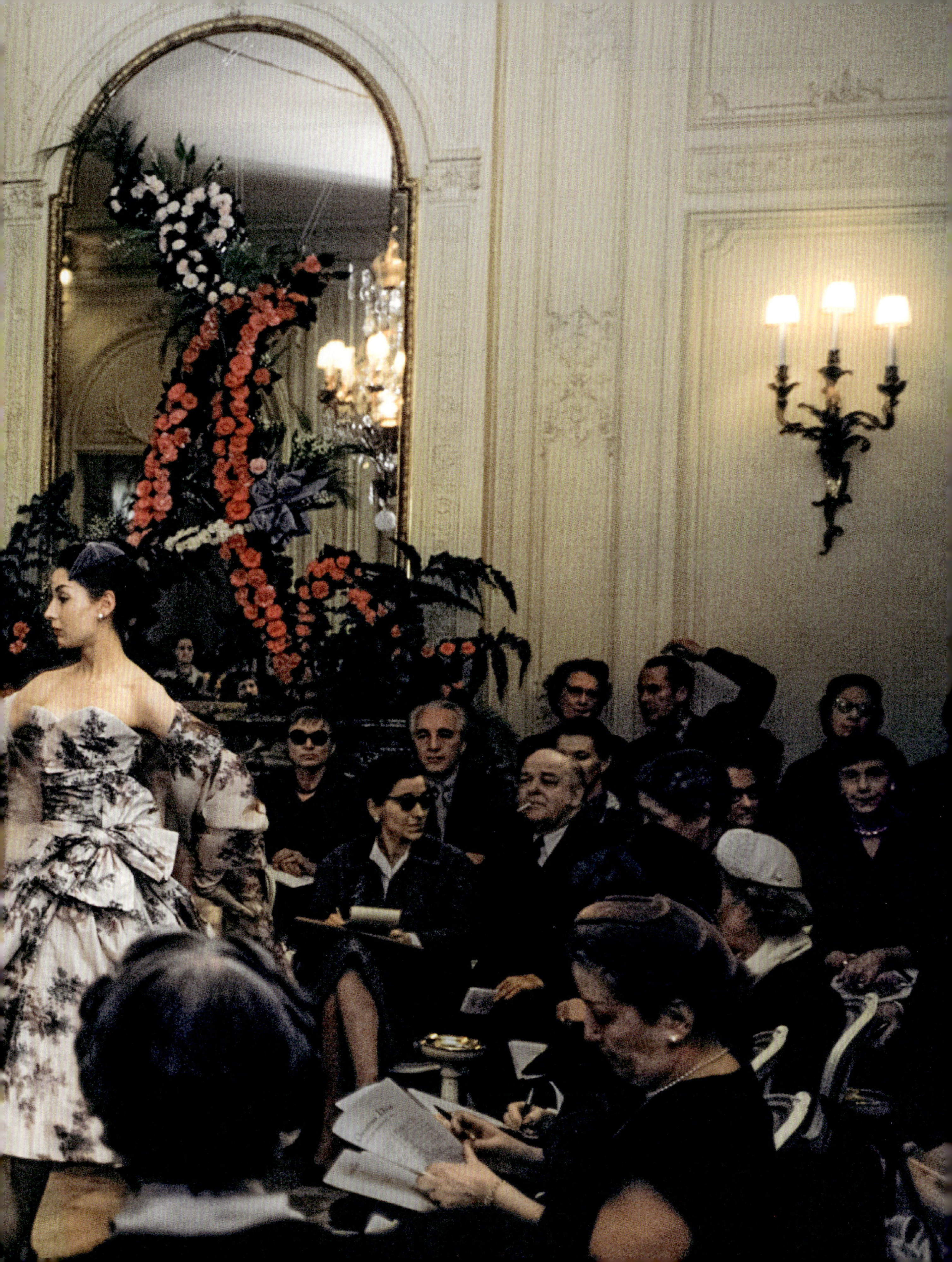

This publication accompanies the exhibition
Azzedine Alaïa's Dior Collection
organized by Christian Dior Couture and the
Fondation Azzedine Alaïa, under the curatorship
of Olivier Saillard, in collaboration with
Gaël Mamine, at La Galerie Dior in Paris, from
November 20, 2025 to May 3, 2026.

This project was made possible with the support of
Bernard Arnault, Chairman and Chief Executive
Officer, LVMH,
Delphine Arnault, Chairman and Chief Executive
Officer, Christian Dior Couture,
Olivier Bialobos, Deputy Managing Director in
charge of Global Communication and Image,
Christian Dior Couture and Parfums Christian Dior.

The House of Dior would like to express its
deep gratitude to Carla Sozzani, Chairman of the
Fondation Azzedine Alaïa, and Olivier Saillard,
the Chief Executive Officer, without whom this
project would not have been possible.

Sincere thanks to Laurence Benaïm and
Alessandra Ronetti for their eloquent
contributions to this catalog, and to the
Dior Ateliers, particularly Maurizio Liotti,
Benoît Hamel, Gaëlle Duval, Nadège Guenin,
and Hong Bo Li for their invaluable help.

Special thanks to Laziz Hamani and
Antoine Tritsch, to Antoine Jean, Marie Marotel,
and Mathieu Delion (Funny Bones), as well
as to Catherine Bonifassi and Vanessa Blondel
(Cassi Edition), for the realization of
this publication.

The House of Dior would also like to thank:

Fondation Azzedine Alaïa
Gaël Mamine,
Miquel Martínez Albero

Christian Dior Couture
Olivier Flaviano, Lucile Desmoulins,
Élisa Jaucourt-Perroy, Dorothée Lacan,
Amélie Lemarchand, Claire Pierson,
Doriane Traverse;
Perrine Scherrer, Solène Auréal-Lamy,
David Da Silva, Joséphine Imbault,
Justine Lasgi, Laura Latapie, Alexandre Mazeau,
Gwenn Meunier, Valérie Mulattieri,
Jessie Rupp, Joana Tosta, Sandra Touraine,
Jennifer Walheim;
Hélène Starkman, Isabelle Rousset,
Alice Lefèvre, Léa Denys;
Daphné Catroux, Charlotte Postic;
and Stéphanie Pélian

Parfums Christian Dior
Frédéric Bourdelier, Vincent Leret,
Inès Allain Balbine

Lastly, thank you to everyone who brought
their support to the preparation, organization,
and promotion of this catalog.

Christian Dior
Cygne noir

Reception dress in silk faille
(detail), Autumn–Winter 1957
haute couture collection, *Fuseau* line.
Paris, Fondation Azzedine Alaïa.

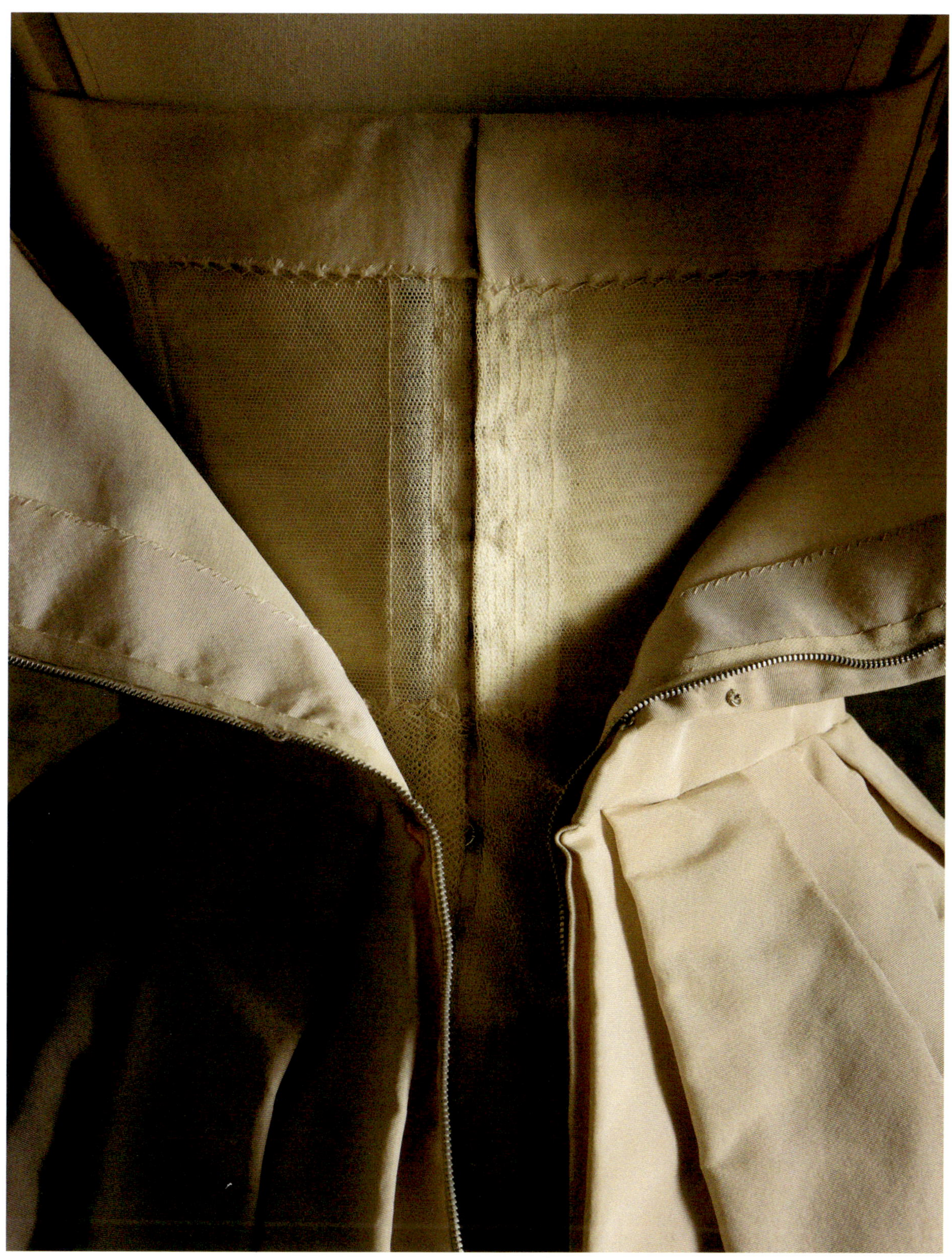

Page 27:
"The collection *Milieu du siècle*, which followed that winter was very expert: it was founded on a system of cutting, based on the internal geometry of the material, straight grain and bias crisscrossed, radiated like windmills."
Christian Dior, *Dior by Dior: The Autobiography of Christian Dior* (London: V&A Publishing, 2025; orig. published in 1957), 183.

Page 45:
"Busts are also rounded, whereas the waist is rather more fitted. Skirts are full at the hips and become narrower further down. The Magnet is in effect the leitmotif which reappears throughout the collection."
Press release, Autumn-Winter 1956 haute couture collection, *Aimant* line.

Page 53:
"It is through the cut that dresses today avoid the insipid overabundance of seams, and in this way are akin to the garments of antiquity, possessing the same apparent simplicity."
Christian Dior, *Conférences écrites par Christian Dior pour la Sorbonne, 1955–1957* (Paris: Éditions de l'Institut français de la mode/Éditions du Regard), 44.

Page 80:
"Red. A very energetic and beneficial color. It is the color of life. I love red and I think it suits almost every complexion. It is good for any time, too."
Christian Dior, *The Little Dictionary of Fashion: A Guide to Dress Sense for Every Woman* (London: V&A Publishing, 2008; orig. published in 1954), 95.

Page 93:
"For late spring and summer, we wanted both the mellowest and the most dazzling tones. Alongside classic *Rouge Dior*, we have a flourishing of *begonia* pink, *azalea* mauve, *hydrangea* blue, *daffodil* yellow, and *soft grass* green."
Press release, Spring-Summer 1952 haute couture collection, *Sinueuse* line.

Page 100:
"Pink. The sweetest of all the colors. Every woman should have something pink in her wardrobe. It is the color of happiness and of femininity."
Dior, *The Little Dictionary of Fashion*, 87.

Page 126:
"It is not sufficiently understood that embroidery is still done by hand, as in the eighteenth century. A ball dress may be entirely covered with millions of *paillettes*, or pearls, each one has to be put on separately as if they had been sewn by fairies."
Dior, *Dior by Dior*, 106.

Page 133:
"The following spring, appeared the *Tulipe* line, marked by the development of the bust and the narrowing of the hips. Little by little the waist was being freed. Colors were inspired by the pictures of the Impressionists, and evoked the fields of flowers dear to Renoir and Van Gogh."
Dior, *Dior by Dior*, 186.

Page 139:
"As the hours go by, the dresses begin to become more elaborate and full, their skirts lengthen, and we imperceptibly shift from the dinner dress to the formal evening gown, which enjoys total freedom in terms of silhouette and volume."
Press release, Spring-Summer 1952 haute couture collection, *Sinueuse* line.

AZZEDINE ALAÏA'S
DIOR
COLLECTION

FIRST PUBLISHED IN THE UNITED STATES
OF AMERICA IN 2025 BY
RIZZOLI INTERNATIONAL PUBLICATIONS, INC.
49 WEST 27TH STREET
NEW YORK, NY 10001
WWW.RIZZOLIUSA.COM

COPYRIGHT ©2025 CHRISTIAN DIOR

TEXTS:
PREFACE AND "THE MANY LIVES OF DRESSES":
OLIVIER SAILLARD
"THE CRAFT OF THE DIOR ATELIERS": LAURENCE BENAÏM
"CHRISTIAN DIOR & THE CULTURE OF COLOR":
ALESSANDRA RONETTI

PHOTOGRAPHS OF THE DIOR LOOKS BY LAZIZ HAMANI,
ASSISTED BY ANTOINE TRITSCH

ALL RIGHTS RESERVED. NO PART OF THIS PUBLICATION
MAY BE REPRODUCED, STORED IN A RETRIEVAL SYSTEM, OR
TRANSMITTED IN ANY FORM OR BY ANY MEANS, ELECTRONIC,
MECHANICAL, PHOTOCOPYING, RECORDING, OR OTHERWISE,
WITHOUT PRIOR CONSENT OF THE PUBLISHER.

PUBLISHER: CHARLES MIERS
EDITORIAL DIRECTOR: CATHERINE BONIFASSI
PRODUCTION DIRECTOR: MARIA PIA GRAMAGLIA
MANAGING EDITOR: LYNN SCRABIS
COPYEDITOR AND PROOFREADER: TRICIA LEVI

ARTISTIC DIRECTION: FUNNY BONES

EDITORIAL COORDINATION: CASSI EDITION
VANESSA BLONDEL, CANDICE GUILLAUME, ABIGAIL GRATER

ISBN: 978-0-8478-7609-9
LIBRARY OF CONGRESS CONTROL NUMBER: 2025938804

IMAGE PROCESSING: FOTIMPRIM, PARIS

PRINTED IN ITALY
2025 2026 2027 2028 / 10 9 8 7 6 5 4 3 2 1

THE AUTHORIZED REPRESENTATIVE IN THE EU
FOR PRODUCT SAFETY AND COMPLIANCE IS
MONDADORI LIBRI S.P.A., VIA GIAN BATTISTA VICO 42,
MILAN, ITALY, 20123
WWW.MONDADORI.IT

VISIT US ONLINE
INSTAGRAM.COM/RIZZOLIBOOKS
FACEBOOK.COM/RIZZOLINEWYORK
YOUTUBE.COM/USER/RIZZOLINY

MIX
Paper | Supporting
responsible forestry
FSC
www.fsc.org   FSC® C013123

COVER

Christian Dior
Élisabeth

Gala dress in embroidered silk velvet
(detail), Autumn–Winter 1952
haute couture collection, *Profilée* line.
Paris, Fondation Azzedine Alaïa.